Direct Access!

With thousands of addresses and thousands of uses, *The Sports Address Book* is the indispensable guide for every sports fan, fanatic, parent, and professional! This information-packed sourcebook can help you to:

- find the right sports camp for your child
- join an amateur team or club
- locate athletic organizations in foreign countries
- get expert information on 53 sports—from archery to wrestling
- sell or buy top-quality sporting equipment
- enter races and tournaments
- confer with experts in athletic medicine
- discover opportunities for the handicapped
- cheer your favorite athletes
- get in touch with the movers, shakers, and stars—at the top of virtually any sport!

If you want to find *anything* in the world of sports, *The Sports Address Book* puts it right in your hands!

THE
SPORTS
ADDRESS
BOOK

SCOTT CALLIS, Editor

POCKET BOOKS

New York   London   Toronto   Sydney   Tokyo

An *Original* publication of POCKET BOOKS

POCKET BOOKS, a division of Simon & Schuster Inc.
1230 Avenue of the Americas, New York, NY 10020

ISBN: 0-671-68842-1

First Pocket Books trade paperback printing July 1988

10 9 8 7 6 5 4 3 2

POCKET and colophon are trademarks
of Simon & Schuster Inc.

Printed in the U.S.A.

CONTENTS ━━━━━━━━━━━━━━

How to Use This Book VII

■ **Directory of Individual Sports:**

■ General Directory

HOW TO USE THIS BOOK ━━━━

You are holding in your hands a unique reference and source book for sports fans. It is a result of the collective efforts of a number of researchers, fans, sports writers, athletes, sports information directors and others who have helped me bring together more than 5,000 addresses in the various sports.

The book is organized in two parts: the sport-by-sport directory and the general or multi-sport directory. Where it seems helpful, I have listed the telephone number with an address. I have attempted to list every sport and every major organization within the sport, especially for the U.S. and Canada. All addresses are as current as possible, but they are, of course, subject to change. And undoubtedly there are omissions, especially in the case of smaller or regional clubs and organizations. If there is a group or club not included whom you wish to contact, my recommendation is to write to a publication or association in that sport and ask for a particular address. If you are interested in contacting foreign organizations, try the country's embassy, delegation or trade mission and ask them for the information, or go through the Olympic committees, which are listed in the book. They are a good source of information.

Individuals in the various sports are listed with an address only. In some cases these are home addresses, in others we have listed the address of their agent or business. In general we have avoided the "c/o" address, but for many individuals this is the preferred way of reaching them for autographs, queries, pictures, information, and so on. If the address of a particular individual is not listed in The Sports Address Book, they can oftentimes be reached by writing in care of their team. This recommendation applies even for retired players, since the teams routinely pass along their mail to them. This is not true in all instances, but I generally found it to be the case.

When trying to contact an individual coach, player or official, it is preferable in every instance to write to them rather than telephoning. These are busy people who cherish their privacy, and most will not respond kindly to someone who intrudes upon their time. A letter, on the other hand, is generally met with openness and responsiveness. These can be handled by a secretary or spouse, or by the player in a time set aside for correspondence. When writing, be straightforward and to the point. If you are writing for an autograph, enclose a 3×5 card and a self-addressed envelope so they can send the card back to you. Don't send six cards for him or her to sign since we were told by a number of athletes that they just throw the extras away. Several said they would not respond to someone who requests more than one autograph, so it is self-defeating to get greedy.

If you are writing to a company or organization for information about products, dates, souvenirs or additional listings, it will also help if you include a self-addressed envelope, but it is not always necessary. Many times I received a response to a written question, even though no return envelope was included. If you are mailing away to a foreign team or organization for a price list with the thought that you will be ordering merchandise from them, you then should include an envelope. If you order a book or souvenir, it is much quicker and ultimately cheaper if you enclose a money order in the country's currency. Most banks should be able to handle this for you, but having said this, it is not always the easiest thing to do. Even in major cities it can be a problem. But if you send a U.S. money order or a check drawn on a U.S. bank, be aware that it can mean a delay of several months.

Camps for various sports are listed under the particular sport. If the camp is for boys or girls only, I have indicated that with a B or G; in the case of tennis and golf I have indicated whether it is for adults (A) or juniors (J); if the camp has more than one location I have listed only the camp's headquarters and noted it with an asterisk(*).

Dates for events, tournaments, races and camps vary from year to year, so don't make plans based on last year's date. Call or write for information regarding the specific time you want to attend.

The *Sports Address Book* is a general information book for the average fan. There are several specialty sport publications that I found invaluable and which contain extensive listings of information. While these are directed more toward the professional reader, they might be helpful if you are looking for more complete information on a particular aspect of sports. The books include *The Sports Market Place* (Sportsguide, P.O. Box 1417, Princeton, N.J. 08542) and *Master's Guide to Sports Camps* (600 Loraine Bldg, 124 East Fulton Street, Grand Rapids, MI 49503). Both are highly recommended.

While changes of address and personnel inevitably occur, I would appreciate it if you would let me know of any corrections, suggestions or added addresses for future editions of this book. You can reach me in care of Pocket Books, 1230 Sixth Avenue, NYC 10020.

A great many people helped me compile *The Sports Address Book*, and I thank them all for their assistance. I especially want to thank Kris Mackerer, Bert Sugar, Jim Bouton, Tim Charlton, Kevin Charlton, Jeff Morey, George Sullivan, Virginia Valenze, Shep Long, Gary Slochowsky and Paul McCarthy for their efforts.

Scott Callis, Editor

AEROBICS

■ ORGANIZATIONS—U.S. &
CANADA

**Aerobics and Fitness
Association of America**
15250 Ventura Boulevard
Sherman Oaks, CA 91403
(818) 905-0040

■ ORGANIZATIONS—
INTERNATIONAL

**International Dance-Exercise
Association (IDEA)**
4501 Mission Bay Drive, Suite 2-F
San Diego, CA 92109
(619) 274-2770

■ PUBLICATIONS

Aerobics and Fitness
15250 Ventura Boulevard
Suite 310
Sherman Oaks, CA 91403

Dance Exercise Today
4501 Mission Bay Drive, Suite 2-F
San Diego, CA 92109

AIR SPORTS

■ ORGANIZATIONS—U.S. &
CANADA

Balloon Federation of America
PO Box 400
Indianola, IA 50125
(515) 961-8809

**Canadian Sport Parachuting
Association**
333 River Road
Ottawa, Ontario, Canada K1L 8H9
(613) 748-5650

**Soaring Society of America,
Inc.**
PO Box E
Hobbs, NM 88241
(505) 392-1177

**Sport Balloon Society of the
U.S.A.**
Menlo Oaks Balloon Field
Drawer 2247
Menlo Park, CA 94026
(415) 326-7679

U.S. Base Association
12619 South Manor Drive
Hawthorne, CA 90250
(213) 678-0163

**U.S. Hang Gliding Association,
Inc.**
12208 Pearlblossom Highway
PO Box 500
Pearlblossom, CA 93553
(805) 944-5333

U.S. Parachute Association
1440 Duke Street
Alexandria, VA 22314
(703) 836-3495

■ PUBLICATIONS

Balloon Life
3381 Pony Express Drive
Sacramento, CA 95834-1422

Hang Gliding
PO Box 500
Pearlblossom, CA 93553

Parachutist
1440 Duke Street
Alexandria, VA 22314

Skydiving Magazine
PO Box 1520
Deland, FL 32721

Soaring Magazine
PO Box E
Hobbs, NM 88241

Sport Flyer
PO Box 98786
Tacoma, WA 98498-0786

■ **EVENTS**

**Albuquerque International Hot
Air Balloon Festival**
3300 Princeton, N.E.
NOS-24
Albuquerque, NM 87101

**U.S. National Hot Air Balloon
Championship**
Indianola Balloons
PO Box 346
Indianola, IA 50125

ARCHERY

■ **ORGANIZATIONS—U.S. &
CANADA**

American Crossbow Association
Route 6, Box 293
Huntsville, AR 72740
(501) 738-6551

**Archery Manufacturers
Association**
200 Castlewood Drive
North Palm Beach, FL 33408
(305) 842-4100

Bowhunters Who Care
PO Box 269
Columbus, NE 68601
(402) 564-7176

Federation of Canadian Archers
333 River Road
Vanier, Ontario, Canada K1L 8H9
(613) 748-5604

**National Archery Association of
the U.S.**
1750 East Boulder Street
Colorado Springs, CO 80909
(303) 578-4576

**National Crossbow Hunter's
Association, Inc.**
118 Main Street
Wadsworth, OH 44281
(216) 336-3568

**National Field Archery
Association**
Route 2, PO Box 514
Redlands, CA 92373
(714) 794-2133

**Professional Archers
Association**
7315 San Anna Drive
Tucson, AZ 85704
(602) 742-5846

■ ORGANIZATIONS—
INTERNATIONAL

**Federation Internationale
Archery**
Via Cerva 30
20122 Milan
Italy

**Professional Archers
Association**
7315 San Anna Drive
Tucson, AZ 85704
(602) 742-5846

■ PUBLICATIONS

Archery Business
11812 Wayzata Boulevard
Suite 100
Minnetonka, MN 55343

Archery World Magazine
11812 Wayzata Boulevard
Suite 100
Minnetonka, MN 55343

Bow & Arrow
PO Box HH
34249 Camino Capistrano
Capistrano Beach, CA 92624

Bowfishing Magazine
PO Box 2005
Wausau, WI 54402-2005

Bowhunters' New Service
7626 West Donges Bay Road
Mequon, WI 53092

N.A.A. Newsletter
1750 East Boulder Street
Colorado Springs, CO 80909

North American Bowhunter
PO Box 5487
Tucson, AZ 85703

The U.S. Archer
7315 North San Anna Drive
Tucson, AZ 85704

Western Bowhunter
PO Box 511
Squaw Valley, CA 93646

BARREL JUMPING

■ ORGANIZATIONS—U.S. &
CANADA

**Canadian Barrel Jumping
Association, Inc.**
10575 Cobourg
Montreal, Nord, Quebec, Canada
HIH 4X3
(514) 323-8147

BASEBALL

■ PROFESSIONAL LEAGUES

MAJOR LEAGUES—AMERICAN

American League
350 Park Avenue
New York, NY 10022
(212) 371-7600
Pres: Dr. Robert Brown
CEO: Robert Fishel
PR Director: Phyllis Merhige

Baltimore Orioles
Memorial Stadium
Baltimore, MD 21218
(301) 243-9800
Owner: Edward Bennet Williams
Pres: Edward Bennet Williams
GM: Roland Hemond
PR Director: Robert Brown

Boston Red Sox
Fedway Park
Boston, MA 02215
(617) 267-9440
Owner: Haywood Sullivan
Pres: Jean R. Yawkey
GM: Lou Gorman
PR Director: Richard Bresciani

California Angels
PO Box 2000
Anaheim, CA 92803
(714) 937-6700
Owner: Gene Autry
Pres: Gene Autry
GM: Mike Port
PR Director: Tim Mead

Chicago White Sox
324 West 35th Street
Chicago, IL 60616
(312) 924-1000
Owners: Jerry Reinsdorf,
        Eddie Einhorn
Pres: Eddie Einhorn
GM: Dave Dombrowski
PR Director: Paul Jensen

Cleveland Indians
Cleveland Stadium
Cleveland, OH 44114
(216) 961-1200
Owner: Patrick O'Neill
Pres: Hank Peters
GM: Dan O'Brien
PR Director: Rick Minch

Detroit Tigers
2121 Trumbull Avenue
Detroit, MI 48216
(313) 962-4000
Owner: Tom Monaghan
Pres: Jim Campbell
GM: Bill Lajoie
PR Director: Dan Ewald

Kansas City Royals
PO Box 419969
Kansas City, MO 64141
(816) 921-2200
Owners: Ewing Kauffman,
        Avron Fogelman
Pres: Joe Burke
GM: John Schuerholz
PR Director: Dean Vogelaar

Milwaukee Brewers
Milwaukee County Stadium
Milwaukee, WI 53214
(414) 933-4114
Owner: Bud Selig
Pres: Bud Selig
GM: Harry Dalton
PR Director: Tom Skibosh

Minnesota Twins
501 Chicago Avenue, South
Minneapolis, MN 55415
(612) 375-1366
Owner: Carl Pohlad
Pres: Howard Fox
GM: Andy MacPhail
PR Director: Tom Mee

New York Yankees
Yankee Stadium
Bronx, NY 10451
(212) 293-4300
Owner: George Steinbrenner
Pres: Gene McHale
GM: Lou Piniella
PR Director: Harvey Greene

Oakland Athletics
Oakland Alameda County Coliseum
Oakland, CA 94621
(415) 638-4900
Owner: Roy Eisenhardt
Pres: Roy Eisenhardt
GM: Sandy Alderson
PR Director: Ray Fosse

Seattle Mariners
PO Box 4100
Seattle, WA 98104
(206) 628-3555
Owner: George Argyros
Pres: Charles Armstrong
GM: Dick Balderson
PR Director: Bob Porter

Texas Rangers
PO Box 1111
Arlington, TX 76010
(817) 273-5222
Owner: Eddie Chiles
Pres: Michael H. Stone
GM: Tom Grieve
PR Director: John Blake

Toronto Blue Jays
Box 7777, Adelaide Street PO
Toronto, Ontario, Canada M5C 2K7
(416) 595-0077
Owners: R. Howard Webster,
   N.E. Hardy
Pres: R. Howard Webster,
   N.E. Hardy
GM: Pat Gillick
PR Director: Howard Starkman

MAJOR LEAGUES—NATIONAL

National League
350 Park Avenue
New York, NY 10022
(212) 371-7300
Pres: A. Bartlett Giamatti
PR Director: Blake Cullen

Atlanta Braves
PO Box 4064
Atlanta, GA 30302
(404) 522-7630
Owner: Ted Turner
Pres: Ted Turner
GM: Bobby Cox
PR Director: Bob DiBiasio

Chicago Cubs
1060 West Addison Street
Chicago, IL 60613
(312) 281-5050
Owner: Stanton Cook
Pres: Stanton Cook
GM: Jim Frey
PR Director: Ned Colletti

Cincinnati Reds
Riverfront Stadium
Cincinnati, OH 45202
(513) 421-4510
Owner: Marge Schott
Pres: Marge Schott
GM: Murray Cook
PR Director: Jim Ferguson

Houston Astros
PO Box 288
Houston, TX 77001
(713) 799-9500
Owner: John McMullen
Pres: Dick Wagner
GM: Dick Wagner
PR Director: Rob Matwick

Los Angeles Dodgers
1000 Elysian Park Avenue
Los Angeles, CA 90012
(213) 224-1500
Owner: Peter O'Malley
Pres: Peter O'Malley
GM: Fred Claire
PR Director: Fred Claire

Montreal Expos
PO Box 500, Station M
Montreal, Que.
Canada H1V 3P2
(514) 253-3434
Owner: Charles Bronfman
Pres: John McHale
GM: Murray Cook
PR Director: Richard Griffin

New York Mets
Shea Stadium
Flushing, NY 11368
(718) 507-6387
Owner: Sterling Doubleday Enterprises
Pres: Fred Wilpon
GM: Frank Cashen
PR Director: Jay Horwitz

Philadelphia Phillies
PO Box 7575
Philadelphia, PA 19101
(215) 463-6000
Owner: Bill Giles
Pres: Bill Giles
GM: Tony Siegle
PR Director: Larry Shenk

Pittsburgh Pirates
Three Rivers Stadium
Pittsburgh, PA 15212
(412) 323-5000
Owner: Mac Prine
Pres: Mac Prine
GM: Syd Thrift
PR Director: Greg Johnson

San Diego Padres
PO Box 2000
San Diego, CA 92102
(619) 283-4494
Owner: Joan Kroc
Pres: Ballard Smith
GM: Jack McKeon
PR Director: Bill Beck

San Francisco Giants
Candlestick Park
San Francisco, CA 94124
(415) 468-3700
Owner: Bob Lurie
Pres: Bob Lurie
GM: Al Rosen
PR Director: Duffy Jennings

St. Louis Cardinals
250 Stadium Plaza
St. Louis, MO 63102
(314) 421-3060
Owner: August Busch, Jr
Pres: August Busch, Jr
GM: Dal Maxvill
PR Director: Jim Toomey

MINOR LEAGUES
American Association (AAA)
1200 Niagara Street
Buffalo, NY 14213
(716) 878-8574

Buffalo Bisons
Aff: Chicago White Sox
War Memorial Stadium
PO Box 538, Station 6
Buffalo, NY 14213
(716) 878-8215

Denver Zephyrs
Aff: Cincinnati Reds
2850 West 20th Avenue
Denver, CO 80211
(303) 433-8645

Indianapolis Indians
Aff: Montreal Expos
Owen J. Bush Stadium
1501 West 16th Street
Indianapolis, IN 46202-2063
(317) 632-5371

Iowa Cubs
Aff: Chicago Cubs
Sec Taylor Stadium
Second & Riverside Drive
Des Moines, IA 50265
(515) 243-6111

Louisville Redbirds
Aff: St. Louis Cardinals
Cardinal Stadium
PO Box 36407
Louisville, KY 40233
(502) 367-9121

Nashville Sounds
Aff: Detroit Tigers
Herschel Greer Stadium
PO Box 23290
Nashville, TN 37202
(615) 242-4371

Oklahoma City Rangers
Aff: Texas Rangers
All Sports Stadium
PO Box 75089
Oklahoma City, OK 73147
(405) 946-8989

Omaha Royals
Aff: Kansas City Royals
Rosenblatt Stadium
PO Box 3665
Omaha, NE 68103
(402) 734-2550

International League (AAA)
PO Box 608
Grove City, OH 43123
(614) 871-1300

Columbus Clippers
Aff: New York Yankees
1155 West Mound Street
Columbus, OH 43223
(614) 462-5250

Maine Guides
Aff: Cleveland Indians
PO Box 287
Old Orchard Beach, ME 04064

Pawtucket Red Sox
Aff: Boston Red Sox
McCoy Stadium
PO Box 2365
Pawtucket, RI 02861

Richmond Braves
Aff: Atlanta Braves
The Diamond
PO Box 6667
Richmond, VA 23230
(804) 359-4444

Rochester Red Wings
Aff: Baltimore Orioles
Silver Stadium
500 Norton Street
Rochester, NY 14621
(716) 467-3000

Syracuse Chiefs
Aff: Toronto Blue Jays
MacArthur Stadium
Syracuse, NY 13208
(315) 474-7833

Tidewater Tides
Aff: New York Mets
PO Box 12111
Norfolk, VA 23502
(804) 461-5600

Toledo Mud Hens
Aff: Minnesota Twins
PO Box 6212
Toledo, OH 43614
(419) 893-9483

Pacific Coast League (AAA)
2101 East Broadway Road, Suite 35
Tempe, AZ 85282
(602) 967-7679

Albuquerque Dukes
Aff: Los Angeles Dodgers
PO Box 26267
Albuquerque, NM 87125
(505) 243-1791

Calgary Cannons
Aff: Seattle Mariners
PO Box 3690, Station B
Calgary, Alberta
Canada T2M 4M4
(403) 284-1111

Edmonton Trappers
Aff: California Angels
12315 Stony Plain Road
Suite 202
Edmonton, Alberta
Canada T5N 3N2
(403) 429-2934

Hawaii Islanders
Aff: Pittsburgh Pirates
320 Ward Avenue, Suite 107
Honolulu, HI 96814
(808) 528-3200

Las Vegas Stars
Aff: San Diego Padres
850 Las Vegas Boulevard
Las Vegas, NV 89101
(702) 386-7200

Phoenix Giants
Aff: San Francisco Giants
5999 East Van Buren Street
Phoenix, AZ 85008
(602) 275-4488

Portland Beavers
Aff: Philadelphia Phillies
PO Box 1659
Portland, OR 97207
(503) 223-2837

Salt Lake City Gulls
Aff: Seattle Mariners
65 West 1300 South
Salt Lake City, UT 84115
(801) 363-7676

Tacoma Tigers
Aff: Oakland A's
PO Box 11087
Tacoma, WA 98411
(206) 752-7707

Tucson Toros
Aff: Houston Astros
PO Box 27045
Tucson, AZ 85726
(602) 325-2621

Vancouver Canadians
Aff: Milwaukee Brewers
Baseball Stadium
4601 Ontario Street
Vancouver, BC
Canada V5V 3H4

Eastern League (AA)
PO Box 716
Plainville, CT 06062
(203) 747-9332

Albany Yankees
Aff: New York Yankees
Albany-Shaker Road
Albany, NY 12211
(518) 869-9236

Glens Falls Tigers
Aff: Detroit Tigers
PO Box 717
Glens Falls, NY 12801
(518) 798-3685

Nashua Pirates
Aff: Pittsburgh Pirates
PO Box 3534
Nashua, NH 03063
(603) 883-2750

New Britain Red Sox
Aff: Boston Red Sox
PO Box 1718
New Britain, CT 06050
(203) 224-8383

Pittsfield Cubs
Aff: Chicago Cubs
PO Box 2246
Pittsfield, MA 01201
(413) 499-0077

Reading Phillies
Aff: Philadelphia Phillies
PO Box 5010
Reading, PA 19612
(215) 375-8469

Vermont Reds
Aff: Cincinnati Reds
104 Church Street
Burlington, VT 05401
(802) 862-6662

Waterbury Indians
Aff: Cleveland Indians
PO Box 172
Waterbury, CT 06720
(203) 756-4491

Southern League (AA)
235 Main Street, Suite 103
Trussville, AL 35173
(205) 655-7062

Birmingham Barons
Aff: Chicago White Sox
PO Box 3972
1137 Second Avenue West
Birmingham, AL 35208
(205) 781-1117

Charlotte O's
Aff: Baltimore Orioles
Crockett Park
400 Magnolia Avenue
Charlotte, NC 28203
(704) 377-3827

Chattanooga Lookouts
Aff: Seattle Mariners
PO Box 11002
Fifth & O'Neal
Chattanooga, TN 37401
(615) 267-2208

Columbus Astros
Aff: Houston Astros
Golden Park
Fourth Street
PO Box 2425
Columbus, GA 31902
(404) 324-3594

Greenville Braves
Aff: Atlanta Braves
1 Braves Avenue
PO Box 16683
Greenville, SC 29606
(803) 299-3456

Huntsville Stars
Aff: Oakland A's
PO Box 14099
Huntsville, AL 35815
(205) 882-2562

Jacksonville Expos
Aff: Montreal Expos
Wolfson Stadium
1201 East Duval Street
PO Box 4756
Jacksonville, FL 32201
(904) 358-2846

Knoxville Blue Jays
Aff: Toronto Blue Jays
Meyer Stadium
633 Jessamine Street
Knoxville, TN 37917
(615) 637-9494

Memphis Chicks
Aff: Kansas City Royals
McCarver Stadium
800 Home Run Lane
Memphis, TN 38104
(901) 272-1687

Orlando Twins
Aff: Minnesota Twins
Tinker Field
287 South Tampa Avenue
PO Box 5645
Orlando, FL 32805
(305) 849-6346

Texas Baseball League (AA)
10201 West Markham Street
Suite 214
Little Rock, AR 72205
(501) 227-7703

Arkansas Travelers
Aff: St. Louis Cardinals
PO Box 5599
Little Rock, AR 72215
(501) 664-1555

Beaumont Golden Gators
Aff: San Diego Padres
PO Box 2707
Beaumont, TX 77704
(409) 832-2255

El Paso Diablos
Aff: Milwaukee Brewers
PO Box 9337
El Paso, TX 79984
(915) 544-1950

Jackson Mets
Aff: New York Mets
PO Box 4209
Jackson, MS 39216
(601) 981-4664

Midland Angels
Aff: California Angels
PO Box 12
Midland, TX 79702
(915) 683-4251

San Antonio Dodgers
Aff: Los Angeles Dodgers
PO Box 28268
San Antonio, TX 78228
(512) 434-9311

Shreveport Captains
Aff: San Francisco Giants
PO Box 3448
Shreveport, LA 71103
(318) 636-5555

Tulsa Drillers
Aff: Texas Rangers
PO Box 4773
Tulsa, OK 74159
(918) 744-5901

California League (A)
1060 Willow, Suite 6
San Jose, CA 95125
(408) 977-1977

Carolina League (A)
4241 United Street
Greensboro, NC 27407
(919) 294-3365

Florida State League (A)
PO Box 414
Lakeland, FL 33802
(813) 683-7233

Midwest League (A)
PO Box 936
Beloit, WI 53511
(608) 364-1188

New York-Pennsylvania League (A)
PO Box 1313
Auburn, NY 13021
(716) 825-0855

Northwest League (A)
PO Box 30025
Portland, OR 97230
(503) 256-0085

South Atlantic League (A)
PO Box 49
Kings Mountain, NC 28086
(704) 739-3466

■ ORGANIZATIONS— INTERNATIONAL

AUSTRALIA
Australian Baseball Federation
3/98 Burbridge Road
Hilton, SA 5033

FRANCE
Federation Francaise de Base-Ball et Soft Ball
23 rue d'Anjou
75008 Paris
France

CARIBBEAN
Caribbean Baseball Conferation
Apartado 1852
Hato Rey, Puerto Rico 00919

DOMINICAN REPUBLIC
Dominican Winter League
Apartado 1246
Santo Domingo
Dominican Republic

JAPAN
Japan Pro Baseball
Imperial Tower
1-1-1 Uchisaiwaicho
Chiyoda-ku, Tokyo 100
Juhei Takeuchi, Commissioner

Japan Central League
Asahi Building, 5F
6-6-7 Ginza
Chuo-ku, Tokyo 104

Chunichi Dragons
4-1-1 Sakae
Naka-ku, Nagoya-shi
Aichi-ken

Hanshin Tigers
Chiyoda Building
2-5-8 Umeida
Kita-ku, Osaka-shi

Hiroshima Toyo Carp
5-25 Motomachi
Hiroshima-shi, Hiroshima-ken

Yakult Swallows
1-1-19 Shimbashi
Minato-ku

Yokohama Taiyo Whales
4-43 Masagocho
Naka-ku, Yokohama-shi

Yomiuri Giants
1-7-1 Otemachi
Chiyoda-ku

Japan Pacific League
Asahi Building, 9F
6-6-7 Ginza
Cho-ku, Tokyo 104

Hankyu Braves
Hankyu Grand Building
8-47 Kakutamachi
Kita-ku, Osaka-shi

Kintetsu Buffaloes
Kintetsu Namba Building
4-1-5 Namba
Minami-ku, Osaka-shi

Lotte Orions
2-2-33 Hyakunincho
Shinjuku-ku

Nankai Hawks
2-8-110 Namba Naka
Naniwa-ku, Osaka-shi

Nippon Ham Fighters
Roppongi Denki Building
6-1-20 Roppongi
Minato-ku

Seibu Lions
Sunshine Building
3-1-1 Higashi-Ikebukuro
Toshima-ku

Japan Collegiate Baseball Association
Natori Building
2-22-8 Shibuya
Shibuya-ku

Tokyo Big Six University Baseball League
Natori Building
2-22-8 Shibuya
Shibuya-ku

MEXICO

Mexican League
Angel Pola #16
Col. Periodista
CP 11220 Mexico, D.F. Mexico

Mexican Pacific League
Pesqueira No. 613-B Sur.
Navojoa, Sonora, Mexico

PUERTO RICO

Puerto Rican Winter League
Avenida Munoz Rivera #1056
Apartado 1852
Hato Rey, PR 00919

UNITED KINGDOM

Baseball Association of Great Britain
78 Connaught Road
Barnet, Herts
England EN5 2PY

British Amateur Baseball and Softball Federation
197 Newbridge Road
Hull
England HU9 2LR

Welsh Baseball Union
42 Heol Hir
Llanishen, Cardiff
(0222) 759474

VENEZUELA

Venezuelan Winter League
Avenida Sorbona
Edif. Marta-2do. Piso, No. 25
Colinas de Bello Monte
Caracas, Venezuela

■ PROFESSIONAL ORGANIZATIONS

Association of Professional Ball Players of America
12062 Valley View Street,
Suite 211
Garden Grove, CA 92645
(714) 892-9900

Baseball Alumni Team
350 Park Avenue
New York, NY 10022
(212) 371-7800

Baseball Commissioner's Office
350 Park Avenue
New York, NY 10022
(212) 371-7800
Commissioner, Peter Ueberroth

Baseball Writers Association of America
36 Brookfield Road
Fort Salonga, NY 11768
(516) 757-0562

Canadian Baseball Hall of Fame
PO Box 4008, Station A
Toronto, Ont M5W 2R1

Major League Baseball Players Alumni Association
2 Skyline Place
5203 Leesburg Pike
Falls Church, VA 22041

Major League Baseball Players Association
805 Third Avenue
New York, NY 10022
(212) 826-0808

Major League Baseball Productions
1212 Avenue of the Americas
New York, NY 10036
(212) 921-8100

Major League Baseball Promotion Corporation
350 Park Avenue
New York, NY 10022
(212) 371-7800

Major League Baseball Umpire
Development Program
Box A
St. Petersburg, FL 33731
(813) 823-1286

Major League Umpires Association
1 Logan Square
Philadelphia, PA 19103
(215) 568-7368

Major League Scouting Bureau
1400 Quail Street, Suite 150
Newport Beach, CA 92660
(714) 752-0712

National Association of Professional Baseball Leagues
PO Box A
201 Bayshore Drive Southeast
St. Petersburg, FL 33731
(813) 822-6937

■ AMATEUR ORGANIZATIONS

All American Amateur Baseball Association
c/o Tom J. Checkush, Secy.
340 Walker Drive
Zanesville, OH 43701
(614) 453-7349

American Amateur Baseball Congress
215 East Green
Marshall, MI 49068
(616) 781-2002

American Baseball Coaches Association
1614 North Lincoln
Urbana, IL 61801
(217) 328-7780

American Legion Baseball
PO Box 1055
Indianapolis, IN 46206
(317) 635-8411

Babe Ruth Baseball
PO Box 5000
1770 Brunswick Avenue
Trenton, NJ 08638
(609) 695-1434

Baseball Canada/Canadian Federation of Amateur Baseball
33 River Road
Ottawa, Ontario, Canada K1L 8H9
(613) 748-5606

Little League Baseball Incorporated
PO Box 3485
Williamsport, PA 17701
(717) 326-1921

National Amateur Baseball Federation
2201 North Townline Road
Rose City, MI 48654
(517) 685-2990

National Association of Leagues, Umpires and Scorers
Box 1420
Wichita, KS 67201
(316) 267-7333

National Baseball Congress
PO Box 1382
Buffalo, NY 14240
(716) 878-8574

Pony Baseball
PO Box 225
Washington, PA 15301
(412) 225-1060

U.S. Baseball Federation
2160 Greenwood Avenue
Trenton, NJ 08609
(609) 586-2381

■ RESEARCH ORGANIZATIONS

Elias Sports Bureau
500 Fifth Avenue
New York, NY 10017
(212) 869-1530

National Baseball Hall of Fame & Museum
Box 590
Cooperstown, NY 13326
(607) 547-9988

Society For American Baseball Research
Administrative Offices:
PO Box 10033
Kansas City, MO 64111
(816) 561-1320
Research Inquiries:
PO Box 1010
Cooperstown, NY 13326

Sports Information Center
1776 Heritage Drive
North Quincy, MA 02171
(617) 328-4674

■ COMPUTING AND BOARD GAMES

Allstar Baseball Solitaire
4820 Westgrove Drive #3207
Dallas, TX 75248
(214) 931-5732

All-Star Baseball
4300 West 47th Street
Chicago, IL 60632
(312) 927-1500

APBA
PO Box 4547
Lancaster, PA 17604
(717) 394-6161

Baseball Challenge
PO Box 47240
Phoenix, AZ 85068
(602) 863-6677

Baseball in Miniature
PO Box 229
Williston Park, NY 11501

Batter Swings
1 Pat Street
Winslow, ME 04901
(207) 873-0711

Big League Baseball
PO Box 16750
Rocky River, OH 44116

Big League Manager
321 East Superior Street
Duluth, MN 55802
(218) 722-1275

Boxscore Baseball
PO Box 610
Sagle, ID 83860
(208) 263-0305

Classic Major League Baseball
1640 Powers Ferry #17
Marietta, GA 30067
(404) 951-8051

Computer Sports Connoisseurs
PO Box 5147
Topeka, KS 66605
(913) 862-9090

Don Mattingly Baseball
3 Drawbridge Court
Baltimore, MD 21228
(301) 747-1422

Dugout Decisions
3116 South 99th Street
Fort Smith, AR 72903
(501) 452-7131

Fanball Sports Leagues
7560 Carlisle Road
Wellsville, PA 17365

Fantasy League Baseball
PO Box 10362
Bainbridge Island, WA 98110
(206) 842-1600

Full Count
PO Box 100594
Nashville, TN 37210
(615) 242-2617

General Manager Baseball League
PO Box 19757
San Diego, CA 92119
(619) 465-BALL

Grand Slam Baseball Trivia Game
Grand Slam Pastimes, Inc.
PO Box 2049
Elizabethtown, KY 42701

Held Sports Games
PO Box 2327
Valparaiso, IN 46384
(219) 465-7082

It's a Hit
8616 Fallsdale Drive
Charlotte, NC 28214
(704) 399-8168

J & J Computer Sports
PO Box 98
East Northport, NY 11731
(516) 266-2622

King of the Diamond
PO Box 3055
Manitowoc, WI 54220
(414) 684-6456

L & L Activities
PO Box 3026
Terre Haute, IN 47803
(812) 238-1601

Micro League Baseball
2201 Drummond Plaza
Newark, DE 19711
(800) PLAY-BAL

National Pastime
5628 North Division #142
Spokane, WA 99207

Pinstripe Glory
PO Box 1288
Woodbridge, NJ 07095

Pro Manager
4517 Harford Road
Baltimore, MD 21214
(301) 254-5300

Pursue the Pennant
PO Box 1045
Brookfield, WI 53008
(414) 784-5066

Realistic Baseball
Box 375
West Point, PA 19486
(215) 641-5202

Replay Baseball
100 Park Avenue
Carmichaels, PA 15320
(412) 966-2559

**Rotisserie League Baseball
Association**
211 West 92nd Street, Box 9
New York, NY 10025
(212) 496-8098

Scoresheet Baseball
21 Avenida Drive
Berkeley, CA 94708
(415) 526-3115

Simulated Sports Services
MacCormack Building #2871
Boston, MA 02101
(800) 832-6777

Statis-Pro Baseball
4517 Harford Road
Baltimore, MD 21214
(301) 254-5300

Stat-Sports Baseball
R.R. 1
Madrid, IA 50156
(515) 795-2617

Strat-O-Matic
46 Railroad Plaza
Glen Head, NY 11545
(516) 671-6566

Sun Sports
PO Box 199
Cheltenham, PA 19012
(215) 663-9460

Super Fan Baseball
3208 North Tucson Boulevard
Tuscon, AZ 85716
(602) 882-2226

True Action Baseball
890 South Cleveland Avenue #8
St. Paul, MN 55116

Walter Mitty Baseball
14881 Dunbarton Place
Miami Lakes, FL 33016
(305) 823-2735

World Series Baseball
PO Box 1145
Carrollton, TX 75006

■ **COLLECTIBLES**

Baseball Hobby News
4540 Kearny Villa Road, Suite 215
San Diego, CA 92123-1573

Big League Cards, Inc.
121 Cedar Lane
Teaneck, NJ 07666-4499
(201) 692-8228

Donruss
975 Kansas Street
Memphis, TN 38106
(901) 775-2960

Fleer
10th and Somerville
Philadelphia, PA 19141
(800) 523-3650

**Major League Marketing
(Sportflics)**
1 Dock Street
Stamford, CT 06902
(203) 359-2999

Sports Collectors Digest
700 East State Street
Iola, WI 54990
(715) 445-2214

Topps
254 36th Street
Brooklyn, NY 11232
(718) 768-8900

■ **PUBLICATIONS**

Amateur Baseball News
215 East Green
Marshall, MI 49068
(616) 781-2002

Baseball America
PO Box 2089
Durham, NC 27702
(800) 845-2726
(919) 682-9635

Baseball Blue Book, Inc.
PO Box 40847
7225 30th Avenue North
St. Petersburg, FL 33743
(813) 334-3545

Baseball Bulletin
PO Box 960
Rochester, MI 48063
(313) 879-1676

Baseball Digest
1020 Church Street
Evanston, Il 60201
(312) 491-6440

Baseball History
Meckler Publishing
11 Ferry Lane
Westport, CT 06880
(203) 226-6967

BaseWoman
PO Box 2292
Glenview, IL 60025

Bullpen
1770 Brunswick Avenue
PO Box 5000
Trenton, NJ 08638
(609) 695-1434

Collegiate Baseball
PO Box 50566
Tucson, AZ 85703
(602) 623-7495

*Japan Pro Baseball Fan
Handbook*
4-19-5 Kichijoji Honcho
Musashino-shi, Tokyo-to
Japan 180
(0422) 22-3208

*Major League Baseball
Yearbook*
1115 Broadway
New York, NY 10010
(212) 807-7100

Major League Monthly
PO Box 355
Jamaica, NY 11415

Pony Baseball Express
300 Clare Drive
Washington, PA 15301
(412) 225-1060

Spitball
6224 Collegevue Place
Cincinnati, OH 45224
(513) 541-4296

Street & Smith's Baseball Yearbook
304 East 45th Street
New York, NY 10017
(212) 880-8698

The National Pastime
c/o John Thorn
18 Virginia Avenue
Saugerties, NY 12477
(914) 246-1102

Who's Who in Baseball
1115 Broadway
New York, NY 10010
(212) 807-7100

■ **PROFESSIONAL CAMPS**

Doyle Baseball School
PO Box 9156, Dept. SN-79
Winter Haven, FL 33883
(813) 293-8994 or
(800) 345-SCOUT

Joe Brinkman Umpire School
1021 Indian River Drive
Cocoa, FL 32922
(305) 639-1515

Major League Baseball Tryout
PO Box 6207
Evanston, IL 60204

New York School of Umpiring
PO Box 238
White Plains, NY 10602
(914) 683-5757

The Baseball School
490 Dotterel Road
Delray Beach, FL 33444
(305) 265-0280

■ **CAMPS**

Roger Smith Baseball Camp
Baseball Office
University of Alabama
PO Box K
University, AL 35486
(205) 348-6161
(B)

NAU Baseball Camp
Northern Arizona University
Box 15400
Flagstaff, AZ 86011-0045
(602) 523-3550
(B)

*Superstar Baseball Camp
5764 Paradise Drive, Suite 7
Corte Madera, CA 94925
(415) 924-8725
(B)

Baseball Camp
University of California-Davis
Davis, CA 95616
1-800-752-0881
(916) 752-0080

Al Ferrer UCSB Baseball Camp
3271 Highway 246
Santa Ynez, CA 93460
(805) 688-6642
(B)

*Falcon Sport Camps
Sports Ticket Office
Jim Hanley, USAFA
Colorado Springs, CO 80840-5461
(303) 472-1895
(B)

Connecticut Professional
Baseball School
2546 Cropsey Avenue
Brooklyn, NY 11214
(718) 728-3799 (in NY)
(203) 754-9055 (in CT)

UCF Summer Baseball Camps
Jay Bergman
Athletic Department
University of Central Florida
Orlando, FL 32816-0555
(B)

Georgia Tech/Jim Morris
Baseball Camp
Georgia Tech Athletic Association
150 Third Street N.W.
Atlanta, GA 30332
(B)

Baseball Camp
Southeastern All-Sports Complex
Bob and Lou Hattaway, General
Managers
Gainesville Street
Carnesville, GA 30521
(404) 384-4516
(B)

Redbird Specialty Baseball
Camp
College of Continuing
Education and Public Service
Illinois State University
Normal, IL 61761
(309) 438-8691
(B)

Midwest Baseball School
Iowa State University
204 State Gym
Ames, IA 50011
(515) 294-4132
(B)

Kansas Jayhawk Baseball Camp
Allen Field House
University of Kansas
Lawrence, KS 66045
(B)

MSU Baseball Camp
c/o Steve Hamilton
Morehead State University
Morehead, KY 40351
(B)

Skip Bertman Baseball Camp
Louisiana State University
PO Box 16355
Baton Rouge, LA 70893
(504) 388-4148
(504) 388-4150
(B)

All American Baseball Camp
6 Ridge Road
Milford, MA 01757
(617) 478-6596
(B)

Baseball Camp
Michigan Campus of Champions
1000 South State Street
Ann Arbor, MI 48109
(313) 763-6767
(B)

Maverick Baseball Camp
Box 28
Mankato State University
Mankato, MN 56001
(507) 389-2689
(501) 389-6111 (day)
(507) 388-9195 (evening)
(B)

Ole Miss Baseball Camp
University of Mississippi
Division of Continuing Education
University, MS 38677
(601) 232-7241
(B)

Sho-Me Baseball Camps
c/o Phil Wilson
Star Route 4
Box 198
Reed Springs, MO 65737
(417) 338-2603
(B)

Baseball U.S.A. Camps
PO Box 1134
Mountainside, NJ 07092
(201) 277-3715
(B)

Baseball Camp
Cornell Summer Sports School
PO Box 729
Cornell University
Ithaca, NY 14851
(607) 255-7333
(B)

West Point Baseball Camp
Bill Permakoff, Director
Athletic Department
Building 639 ODIA
West Point, NY 10996
(B)

Baseball Camp
UNC-W Athletic Dept.
University of North Carolina at
Wilmington
601 South College Road
Wilmington, NC 28403-3297
(B)

Baseball Camp
Dick Finn or Joe Carbone
Baseball Office
Ohio State University
Room 212
St. John Arena
410 Woody Hayes Drive
Columbus, OH 43210
(B)

Baseball Camp
Xavier Summer Camps
Xavier University
O'Connor Sports Center
Cincinnati, OH 45207
(513) 745-3208
(B)

Enos Semore Baseball Camp
University of Oklahoma
401 W. Imhoff
Norman, OK 73069
(405) 325-8201
(405) 325-8271
(B)

Boys Baseball Camp
The Pennsylvania State University
410 Keller Conference Center
University Park, PA 16802
(814) 865-7557
(B)

Baseball Camp
Coach Bill Wilhelm
102 Berry Street
Clemson, SC 29631
(803) 654-5801
(B)

UT Baseball Camp
Box 47
Knoxville, TN 37901
(615) 974-1261
(B)

Red Raider Baseball Camp
c/o Division of Continuing
Education
Box 4110
Texas Tech University
Lubbock, TX 79409-4110
(806) 742-2352

Baseball Camp
Brigham Young University
Summer Sports Camps
Conferences and Workshops
154 HCEB
Provo, UT 84602
(801) 378-4903

Hitter's Camp
Sports Camps, Inc.
RR 1, Box 213
River Falls, WI 54022
(715) 425-3135
(B)

*Golden Bear and Panda
Summer Sports Programs
Department of Athletic Services
Pavillion 220
University of Alberta
Edmonton, Alberta
Canada T6G 2H9
(403) 432-3534
(B)

■ INDIVIDUALS

Hank Aaron
1611 Adams Drive, SW
Atlanta, GA 30311

Joe Adcock
Box 385
Coushatta, LA 71019

Dick Allen
PO Box 204
Sellersville, PA 18960

Sparky Anderson
4077 N. Verde Vista Drive
Thousand Oaks, CA 91360

Joaquin Andujar
Juan Deacosta #10A
San Pedro De Marcoris
Dominican Republic

Luis Aparicio
Calle 67 #26-82
Maracaibo, Venezuela

Luke Appling
RR 7
Bragg Road
Cummings, GA 30130

Tony Armas
Los Mercedes #37
P. Piritu Edo
Venezuela

Richie Ashburn
Ardmore, Pa 19003

Earl Averill
1806 19th Drive, Northeast
Auburn, WA 98002

Roberto Avila
Navegantes Fr-19 Reforma
Veracruz, Mexico

Wally Backman
160 Southeast 39th Street
Hillsboro, OR 97123

Jim Bagby, Jr.
1910 South Cobb Drive #4B
Marietta, GA 30060

Harold Baines
107 Trusty Street
Saint Michael, MD 21663

Dusty Baker
24525 Palermo Drive
Calabasas, CA 91302

Steve Balboni
28 Celeste Street
Manchester, NH 03103

George Bamberger
455 North Bath Club Boulevard
Redington Beach, FL 33708

Sal Bando
104 West Juniper Lane
Mequon, WI 53092

Ernie Banks
10660 Wilshire Boulevard #408
West Los Angeles, CA 90024

Steve Barber
Toyota West
2025 South Decatur Boulevard
Las Vegas, NV 89102

Larry Barnett
6464 Hughes Road
Prospect, OH 43342

Kevin Bass
1971 Byers Drive
Menlo Park, CA 94025

Don Baylor
250 Truman
Box 476
Cresskill, NJ 07626

Glenn Beckert
870 Virginia Lake Court
Palatine, IL 60067

Mark Belanger
2028 Pot Spring Road
Timonium, MD 21093

Bo Belinsky
53567 Kam Highway #111
Hauula, HI 96717

Buddy Bell
6485 Hunters Trail
Cincinnati, OH 45243

Gus Bell
Minuteman
1010 Race Street
Cincinnati, OH 45202

James "Cool Papa" Bell
3034 Dickson Street
St. Louis, MO 63106

Johnny Bench
Box 2486
Cincinnati, OH 45201

Yogi Berra
19 Highland Avenue
Montclair, NJ 07042

Bill Bevens
5067 8th Avenue NE
Salem, OR 97303

Ewell Blackwell
84 Uloque Court
Brevard, NC 28712

John Blanchard
15541 Larkin Drive
Minnetonka, MN 55343

Vida Blue
PO Box 14438
Oakland, CA 94614

Bert Blyleven
18992 Canyon Drive
Villa Park, CA 92667

Mike Boddicker
Box 21
Norway, IA 52318

Wade Boggs
599 Marmora Avenue
Tampa, FL 33606

Ray Boone
15420 Olde Highway 80 #137
El Cajon, CA 92021

Lou Boudreau
15600 Ellis Avenue
Dolton, IL 60419

Jim Bouton
6 Myron Court
Teaneck, NJ 07666

Larry Bowa
315 Magnolia Drive
Clearwater, FL 33516

Dennis "Oil Can" Boyd
1611 20th Street
Meridian, MS 39301

Clete Boyer
695 Clearwater Harbor Drive
Largo, FL 33540

Ralph Branca
791 North Street
White Plains, NY 10605

George Brett
3201 West 98th Street
Leawood, KS 66206

Greg Brock
427 Windflower
Placentia, CA 92670

Lou Brock
12595 Durbin Drive
St. Louis, MO 63141

Hubie Brooks
1502 Spring Avenue
Compton, CA 90221

Tom Brunansky
1319 South Hillward Avenue
West Covina, CA 91791

Al Bumbry
28 Tremblant Court
Lutherville, MD 21093

Lew Burdette
2837 Gulf of Mexico Drive
Longboat Key, FL 33548

Smokey Burgess
717 Carollen Road
Forest City, NC 28043

Rick Burleson
270 East Mira Verde Drive
Lahabra Heights, CA 90631

Jeff Burroughs
6155 Laguna Court
Long Beach, CA 90803

Brett Butler
2236 Lunceford Lane
Lilburn, GA 30247

Dolph Camilli
2831 Hacienda Street
San Mateo, CA 94403

Roy Campanella
6213 Capistrano
Woodland Hills, CA 9167

Bert Campaneris
1021 Southwest First Avenue #2
Miami, FL 33130

José Canseco
2530 Southwest 102nd Avenue
Miami, FL 33165

Bernie Carbo
908 Winchester
Lincoln Park, MI 48146

Rod Carew
5144 Crescent Drive
Anaheim, CA 92807

Steve Carlton
16240 Holts Lake Drive
Chesterfield, MO 63017

Gary Carter
2259 Conego Lane
Fullerton, CA 92623

Norm Cash
4522 Rolling Pines Court
West Bloomfield, MI 48033

Phil Cavarretta
2206 Portside Passage
Palm Harbor, FL 33563

Cesar Cedeno
77 Carpenter Ridge
Blue Ash, OH 45241

Orlando Cepeda
1916 Church Street #A
Burbank, CA 91504

Rick Cerone
63 Eisenhower Avenue
Cresskill, NJ 07626

Chris Chambliss
54 Ivy Chase
Atlanta, GA 30342

Albert "Happy" Chandler
191 Elm Street
Versailles, KY 40383

Joe Charboneau
44 High Street
Lockport, NY 14094

Jim Clancy
6147 Robroy Street
Oak Forest, IL 60452

Jack Clark
602 Cornwallis
Foster City, CA 94404

Roger Clemens
10131 Beekman Place Drive
Houston, TX 77043

Rocky Colavito
Box 1969
Kansas City, MO 64141

Nate Colbert
17369 Ruetto Beto
San Diego, CA 92127

Vince Coleman
3810 North Canal Street #207
Jacksonville, FL 32209 (old)

Eddie Collins
Box 206
Kennet Square, PA 19348

Dave Concepcion
Urb. Los Caobos Botalon 5D
5 Piso-Marcay, Venezuela

Tony Conigliaro
339 Nahant Road
Nahant, MA 01908

Jocko Conlan
7810 East Mariposa Drive
Scottsdale, AZ 85251

Gene Conley
4 Birchtree Road
Foxboro, MA 02035

Chuck Conners
Star Route Box 4400-73
Tehachapi, CA 93561

Cecil Cooper
Box 213
Sealy, TX 77474

Roger Craig
2453 Canora Avenue
Alpine, CA 92331

Jose Cruz
B-15 Jardines Lafayette
Arroyo, Puerto Rico 00615

Mike Cuellar
Block-5 Drive Villalobos Street
Levittown Lakes, Puerto Rico 00632

Alvin Dark
103 Cranberry Way
Easley, SC 29640

Ron Darling
19 Woodland Street
Millbury, MA 01527

Eric Davis
6606 Denver Avenue #1
Los Angeles, CA 90044

Glenn Davis
PO Box 14025
Savannah, GA 31416

Tommy Davis
9767 Whirlaway
Alta Loma, CA 91701

Willie Davis
4419 Buena Vista #203
Dallas, TX 75202

Andre Dawson
6295 Southwest 58th Place
Miami, FL 33143

Doug DeCinces
9411 Hazel Circle
Villa Park, CA 92667

Rob Deer
230 Hillcrest Street
Anaheim, CA 92807

Bucky Dent
17 West 544 Sutton Place
Westmont, IL 60559

Bill Dickey
114 East 5th Street
Little Rock, AR 72203

Dom DiMaggio
162 Point Road
Marion, MA 02738

Joe DiMaggio
2150 Beach Street
San Francisco, CA 94123

Larry Doby
Nishuane Road-45
Montclair, NJ 07042

Bobby Doerr
33705 Illamo Agness Road
Agness, OR 97406

Moe Drabowsky
530 Audubon Place
Highland Park, IL 60035

Walt Dropo
65 East India Row #31C
Boston, MA 02109

Don Drysdale
78 Colgate
Rancho Mirage, CA 92270

Bill Duran
5309 East Knoll Court #517
Cincinnati, OH 45239

Leon Durham
3932 Dickson Avenue
Cincinnati, OH 45229

Leo Durocher
1400 East Palm Canyon #210
Palm Springs, CA 92262

Lenny Dykstra
2701 Shenandoah Drive
Laguna Hills, CA 92653

Mike Easler
14901 Milverton
Cleveland, OH 44120

Dennis Eckersly
263 Morse Road
Sudbury, MA 01776

Dock Ellis
121 East 139th Street
Los Angeles, CA 90061

Del Ennis
712 Woodside Road
Jenkintown, PA 19046

Darrell Evans
354 Provencal
Detroit, MI 48231

Dwight Evans
3 Jordan Road
Lynnfield, MA 01940

Roy Face
608 Della Drive #5F
North Versaille, PA 15137

Ron Fairly
23140 Park Sorrento
Calabasas, CA 91302

Bob Feller
Box 157
Gates Mills, OH 44040

Sid Fernandez
992C Awaawaanoa Place
Honolulu, HI 96825

Rick Ferrell
2199 Golfview #203
Troy, MI 48084

Mark Fidrych
259 Crawford
Northborough, MA 01532

Rollie Fingers
1268 Hidden Mountain Drive
El Cajon, CA 92020

Carlton Fisk
16612 Catawba Road
Lockport, IL 60441

Mike Flanagan
35 Eagle Rock
Amherst, NH 03031

Curt Flood
2368 Monticello Avenue
Oakland, CA 94611

Whitey Ford
38 Schoolhouse Lane
Lake Success, NY 11020

Bob Forsch
428 Hickory Glen Lane
St. Louis, MO 63141

Julio Franco
Cf 16 B. Libre Ing Cons.
San Pedro De Macoris
Dominican Republic

Bill Freehan
4248 Sunningdale
Bloomfield Hills, MI 48013

Jim Fregosi
18772 Winnwood Lane
Santa Ana, CA 92705

Jim Frey
1805 Reuter Road
Timonium, MD 21093

Woodie Fryman
RR 1 Box 21
Ewing, KY 41039

Carl Furillo
1415 Carsonia Avenue
Stony Creek Mills, PA 19606

Joe Garagiola
6221 East Huntress Drive
Paradise Valley, AZ 85253

Phil Garner
Box 288
Houston, TX 77001

Ralph Garr
7819 Chaseway Drive
Missouri City, TX 77459

Ned Garver
Box 114
Ney, OH 43549

Steve Garvey
4320 Lajolla Village Drive
San Diego, CA 92122

Charlie Gehringer
32301 Lasher Road
Birmingham, MI 48010

Cesar Geronimo
Tefada Flo. #56
Santo Domingo,
Dominican Republic

Bob Gibson
215 Belleview Boulevard South
Belleview, NE 68005

Al Gionfriddo
64 Bristol Place
Goleta, CA 93117

Dan Gladden
888 Brook Grove Lane
Cupertino, CA 05014

Lefty Gomez
26 San Benito Way
Novato, CA 94947

Dwight Gooden
3101 East Elm Street
Tampa, FL 33610

Rich Gossage
10565 Viacha Way
San Diego, CA 92124

Pete Gray
203 Phillips Street
Nanticoke, PA 18634

Hank Greenberg
1129 Miradero Road
Beverly Hills, CA 90210

Alfredo Griffin
B#3 B Hatomayor Ing Cons
San Pedro De Macoris
Dominican Republic

Ross Grimsley
39 Judges Lane
Towson, MD 21204

Dick Groat
320 Beach Street
Pittsburgh, PA 15218

Jerry Grote
148-26 Willow Bend
San Antonio, TX 78232

Ron Guidry
109 Conway
Lafayette, LA 70507

Harvey Haddix
4001 Vernon Ashbury Road
South Vienna, OH 45369

Mel Hall
RR1 Route 90
Cayaga, NY 13034

Bill Haller
2013 South Lake Drive
Vandalia, IL 62471

Mel Harder
130 Center Street #6A
Chardon, OH 44024

Tommy Harper
3 Christopher Drive
Stoughton, MA 02072

Toby Harrah
824 Chapparral
Bedford, TX 76021

Bud Harrelson
31 Falcon Drive
Hauppauge, NY 11787

Richie Hebner
510 Nathan Street
Norwood, MA 02062

Woodie Held
Big Diamond Ranch
Dubois, WY 82513

Rickey Henderson
10561 Englewood Drive
Oakland, CA 94621

Elrod Hendricks
3707 Brownbrook Court
Randallstown, MD 21133

Billy Herman
3111 Garden East #33
Palm Beach Gardens, FL 33410

Keith Hernandez
1300 Christmas Valley
Chesterfield, MD 63017

Willie Hernandez
Bo Espina Calle C Box 125
Aguada, Puerto Rico 00602

Tommy Herr
1077 Old Forge Crossing
Lancaster, PA 17601

Whitey Herzog
3613 South Forest
Independence, MO 64052

John Hiller
Star Route 1, Box 176
Iron Mountain, MI 49801

Larry Hisle
PO Box 84 c/o Ferguson
Portsmouth, OH 45662

Butch Hobson
1422 Clarendon Avenue
Bessemer, AL 35020

Ken Holtzman
933 Providence Street
Buffalo Grove, IL 60089

Bob Horner
1660 Chevron Way
Dunwoody, GA 30338

Willie Horton
19312 Steel Street
Detroit, MI 48235

Ralph Houk
2941 Northeast 23rd Court
Pompano Beach, Fl 33062

Carl Hubbell
Suncrest Apartment #8
130 North Leseuer #1
Mesa, AZ 83205

Ron Hunt
2806 Jackson Road
Wentsville, MO 63385

Catfish Hunter
RR 1 Box 895
Hertford, NC 27944

Bruce Hurst
539 Churchill Drive
St. George, UT 84770

Monte Irvin
104 Sycamore Circle
Homosassa, FL 32646

Bo Jackson
PO Box 2517
Auburn, AL 36831-2517

Danny Jackson
31 Newark #C
Aurora, CO 80012

Reggie Jackson
22 Yankee Hill
Oakland, CA 94616

Travis Jackson
101 South Olive Street
Waldo, AR 71770

Julian Javier
B#12 Urb. Pina
San Francisco de Macoris
Dominican Republic

Ferguson Jenkins
Box 275
Blenheim, Ontario
Canada

Tommy John
3133 North 16th Street
Terre Haute, IN 47804

William "Judy" Johnson
3701 Kiamensi
Marshalltown, DE 19808

Randy Jones
15358 Midland Road
Poway, CA 92064

Billy Jurges
7001 142nd Avenue #74
Largo, FL 33541

Jim Kaat
Box 86
Glen Mills, PA 19342

Al Kaline
945 Timberlake Drive
Bloomfield Hills, MI 48013

George Kell
Box 158
Swifton, AR 72471

Ken Keltner
3220 King Arthur's Court West
Greenfield, WI 53221

Steve Kemp
32151 Sea Island #1
Laguna Niguel, CA 92677

Don Kessinger
2771 Clark Road
Memphis, TN 38115

Harmon Killebrew
Box 626
Ontario, OR 97914

Ralph Kiner
17 Legrande Avenue #17
Greenwich, CT 06830

Dave Kingman
818 West Busse Avenue
Mount Prospect, IL 60056

Ted Kluszewski
8353 Island Lane
Maineville, OH 45039

Ray Knight
RR 2 Box 380C
Albany, GA 31707

Sandy Koufax
PO Box BB
Carpenteria, CA 93013

Ed Kranepool
133-09 Blossom Avenue
Flushing, NY 11355

Tony Kubek
3311 North McDonald
Appleton, WI 54911

Harvey Kuenn
17406 Country Club
Sun City, AZ 85373

Bowie Kuhn
320 Murray Avenue
Ridgewood, NJ 07450

Clement Labine
Box 643
Woonsocket, RI 02895

Don Larsen
17090 Copper Hill Drive
Morgan Hill, CA 95037

Tom Lasorda
1473 West Maxzim
Fullerton, CA 92633

Cookie Lavagetto
46 Tara Road
Orinda, CA 94563

Rudy Law
10712 Felton Street
Inglewood, CA 90304

Vern Law
3885 West Little Rock Drive
Provo, UT 84601

Charlie Lea
4237 Fairmont Avenue
Memphis, TN 38108

Ron LeFlore
5126 Iroquois
Detroit, MI 48213

Bob Lemon
1141 Claiborne Drive
Long Beach, CA 90807

Buck Leonard
605 Atlantic Avenue
Rocky Mount, NC 27801

Dennis Leonard
4102 Evergreen Lane
Blue Springs, MO 64015

Mickey Lolich
6252 Robinhill
Washington, MI 48094

Jim Lonborg
498 First Parish Road
Scituate, MA 02066

Eddie Lopat
99 Oak Trail Road
Hillsdale, NJ 07642

Davey Lopes
16984 Avenue De Santa Ynez
Pacific Palisades, CA 90272

Al Lopez
3601 Beach Drive
Tampa, FL 33609

Sparky Lyle
107 Pine Terrace Drive
Demarest, NJ 07627

Fred Lynn
6961 East Via El Estribo
Anaheim Hills, CA 92807

Ted Lyons
1401 Loree Street
Vinton, LA 70668

Hal Macrae
1312 63rd Street NW
Bradenton, FL 33505

Bill Madlock
453 East Decatur Street
Decatur, IL 62521

Sal Maglie
77 Morningside Drive
Grand Island, NY 14072

Candy Maldonado
Buzon G-27, Bo. Dominguito
Arecibo, Puerto Rico 00612

Jim Maloney
2217 West Keats
Fresno, CA 93705

Frank Malzone
16 Aletha Road
Needham, MA 02192

Mickey Mantle
5730 Watson Circle
Dallas, TX 75225

Juan Marichal
Ed.Hache 3, Piso Este,
Kennedy Avenue
Santo Domingo,
Dominican Republic

Billy Martin
417 South Broad Street
New Orleans, LA 70119

Jon Matlack
8100 Shelton Drive
Fort Worth, TX 76112

Eddie Matthews
13744 Recuerdo Drive
Del Mar, CA 92014

Don Mattingly
Box 110 Browning Road
Evansville, IN 47711

Gene Mauch
46 La Ronda Drive
Rancho Mirage, CA 92270

Willie Mays
51 Mount Vernon Lane
Atherton, CA 94025

Bill Mazeroski
RR 6 Box 130
Greensburg, PA 15601

Lee Mazzilli
12 Carpenters Dark Road
Greenwich, CT 06830

Tim McCarver
1518 Youngford Road
Gladwynne, PA 19035

Willie McCovey
220 Crest Road
Woodside, CA 94062

Lindy McDaniel
5024 South Osage
Kansas City, MO 64133

Sam McDowell
7727 St. Lawrence Avenue
Pittsburgh, PA 15218

Willie McGee
2081 Lupine Road
Hercules, CA 94547

Tug McGraw
Colehill Rose Valley Road
Media, PA 19063

Dave McNally
3305 Ramada Drive
Billings, MT 59102

Kevin McReynolds
Camp Robinson
North Little Rock, AR 72118

Bill Melton
285 Beverly
Laguna Beach, CA 92651

Andy Messersmith
200 Lagunita Drive
Soquel, CA 95073

Gene Michael
30 Farrington Street
Closter, NJ 07624

Orestes Minoso
4250 Marin Drive
Chicago, IL 60613

Johnny Mize
Box 112
Demorest, GA 30535

Bill Monbouquette
271 Clark Hill Road
New Boston, NH 03070

Rick Monday
1056 Rashford Drive
Placentia, CA 92670

Wally Moon
Joe Courtney Insurance
Box 10088
College Station, TX 77840

Joe Morgan
5588 Fernhoff Road
Oakland, CA 94619

Lloyd Moseby
3400 Kingmont Drive
Loomis, CA 95650

Manny Mota
27 De Fabrero #445
Santa Domingo
Dominican Republic

Bobby Murcer
3244 Whippoorwill
Oklahoma City, OK

Dale Murphy
12055 Houze Road
Roswell, GA 30076

Eddie Murray
711 40th Street #450
Baltimore, MD 21211

Stan Musial
85 Trent Drive
Ladue, MO 63124

Ray Narleski
1183 Chews Landing Road
Laurel Springs, NJ 08021

Graig Nettles
13 North Lane
Del Mar, CA 92014

Hal Newhouser
2584 Marcy
Bloomfield Hills, MI 48013

Joe Niekro
214 Ash Lane
Lakeland, FL 33801

Phil Niekro
4781 Castlewood Drive
Lilburn, GA 30247

Jim Northrup
1326 Otter Drive
Pontiac, MI 48054

Joe Nuxhall
5706 Lindenwood Lane
Fairfield, OH 45014

Blue Moon Odom
10337 Slater Avenue #206
Fountain Valley, CA 92708

Ben Ogilvie
917 Bodark Lane
Austin, TX 78745

Bob Ojeda
14884 Road 312
Visalia, CA 93277

Tony Oliva
212 Spring Valley Drive
Bloomington, MN 55420

Jesse Orosco
1359 Tomol Road
Carpinteria, CA 93013

Claude Osteen
RR3 Box 453
Annville, PA 17003

Amos Otis
1327 Fairway Circle
Blue Springs, MO 64015

Tom Paciorek
2872 North Deshon Road
Stone Mountain, GA 30087

Andy Pafko
1420 Blackhawke Drive
Mount Prospect, IL 60056

Jim Palmer
Box 145
Brooklandville, MD 21022

Wes Parker
2140 Colorado Avenue
Santa Monica, CA 90404

Mel Parnell
700 Turquoise Street
New Orleans, LA 70124

Lance Parrish
960 West Hardsale
Bloomfield Hills, MI 48013

Freddie Patek
965 East Weinert Street
Sequin, TX 78155

Joe Pepitone
Lighthouse Road
Saugerties, NY 12477

Tony Perez
Los Flores 113
Santurce, Puerto Rico 00911

Ron Perranoski
18731 Martha Street
Tarzana, CA 91356

Gaylord Perry
RR 3 Box 565
Williamston, NC 27892

Jim Perry
5744 Duncan Lane
Minneapolis, MN 55436

Johnny Pesky
25 Parsons Drive
Swampscott, MA 01907

Gary Peters
2626 Espanola Avenue
Sarasota, FL 33580

Rico Petrocelli
19 Townsend Road
Lynnfield, MA 01940

Jimmy Piersall
1105 Oakview Drive
Wheaton, IL 60187

Lou Piniella
103 McIntyre Lane
Allendale, NJ 07401

Johnny Podres
1 Colonial Court
Glens Falls, NY 12801

Darrell Porter
3833 West 73rd Street
Milwaukee, WI 53216

Boog Powell
U.S. Anglers Marine
Key West, FL 33040

Kirby Puckett
7921 South Wolcott
Chicago, IL 60620

Dan Quisenberry
12208 Buena Vista
Leawood, KS 66209

Dick Radatz
830 West Chestnut Street
Brockton, MA 02401

Tim Raines
2316 Airport Boulevard
Sanford, FL 32771

Willie Randolph
648 Juniper Place
Franklin Lakes, NJ 07417

Johnny Ray
RR 1 Box 64
Chauteau, OK 74337

Pee Wee Reese
3211 Beals Branch Road
Louisville, KY 40206

Dusty Rhodes
245 Dixon Avenue
Staten Island, NY 10303

Jim Rice
RR 8 Box 686
Anderson, SC 29621

J. R. Richard
10235 Sagedale
Houston, TX 77089

Bobby Richardson
47 Adams
Sumter, SC 29150

Dave Righetti
1574 Koch Lane
San Jose, CA 95125

Cal Ripken Sr.
410 Clover Street
Aberdeen, MD 21001

Cal Ripken Jr.
410 Clover Street
Aberdeen, MD 21001

Phil Rizzuto
912 Westminster Avenue
Hillside, NJ 07205

Robin Roberts
504 Terrace Hill Drive
Temple Terrace, FL 33617

Brooks Robinson
1506 Sherbrook Road
Lutherville, MD 21093

Frank Robinson
15557 Aqua Verde Drive
Los Angeles, CA 90077

Preacher Roe
204 Wildwood Terrace
West Plains, MO 65775

Steve Rogers
2335 East Berkeley
Springfield, MO 65804

Cookie Rojas
15245 Melrose Drive
Stanley, KS 66221

Al Rosen
Box 24308
San Francisco, CA 94124

Edd Roush
122 39th Street Court NW
Bradenton, FL 33505

Joe Rudi
RR 1 Box 66
Baker, OR 97814

Pete Runnels
1106 Wilma-Lois Street
Pasadena, TX 77502

Nolan Ryan
719 Dezzo Drive
Alvin, TX 77511

Bret Saberhagen
19229 Arminta Street
Reseda, CA 91335

Johnny Sain
2 South 707 Avenue Latour
Oakbrook, IL 60521

Juan Samuel
Calle 1 #22 Restauracion
San Pedro De Marcoris
Domincan Republic

Ryne Sandberg
106 1/2 First Street Southwest
Brewster, WA 98812

Steve Sax
11 Westport
Manhattan Beach, CA 90266

Mike Schmidt
24 Lakewood Drive
Media, PA 19063

Red Schoendienst
331 Ladue Woods Court
Creve Couer, MO 63141

George Scott
1316 Goodrich Street
Greenville, MS 38701

Tom Seaver
Larkspur Lane
Greenwich, CT 06830

Joe Sewell
1618 Dearing Place
Tuscaloosa, AL 35401

Rip Sewell
827 Russell Drive
Plant City, FL 33566

Bobby Shantz
152 Mount Pleasant Avenue
Ambler, PA 19002

Lawrence Sherry
27181 Arena Lane
Mission Viejo, CA 92675

Ken Singleton
5 Tremblant Court
Lutherville, MD 21093

Bill Skowron
1118 Beachcomber Drive
Schaumburg, IL 60193

Enos Slaughter
RR 2
Roxboro, NC 27573

Reggie Smith
6157 Ellenview
Woodland Hills, CA 91367

Ozzie Smith
8004 Hillandale
San Diego, CA 92120

Duke Snider
3037 Lakemont Drive
Fallbrook, CA 92028

Warren Spahn
RR 2
Hartshorne, OK 74547

Eddie Stanky
2100 Spring Hill Road
Mobile, AL 36607

Willie Stargell
7232 Thomas Boulevard
Pittsburgh, PA 15208

Rusty Staub
1271 Third Avenue
New York, NY 10021

Dave Stieb
160 Sheffield Circle East
Palm Harbor, FL 33563

Steve Stone
4333 North Brown Avenue
Scottsdale, AZ 85251

Mel Stottlemyre
5804 West Chestnut Street
Yakima, WA 98908

Darryl Strawberry
1419 Red Bluff Court
San Dimas, CA 91773

Dick Stuart
c/o Thomas George
202 East Main Street
Huntington, NY 11743

B. J. Surhoff
239 Purchase Street
Rye, NY 10580

Rick Sutcliffe
313 NW North Shore Drive
Parkville, MO 64151

Bruce Sutter
1368 Hamilton Road
Kennesaw, GA 30144

Don Sutton
25442 Gallup Circle
Laguna Hills, CA 92653

Ron Swoboda
603 East Lamarche
Phoenix, AZ 85022

Frank Tanana
129 38th Street
Newport Beach, CA 92660

Chuck Tanner
34 Maitland Lane East
New Castle, PA 16101

Danny Tartabull
3912 Walnut Street
Tampa, FL 33607

Birdie Tebbetts
229 Oak Avenue
Anna Maria, FL 33501

Kent Tekulve
1531 Sequoia
Pittsburgh, PA 15241

Gary Templeton
13552 Del Pominte Road
Poway, CA 92064

Bill Terry
Box 2177
Jacksonville, FL 32203

Bobby Thomson
122 Sunlit Drive
Watchung, NJ 07060

Andre Thornton
Box 395
Chagrin Falls, OH 44022

Marv Throneberry
12102 Macon Road
Collierville, TN 38017

Louis Tiant
2495 Starmount Way
El Dorado Hills, CA 95630

Joe Torre
3088 Greenfield Road
Marietta, GA 30067

Mike Torrez
208 North Lake Street
Topeka, KS 66616

Cesar Tovar
Calle Real Prado Maria #58
Caracas, Venezuela

Tom Tresh
4206 East Wing Road, RR 6
Mount Pleasant, MI 48858

Virgil Trucks
RR 3, #5 Greenvalley
Leeds, AL 35094

Bob Ueker
N60W15734 Hawthorne Drive
Menomonee Falls, WI 53051

Willie Upshaw
Box 395
Blanco, TX 78606

Bobby Valentine
791 North Street
White Plains, NY 10605

Fernando Valenzuela
3004 North Beachwood Drive
Hollywood, CA 90068

Elmer Valo
571 Columbia Avenue
Palmerton, FL 33562

John Vandermeer
4005 Leona Avenue
Tampa, FL 33606

Bob Veale
1502 Lomb Avenue West
Birmingham, AL 35208

Mickey Vernon
100 East Rose Valley Road
Wallingford, PA 19086

Zoilo Versalles
8645 Fremont South
Bloomington, MN 55420

Bill Virdon
1311 River Road
Springfield, MO 65804

Bob Watson
215 Bolling Road
Atlanta, GA 30305

Earl Weaver
19016 West Lake Drive
Hialeah, FL 33015

Lou Whitaker
803 Pipe
Martinsville, VA 24112

Frank White
8925 Lambert Drive
Lee's Summit, MO 64063

William White
71 Callowhill Road
Chalfont, PA 18914

Hoyt Wilhelm
Box 2217
Sarasota, FL 33578

Billy Williams
586 Prince Edward Road
Glen Ellyn, IL 60137

Ted Williams
Box 481
Islamorada, FL 33036

Maury Wills
245 Fowling
Playa Del Rey, CA 90291

Mookie Wilson
150 Highland Avenue
Staten Island, NY 10301

Willie Wilson
5 Glenwood Place
Summit, NJ

Bobby Wine
2612 Woodland Avenue
Norristown, PA 19401

Dave Winfield
367 West Forest
Teaneck, NJ 07666

Rick Wise
RR 2 Box 317
Hillsboro, OR 97123

Wilbur Wood
8 Wachusett Drive
Lexington, MA 02173

Todd Worrell
306 Harvard Drive
Arcadia, CA 91006

Butch Wynegar
528 Spring Creek Drive
Longwood, FL 32779

Early Wynn
Box 218
Nokomis, FL 33551

Jim Wynn
932 1/2 East 41st Place
Los Angeles, CA 90053

Carl Yastrzemski
4621 South Ocean Boulevard
Highland Beach, FL 33431

Steve Yeager
5225 White Oak #4
Encino, CA 91316

Eddie Yost
35 Crown Ridge Road
Wellesley, MA 02181

Robin Yount
8140 East Sands Drive, Box 545
Scottsdale, AZ 85255

Don Zimmer
10124 Yacht Club Drive
St. Petersburg, FL 33706

BASKETBALL

■ PROFESSIONAL LEAGUES

MAJOR LEAGUE

National Basketball Association
645 Fifth Avenue
New York, NY 10022
(212) 826-7000
Commissioner: David J. Stern

Atlanta Hawks
100 Techwood Drive NW
Atlanta, GA 30303
(404) 681-3600
Directors: Ted Turner, Bud Seretean, Bruce Wilson, J. Michael Gearon, Stan Kasten, Michael Fratello
Pres: Stan Kasten
GM: Stan Kasten
PR Director: Bill Needle

Boston Celtics
Boston Garden at North Station
Boston, MA 02114
(617) 523-6050
Chmn: Don Gaston
Pres: Red Auerbach
GM: Jan Volk
PR Director: Jeff Twiss

Charlotte Hornets
1 Television Place
Charlotte, NC 28205
(704) 376-6430
Pres: George Shinn
GM: TBA
PR Director: TBA

Chicago Bulls
980 North Michigan Avenue
Chicago, IL 60611
(312) 943-5800
Chmn: Jerry Reinsdorf
GM: Jerry Krause
PR Director: Tim Hallman

Cleveland Cavaliers
The Coliseum
Richfield, OH 44286
(216) 659-9100
Chmn: George Gund and
     Gordon Gund
Pres: Thaxter Trafton
GM: Wayne Embry
PR Director: Bob Price

Dallas Mavericks
Reunion Arena
777 Sports Street
Dallas, TX 75207
(214) 748-1808
Owner: Donald Carter
Pres: Donald Carter
GM: Norm Sonju
PR Director: Kevin Sullivan

Denver Nuggets
PO Box 4286
Denver, CO 80204
(303) 893-6700
Owner: Sidney Shlenker
Pres: Vince Boryla and
     Dean Bonham
GM: Pete Babcock
PR Director: Harve Kirkpatrick

Detroit Pistons
Pontiac Silverdome
1200 Featherstone Road
Pontiac, MI 48057
(313) 338-4500
Managing Partner: William
Davidson
CEO: Thomas Wilson
GM: Jack McCloskey
PR Director: Matt Dobeck

Golden State Warriors
The Oakland Coliseum Arena
Nimitz Freeway and
Hegenberger Road
Oakland, CA 94621
(415) 638-6300
Chmn: James Fitzgerald
Pres: Dan Finnane
PR Director: Cheri White

Houston Rockets
The Summit
Houston, TX 77046
(713) 627-0600
Chmn: Charlie Thomas
Pres: Ray Patterson
GM: Ray Patterson
PR Director: Jay Goldberg

Indiana Pacers
2 West Washington
Indianapolis, IN 46204
(317) 263-2100
Owners: Melvin Simon and
        Herbert Simon
GM: Don Walsh
PR Director: Dale Ratermann

Los Angeles Clippers
LA Memorial Sports Arena
3939 South Figueroa
Los Angeles, CA 90037
(213) 748-6131
Owner: Donald Sterling
Pres: Alan Rothenberg
GM: Elgin Baylor
PR Director: Jack Gallagher

Los Angeles Lakers
PO Box 10
Inglewood, CA 90306
(213) 674-6000
Owner: Dr. Jerry Buss
Pres: Bill Sharman
GM: Jerry West
PR Director: Josh Rosenfeld

Miami Heat
Miami Center
100 Chopin Place Suite 200
Miami, FL 33131
(305) 577-HEAT
Pres: Lewis Schaffel
GM: TBA
PR Director: TBA

Milwaukee Bucks
901 North Fourth Street
Milwaukee, WI 53203
(414) 272-6030
Pres: Herb Kohl
GM: John Steinmiller
PR Director: Bill King

Minnesota Timberwolves
5525 Cedar Lake Road
Minneapolis, MN 55416
(612) 544-3865
Pres: Robert Stein
GM: TBA
PR Director: TBA

New Jersey Nets
Brendan Byrne Arena
East Rutherford, NJ 07073
(201) 935-8888
CEO: Alan Aufzien
Pres: Bernie Mann
GM: Harry Weltman
PR Director: John Mertz

New York Knickerbockers
Four Penn Plaza
New York, NY 10001
(212) 563-8000
Pres: Richard Evans
GM: Al Bianchi
PR Director: John Cirillo

Orlando Magic
13 West Pine
Orlando, FL 32801
(305) 422-7433
Pres: Pat Williams
GM: TBA
PR Director: TBA

Philadelphia 76ers
The Spectrum
PO Box 25040
Philadelphia, PA 19147
(215) 339-7600
Pres: Harold Katz
GM: John Nash
PR Director: Dave Coskey

Phoenix Suns
2910 North Central
PO Box 1369
Phoenix, AZ 85001
(602) 266-5753
Chmn: Richard Bloch
Pres: Donald Pitt
GM: Jerry Colangelo
PR Director: Tom Ambrose

Portland Trail Blazers
700 Northeast Multnomah Street
Suite 950, Lloyd Building
Portland, OR 97232
(503) 234-9291
Chmn: Lawrence Weinberg
Pres: Harry Glickman
GM: Jon Spoelstra
PR Director: John Lashway

Sacramento Kings
1515 Sports Drive
Sacramento, CA 95834
(916) 648-0000
Owners: Joseph Benvenutti, Gregg
Lukenbill, Frank Luckenbill, Bob
Cook and Stephen Cippa
Pres: Joe Axelson
GM: Joe Axelson
PR Director: Julie Fie

San Antonio Spurs
HemisFair Arena
PO Box 530
San Antonio, TX 78292
(512) 224-4611
Chmn: Angelo Drossos
GM: Bob Bass
PR Director: Wayne Witt

Seattle Supersonics
C-Box 900911
Seattle, WA 98109
(206) 281-5800
Chmn: Barry Ackerly
Pres: Bob Whitsitt
GM: Bob Whitsitt
PR Director: Jim Rupp

Utah Jazz
5 Triad Center
Salt Lake City, UT 84180
(801) 575-7800
Owner: Larry Miller
Pres: Dave Checketts
GM: Dave Checketts
PR Director: Bill Kreifert

Washington Bullets
One Harry S. Truman Drive
Landover, MD 20786
(301) 350-3400
Pres: Abe Pollin
GM: Bob Ferry
PR Director: Mark Pray

MINOR LEAGUES

Continental Basketball Association
425 South Cherry Street
Denver, CO 80222
(303) 331-0404

Albany Patroons
112 State Street, 2nd Floor
Albany, NY 12207
(518) 434-1005

Charleston Gunners
PO Box 6809
Charleston, WV 25302
(304) 346-9495

Cincinnati Slammers
Cincinnati Gardens
2250 Seymour Avenue
Cincinnati, OH 45212
(513) 631-7793

La Crosse Catbirds
312 State Street
La Crosse, WI 54601
(608) 782-4700

Pensacola Tornados
201 East Gregory Street
Pensacola, FL 32501
(904) 433-7933

Rockford Lightning
300 Elm Street
Rockford, IL 61101
(815) 968-5600

Savannah Spirits
321 West York Street
Savannah, GA 31401
(912) 236-1200

Tampa Bay Thrillers
100 West Kennedy Boulevard
Suite 355
Tampa, FL 33602
(813) 221-2777

Topeka Sizzlers
PO Box 559
Topeka, KS 66601
(913) 357-8300

Wisconsin Flyers
PO Box 1025
Neenah, WI 54956
(414) 738-6633

Wyoming Wildcatters
800 North Poplar Street, Suite 109
Casper, WY 82601
(307) 577-9453

International Basketball Association
(6'4" and under)
658 East Commonwealth Avenue
Fullerton, CA 92631
(714) 447-3397

Fresno Flames
317 North Van Ness
Fresno, CA 93701
(209) 264-5314

Rucker Professional League
2340 Third Avenue
New York, NY 10037
(212) 410-3240

U.S. Basketball League
117 North Broad Street
Milford, CT 06460
(203) 877-9508

■ ORGANIZATIONS

**Amateur Basketball Association
of the United States of America**
1750 East Boulder Street
Colorado Springs, CO 80909
(303) 632-7687

Harlem Globetrotters
6121 Santa Monica
Los Angeles, CA 90038
(818) 906-1234

**International Association of
Approved Basketball Officials**
61 South Main Street
West Hartford, CT 06107
(203) 232-7530

**Metropolitan Intercollegiate
Basketball Association**
c/o Peter A. Carlesimo
330 Park Street
Montclair, NJ 07043
(201) 783-5577

**Naismith Memorial Basketball
Hall of Fame**
PO Box 179, Highland Station
1150 West Columbus Avenue
Springfield, MA 01101-0179
(413) 781-6500

**National Association of
Basketball Coaches**
PO Box 307
Branford, CT 06405
(203) 488-1232

**National Association of
Basketball Referees**
475 Park Avenue South
New York, NY 10016
(212) 725-1800

**National Wheelchair Basketball
Association**
110 Seaton Building
University of Kentucky
Lexington, KY 40506
(606) 257-1623

**National Women's Basketball
Association**
PO Box 240298
Charlotte, NC 28824

NBA Properties, Inc.
437 Madison Avenue
New York, NY 10022
(212) 826-7003

**Professional Basketball Writers'
Association of America**
c/o Dan Blumenthal
434 West 120th Street
New York, NY 10027
(212) 666-6352

■ ORGANIZATIONS—INTERNATIONAL

AUSTRALIA

Australian Basketball Federation, Inc.
203 New South Head Road
Edgecliff, NSW Z027
Australia
(02) 326 1144

National Basketball League
140 William Street
Kings Cross, NSW Z011
Australia
(02) 356 3950

CANADA

Basketball Canada
333 River Road, Tower A
11th Floor
Vanier, Ontario, Canada
K1L 8H9
(613) 748-5607

FRANCE

Federation Francaise de Basket-Ball
82 rue d'Hauteville
75010 - Paris
France
(1) 770.33.55

GERMANY

Deutscher Basketball-bund
Stresemannstrasse 12
Postfach 708
5800 Hagen
West Germany

IRELAND

Irish Basketball Association
53 Middle Abbey Street
Dublin 1
Ireland
733476

UNITED KINGDOM

British and Irish Basketball Federation
Calomax House
Lupton Avenue
Leeds LS9 7EE
England
(0532) 496044

English Basketball Association
Calomax House
Lupton Avenue
Leeds LS9 7EE
England
(0532) 496044

Scottish Basketball Association
8 Frederick Street
Edinburgh EH2 2HB
Scotland
031-225 7143

■ PUBLICATIONS

Basketball Times
PO Box 960
Rochester, MI 48063

CBA Newsweekly
425 South Cherry Street, Suite 230
Denver, CO 80222

CBA Official Guide
425 South Cherry Street, Suite 230
Denver, CO 80222

Eastern Basketball Magazine
7 May Court
West Hempstead, NY 11552

International Basketball
320 East 23rd Street, Suite 9C
New York, NY 10010

National Recruiter's Cageletter
PO Box 2086
Cedar Rapids, IA 52406

NCAA Basketball Programs
546 East Main Street
Lexington, KY 40502

The Basketball Clinic
117 Cuttermill Road
Great Neck, NY 11021

■ **CAMPS**

UAB Basketball Camp
Athletic Department
University of Alabama-Birmingham
University Station
Birmingham, AL 35294
(205) 934-3402
(B)

Basketball Camp
Jim Hamey
3291 Douglas Highway
Juneau, AK 99801
(907) 586-1497

Northwest Basketball Camp
Box 234
Sundre, Alberta, Canada
T0M IXO

Basketball Camp
Arizona State University
Tempe, AZ 85287
(602) 965-3261 (B)
(602) 965-2603 (G)

Basketball Camps and Officiating Camp
*Sportsworld
5764 Paradise Drive
Suite 7
Corte Madera, CA 94925
1-800-542-6005

Bill Cartwright Basketball Camp
PO Box 789
Elk Grove, CA 95624
(916) 972-0857

Billie Moore Girls' Basketball Camp
2801 "B" Ocean Park Boulevard
Suite 291
Santa Monica, CA 90405
(213) 825-8699
(G)

Basketball Camp
University of San Diego
Sports Center
Alcala Park
San Diego, CA 92110
(619) 260-4803

Basketball Camp
Campus Box 378
Boulder, CO 80309
(303) 492-6086

Pistol Pete All-Star Basketball Camp
P.O. Box 612
Clearwater, FL 33517
(813) 446-6162

Bill Cronauer
B/C Basketball Camp Director
6370-90th Avenue North
Pinellas Park, FL 33565
(404) 384-4516 (SE Athletic
Complex)
(813) 545-5882 (Bill Cronauer)

Mike Glenn Basketball Camp for the Hearing Impaired
3166 Big Spring Court
Decatur, GA 30034

Georgia Tech/Bobby Cremins Basketball School
Georgia Tech Athletic Association
150 Third Street, Northwest
Atlanta, GA 30332
(B)

Basketball Camp
1910 University Drive
Boise, ID 83725
(208) 385-1288 (B)
(208) 385-1760 (G)

Bradley Basketball Camps, Inc.
Haussler Hall
Bradley University
Peoria, IL 61625
(309) 676-7611

Basketball Camp
Ray Meyer
DePaul University
1011 Beld Avenue
Chicago, IL 60614
(312) 341-8290
(715) 546-3546 (Camp Phone)
(B)

Dick Baumgartner's Basketball Shooting Camp
549 Meadowbrook Lane
Richmond, IN 47347
(317) 966-4994

Basketball Camp
Woody Wilson
1800 Lincoln Avenue
University of Evansville
Evansville, IN 47722
(812) 479-2762

Ron Greene Basketball Camp
Attn: Mark Atherton
Indiana State University
Terre Haute, IN 47809
(812) 237-4002
(B)

Basketball Camp
The University of Iowa Sports
Camps
E216 Field House
Iowa City, IA 52242
(319) 353-3149
(B)

Basketball Camp
Mark Freidinger
Allen Fieldhouse
University of Kansas
Lawrence, KS 66045
(913) 864-3056

Basketball Camp
Memorial Coliseum
University of Kentucky
Lexington, KY 40506-0019
(606) 257-1916 (B)
(606) 257-6046 (G)

Cardinal Basketball Camp
University of Louisville
Louisville, KY 40292
(502) 588-6531
(B)

Dale Brown/LSU Basketball Camp
650 North Ardenwood
Building 5
Baton Rouge, LA 70806
(504) 927-5552

Basketball Camp
Alex Robinson
General Manager
111 Robin Hill Road
PO Box 122
South Chelmsford, MA 01824
(617) 256-9206
(B)

Basketball Camp
Michigan Camps of Champions
1000 South State Street
Ann Arbor, MI 48109
(313) 763-6767

Basketball Camp
Gary Center
Western Michigan University
Kalamazoo, MI 49008-3899
(616) 383-0354 (B)
(616) 383-1423 (G)

*Otter Camps, Inc.
Box 795
Dent, MN 56528
(218) 758-2112
(218) 346-5036

Tiger Basketball Camp
c/o Norm Stewart
2409 Beachview Drive
Columbia, MO 65203
(314) 882-6501
(B)

Creighton Girls Basketball Camp
Bruce Rasmussen
2500 California Street
Omaha, NE 68134
(G)

Creighton Basketball Camp
Tony Barone
P.O. Box 34296
Omaha, NE 68134
(B)

Oglivie's Lobo Team Camp
c/o Basketball Office
University of New Mexico
South Athletic Complex
Albuquerque, NM 87131
(505) 277-6372

Hoop du Jour Basketball Camp
c/o Basketball Office
Fordham University
Bronx, NY 10458
(212) 579-2460
(B)

Empire State Basketball Camp for Girls
12 Carlton Terrace
Loudonville, NY 12211
(518) 459-5210
(G)

"The Big Guy" Basketball Camp
Don Flewelling, Director
Oneonta State University
Oneonta, NY 13820
(607) 431-3595
(B)

Bulls Basketball Camp
Richard Jacob
SUNY at Buffalo
Alumni Arena
Buffalo, NY 14260
(716) 636-3141
(B)

Basketball Camp
Will Klein
569 Kimball Avenue
Yonkers, NY 10704
(914) 237-1306
(212) 246-3064

Syracuse University
Basketball Camps
Manley Field House
Syracuse University
Syracuse, NY 13210
(315) 423-2082

Davidson College
Basketball Camp
Basketball Office
Davidson, NC 28036
(704) 892-2000

Basketball Camp
Coach Mike Krzyzewski
P O Box 4704 Duke Station
Durham, NC 27706
(919) 684-3777

Basketball Camp
Jim Valvano
Box 1409
Cary, NC 27511
(919) 737-2105
(B)

Basketball Camp
Dave Gunther
University of North Dakota
Grand Forks, ND 58202

Bill Sudeck/Case Western Reserve Basketball Camp
Athletic Department
Emerson Gym
Cleveland, OH 44106
(216) 368-2865
(B)

Basketball Camp
Randy Montgomery
Triway High School
Gambier, OH 43022
(216) 264-8685
(614) 427-2244

Basketball Camp
Summer Sports School
Miami University
220 Millett Hall
Oxford, OH 45056
(513) 529-3924

Basketball Camp
Xavier University Basketball Office
3800 Victory Parkway
Cincinnati, OH 45207
(513) 745-3418 (B)
(513) 745-3413 (G)

Golden Hurricane Basketball Camp
University of Tulsa
600 South College Avenue
Tulsa, OK 74104
(918) 592-6000

Cathy Rush Sports Camps
P.O. Box 436
Wayne, PA 19087
(215) 688-1572
After June 15, 1987:
c/o Delaware Valley College
Doylestown, PA 18901
(215) 345-8314
(G)

76ers Basketball Camp
Box 1073
Bala Cynwyd, PA 19004
(215) 649-4499

Lafayette College
Basketball Camp
Basketball Office
Kirby Field House
Easton, PA 18042
(215) 250-5475
(212) 250-5477

Basketball Office
University of Pittsburgh
P.O. Box 7436
Pittsburgh, PA 15213
(412) 624-4585

Kevin Porter Basketball Camp
Saint Francis College
Loretto, PA 15940
(814) 472-7000
Ext. 621, 622, or 626
(B)

Providence College
Basketball Office
Providence, RI 02918
(401) 865-2266
(B)

Basketball Camp Director
UTAD, Box 47
Knoxville, TN 37901
(615) 974-1206
(B)

Basketball Camp
Baylor University Athletic
Department
P.O. Box 6427
Waco, TX 76706
(817) 754-4648

Dave Bliss Mustang Basketball Camp
Moody Coliseum
Southern Methodist University
Dallas, TX 75275
(214) 692-3501

The University of Texas Basketball Camp
P.O. Box 7399
Austin, TX 78713
(512) 471-5816
(512) 471-4265
(B)

Ralph Sampson Basketball School
PO Box 1038
Harrisonburg, VA 22801
(703) 879-2466

Terry Hollands's Basketball Camp
109 E. Jefferson Street
Charlottesville, VA 22901
(804) 924-7751
(B)

Wildcat Basketball Camp
Nicholas Pavilion
Central Washington University
Ellensburg, WA 98926

Cougar Cage Camp
114 Bohler Gym
Washington State University
Pullman, WA 99164-1610
(509) 335-0311

MacGregor/Milwaukee Bucks Basketball Camps
2236 West Blue Mound Road
Suite B
Waukesha, WI 53186-2916
1-800-633-2823 (outside WI)
(414) 786-0366

*Summercamps
University of Wisconsin-La Crosse
Office of Extended Education
1725 State Street
La Crosse, WI 54601
(608) 785-8819
(608) 785-8565

University of Wisconsin
Oshkosh Sports Camps
Department of Residence Life
270 S. Gruenhagen
Oshkosh, WI 54901
(414) 424-3212

■ **INDIVIDUALS**

Kareem Abdul-Jabbar
11050 Santa Monica Boulevard
Los Angeles, CA 90025

Red Auerbach
4200 Massachusetts Avenue, N.W.
Washington, DC 20016

Gene Bartow
2636 Creekview
Birmingham, AL 35226

Dr. Jerry Bass
1143 Summit Drive
Beverly Hills, CA 90210

Larry Bird
150 Causeway Street
Boston, MA 02114

Senator Bill Bradley
731 Hart Office Building
Washington, DC 20510

Carl Braun
5604 SE Foxcross Place
Stuart, FL 33497

Dale Brown
Basketball Office
Louisiana State University
Baton Rouge, LA 70894

Lawrence Brown
Allen Fieldhouse
University of Kansas
Lawrence, KS 66045

Lou Carnesecca
St. John's University
Basketball Office
Jamaica, NY 11439

Wilt Chamberlain
15216 Antelo Place
Los Angeles, CA 90024

Bob Cousy
459 Salisbury Street
Worcester, MA 01609

Denny Crum
2301 South 3rd Street
Louisville, KY 40292

Ernie DiGregeorio
60 Chestnut Avenue
Narragansett, RI 02882

Julius Erving
Box 25040, Southwest Station
Philadelphia, PA 19147

Walt Frazier
675 Flamingo Drive
Atlanta, GA 30311

Tom Gola
15 Kings Oak Lane
Philadelphia, PA 19115

Cliff Hagan
c/o University of Kentucky
Lexington, KY 40506

Harlem Globetrotters
15301 Ventura Boulevard #430
Sherman Oaks, CA 91403

Gail Goodrich
601 26th Street
Santa Monica, CA 90402

Magic Johnson
1498 Moraga Drive
Los Angeles, CA 90049

Sam Jones
9200 Sunset Boulevard #808
Los Angeles, CA 90069

John "Red" Kerr
c/o WMAQ,AM Radio
Chicago, IL 60604

Bobby Knight
Indiana University
Basketball Assembly Hall
Bloomington, IN 47405

Meadowlark Lemon
Box 398
Sierra Vista, AZ 85636

Jerry Lucas
3260 Wakefield Drive
Decatur, GA 30034

Pete Maravich
304 West 23rd Avenue
Covington, LA 70433

Slater Martin
4119 Plaud
Houston, TX 77022

Roland Massimino
Villanova University
Lancaster & Ithan Avenues
Villanova, PA 19085

Raymond Meyer
2518 Cedar Glen Drive
Arlington Hts, IL 60005

George Miken
801 Marquette Avenue
Minneapolis, MN 55402

Earl (The Pearl) Monroe
113 West 88th Street
New York, NY 10025

Norm Nixon
2265 Westwood Boulevard #469
Los Angeles, CA 90064-2016

Lute Olson
University of Arizona
McKale Center
Tuscon, AZ 85721

Bob Pettit
Chairman of the Board of Directors
Jefferson Guaranty Bank
3525 North Causeway Boulevard
Matairie, LA 70002

Oscar Robertson
6 East 4th Street
Cincinnati, OH 45202

Bill Russell
PO Box 58
Mercer Island, WA 98040

Dolph Schayes
5 North Ridge
Dewitt, NY 13214

William Sharman
PO Box 10
Inglewood, CA 90306

Dean Smith
PO Box 2126
Chapel Hill, NC 27514

Jerry Tarkanian
University of Nevada-Las Vegas
Las Vegas, NV 89154

John Thompson
Georgetown University
Basketball Office
Washington, DC 20057

Wes Unseld
2210 Cedar Circle Drive
Baltimore, MD 21228

Jim Valvano
North Carolina State University
Campus Box 8501
Raleigh, NC 27695-8601

Butch van Breda Kolff
c/o Athletic Department
Lafayette College
Easton, PA 18042

Ernest (Kiki) Vanderweighe III
275 Bentley Circle
Los Angeles, CA 90049

Jamaal Wilkes
7846 West 81st Street
Playa del Ray, CA 90291

John Wooden
17711 Margate Street #102
Encino, CA 91316

BILLIARDS

■ ORGANIZATIONS—U.S. & CANADA

American Billiard Association
1660 Lin Lor Court
Elgin, IL 60123
(312) 741-6836

Billiard Congress of America
9 South Linn Street
Iowa City, IA 52240
(319) 351-2112

■ PUBLICATIONS

Billiards Digest
875 North Michigan Avenue
Suite 1801
Chicago, IL 60611
(312) 266-7179

■ INDIVIDUALS

Willie Mosconi
1804 Prospect Ridge
Hidden Heights, NJ 08035

BOATING

■ ORGANIZATIONS—U.S. & CANADA

American Canoe Association
PO Box 248, Lorton
Lorton, VA 22079
(703) 550-7523

American Power Boat Association
17640 East Nine Mile Road
East Detroit, MI 48021
(313) 773-9700

America's Cup
Sail America
1904 Hotel Circle North
San Diego, CA 92108-2809
(619) 296-9224

Canadian Amateur Rowing Association
333 River Road, Tower C, 10th Floor
Ottawa, Ontario, Canada
K1L 8H9
(613) 748-5656

Canadian Canoe Association
10th Floor, Tower C
333 River Road
Ottawa, Ontario, Canada
K1L 8H9
(613) 748-5623

Canadian Yachting Association
333 River Road
Ottawa, Ontario, Canada
K1L 8H9
(613) 748-5687

Marine Retailers Association of America
15 North Michigan Ave., Suite 523
Chicago, IL 60601
(312) 938-0359

National Marine Manufacturerers Association
401 North Michigan Avenue
Chicago, IL 60611
(312) 836-4747

National Rowing Foundation
PO Box 6030
Arlington, VA 22206
(703) 379-2974

New York Yacht Club
37 West 44th Street
New York, NY 10036
382-1000

San Diego Yacht Club
1011 Anchorage Lane
San Diego, CA 92106
(619) 222-1103

Scholastic Rowing Association of America
c/o Msgn. Glendon E. Robertson
Kresson Road, Route 541
Gibbsboro, NJ 08026
(609) 784-3878

U.S. Yacht Racing Union
PO Box 209
Newport, RI 02840
(401) 849-5200

■ ORGANIZATIONS— INTERNATIONAL

Federation Internationale Des Rowing
c/o Thomas Keller, Pres
Talstrasse 65
Postfach 4822
CH-8022 Zurich
Switzerland

International Canoe Federation
c/o Caslav Veljic
Sarajevska 22-I, 11000 Belgrade
Yugoslavia

Internationale Yacht Racing
Union
60 Knightsbridge
London SWIX 7JX England

Union Internationale Motor
Union Int. Motonautique
C.C.N. Bruxelles 21
Botle Postale 21
B-1000 Belgium

U.S. Rowing Association
251 N. Illinois St, Suite 980
Indianapolis, IN 46204
(317) 237-2769

■ PUBLICATIONS

American Rowing
251 North Illinois Street
Suite 980
Indianapolis, IN 46204

Board & Sail Magazine
PO Box 8108
Sacramento, CA 95818

Canoe Magazine
10526 N.E. 68th Street, Number 5
Kirkland, WA 98083

Sailboard News
Two South Park Place
PO Box 159
Fair Haven, VT 05743

Sailing Magazine
125 East Main Street
Port Washington, WI 53074

The American Canoeist
PO Box 248
Lorton, VA 22079

*Yacht Racing & Cruising
Magazine*
111 East Avenue
Norwalk, CT 06851

■ CAMPS

ROWING/SCULLING
Culver Summer Camps
Office of Admissions
Culver, IN 46511
(219) 842-8207

SAILING
Annapolis Sailing School
601 Sixth Street
PO Box 3334
Annapolis, MD 21403
(301) 267-7205 (in MD)
1-800-638-9192

Myles Gordon's Sailing Center
235 Main Street
Kingston, NY 12401
(914) 338-7313

Sailing School
Capt. Carl Selin
Box 84
Key Colony Beach, FL 33051
(305) 743-4676
1-800-845-CAMP
Summer Address:
Capt. Carl Selin
Deer Isle Sailing Center
Box 62
Deer Isle, ME 04627
(207) 348-2339

Summer Camp Programs
Christchurch School
Christchurch, VA 23031
(804) 758-2306

Wind Works Sailing School
Shilshole Bay Marina
7001 Seaview Avenue N.W.
Seattle, WA 98117
(206) 784-9386

■ **INDIVIDUALS**

Dennis Conner
401 West A Street #615
San Diego, CA 92101

Ted Turner
1050 Techwood Drive
Atlanta, GA 30318

BOCCE

■ **ORGANIZATIONS—U.S. & CANADA**

U.S. Bocce Federation
1065 South Sheridan
Denver, CO 80226
(303) 934-7211

■ **ORGANIZATIONS— INTERNATIONAL**

International Bocce Association
400 Rutger Street
PO Box 170
Utica, NY 13503-0170
(315) 733-9611

BODY BUILDING

■ **ORGANIZATIONS—U.S. & CANADA**

Canadian Weightlifting Federation
333 River Road
Ottawa, Ontario, Canada K1L 8H9
(613) 748-5684

National Gym Association
65-06 Fresh Pond Road
Ridgewood, NY 11385
(718) 848-0789

National Strength and Conditioning Association
PO Box 81410
Lincoln, NE 68501
(402) 472-3000

U.S. Powerlifting Federation, Inc.
2103 Langley Avenue
PO Box 18485
Pensacola, FL 32504
(904) 477-4863

U.S. Weightlifting Federation
1750 East Boulder Street
Colorado Springs, CO 80909
(303) 578-4508

■ **ORGANIZATIONS—
INTERNATIONAL**

**International Federation of
Body Builders**
2875 Bates Road
Montreal, Quebec
Canada H3S 1B7
(514) 731-3783

**International Powerlifting
Federation**
PO Box 6007
S-126 06 Hagerstern
Sweden

**International Weightlifting
Federation**
1374 Budapest, pf. 614
Hungary

■ **PUBLICATIONS**

Flex
21100 Erwin Street
Woodland Hills, CA 91367

Muscle and Body Builder
Charlton Building
Derby, CT 06418

Muscle & Fitness
21100 Erwin Street
Woodland Hills, CA 91367

Powerlifting USA Magazine
Box 467
Camarillo, CA 93011

Strength & Health
Box 1707
York, PA 17405

*Women's Physique World
Magazine*
19127 Wiersma Street, Suite 1
Cerritos, CA 90701

■ **INDIVIDUALS**

Lou Ferrigno
621-17th Street
Santa Monica, CA 90402

Arnold Schwarzenegger
321 Hampton Drive
Venice, CA 90291

BOOMERANG

■ **ORGANIZATIONS—
INTERNATIONAL**

AUSTRALIA

**Boomerang Association of
Australia**
P.O. Box 155
Barooga via Cobram, NSW 3644
Australia
(058) 734463

BOWLING

ORGANIZATIONS—U.S. & CANADA

American Blind Bowling Association
3500 Terry Drive
Norfolk, VA 23518
(804) 857-7267

American Bowling Congress
5301 South 76th Street
Greendale, WI 53129
(414) 421-6400

Billiard and Bowling Institute of America
200 Castlewood Drive
North Palm Beach, FL 33408
(305) 842-4100

Bowling Proprietors' Association of America
PO Box 5802
Arlington, TX 76005
(817) 649-5105

Bowling Writers Association of America
6357 Siena Street
Centerville, OH 45459

BVL Fund
1919 Penn Avenue Northwest
Washington, DC 20006
(301) 942-5880

Canadian 5 Pin Bowlers' Association
No. 505, 200 Isabella Street
Ottawa, Ontario, Canada K1S 1V7
(613) 230-6394

Ladies Pro Bowlers Tour
7171 Cherryvale Boulevard
Rockford, IL 61112
(815) 332-5756

National Bowling Association
377 Park Avenue South
7th Floor
New York, NY 10016
(212) 689-8308

National Bowling Council
1919 Penn Avenue, N.W.
Suite 504
Washington, DC 20006
(202) 659-9080

National Bowling Hall of Fame and Museum
111 Stadium Plaza
St. Louis, MO 63102
(314) 231-6340

National Deaf Bowling Association
9244 East Mansfield Avenue
Denver, CO 80237
(303) 771-9018 TDD only

National Duckpin Bowling Congress
Fairview Avenue
Baltimore-Linthicum, MD
21090-1466
(301) 636-2695

Professional Bowlers Association of America
1720 Merriman Road
Akron, OH 44313
(216) 836-5568

Tri State Bowling Conference
c/o Dick Burns, Secy/Treas
Western New England College
1215 Wilbraham Road
Springfield, MA 01119
(413) 782-1333

Young American Bowling Alliance
5301 South 76th Street
Greendale, WI 53129
(414) 421-4700

■ **ORGANIZATIONS— INTERNATIONAL**

Federation Internationale des Quilleurs
5301 South 76th Street
Greendale, WI 53129-0050

Women's International Bowling Congress, Inc.
5301 South 76th Street
Greendale, WI 53129
(414) 421-9000

■ **PUBLICATIONS**

Bowler's Journal
875 North Michigan Avenue
Chicago, IL 60611

Bowlers News
PO Box 136
Oswego, NY 13827

Bowling Digest
1020 Church Street
Evanston, IL 60201

Bowling Proprietor
615 Six Flags Drive
Arlington, TX 76011

Bowling World
PO Box 855
Danville, CA 94526

California Bowling News
PO Box 7128
Burbank, CA 91510

St. Louis Bowling Review
400 Brookes-Suite 100
Hazelwood, MO 63042

Ten Pin Journal
5228 North 88th Court
Milwaukee, WI 53225

The Chicago Bowler
10450 Cermak Road
PO Box 7008
Westchester, IL 60153

The Deaf Bowler
9244 East Mansfield Avenue
Denver, CO 80237

■ **CAMPS**

Professional Bowling Camps, Inc.
5901 Warner Avenue, Suite 82
Huntington Beach, CA 92649
(714) 848-6610

BOXING

■ ORGANIZATIONS— U.S. & CANADA

Canadian Boxing Association
333 River Road
Ottawa, Ontario, Canada K1L 8H9
(613) 748-5611

Canadian Professional Boxing Federation
City Hall, 2nd Floor
Edmonton Alberta Canada
T5J 2R7
(403) 428-5457

Golden Gloves Association of America, Inc.
9910 Indian School Road, NE
Albuquerque, NM 87112
(505) 294-8659

International Boxing Hall of Fame
PO Box 425
Canastota, NY 13032
(315) 697-7095

USA Amateur Boxing Federation
1750 East Boulder Street
Colorado Springs, CO 80909
(303) 632-5551

■ ORGANIZATIONS— INTERNATIONAL

International Amateur Boxing Association
135 Westervelt Place
Cresskill, NJ 07626

International Boxing Federation
30 Clinton Street
Newark, NJ 07102
(201) 621-7200

International Boxing Research Organization
Box 84
Guilford, NY 13780
(607) 335-2240 (Work)
(607) 895-6846

International Boxing Writers Association
Box 610
Millwood, NY 10546
(914) 359-6334
(914) 694-5040

International Veteran Boxers' Association
94 Crescent Avenue
New Rochelle, NY 10801
(914) 235-6820

World Boxing Council
Genova 33-DESP 503
Mexico D.F. 06600 Mexico
(905) 525-37-87
(905) 569-19-11

AUSTRALIA

Amateur Boxing Union of Australia
27 South Avenue
Double Bay, NSW 2028
(02) 32 3129

FRANCE

Federation Francaise de Boxe Anglaise
62 rue Nollet
75017 - Paris
France
(1) 627.52.45

Federation Francaise de Boxe Francaise, Savate, et Disciplines Assmilees
25 Boulevard des Italiens
75002 - Paris
(1) 742.82.27

GERMANY, FEDERAL REPUBLIC OF
Deutscher Amateur-Box-Verband
Pfannkuchstrasse 16
Postfach 710166
6000 Frankfurt 71
West Germany
069/6606-0

IRELAND
Irish Amateur Boxing Association
National Stadium
South Circular Road
Dublin 8
Ireland
753371-2

UNITED KINGDOM
Amateur Boxing Association of England
Francis House, Francis Street
London SW1P 1DE
England
01-828 8571

Scottish Amateur Boxing Association
60 St. Andrews Gardens
Dalry, Ayrshire KA24 4J2
Scotland
(029483)2748

Welsh Amateur Boxing Association
8 Erw Wen
Rhiwbina, Cardiff CF4 6JW
England
(0222)623566

■ **PUBLICATIONS**

Boxing Illustrated
PO Box 304
Pleasantville, NY 10570

International Boxing
PO Box 48
Rockville Centre, NY 11571

Ring Magazine
130 West 37th Street
New York, NY 10018

The Amateur Boxer
PO Box 249
Cobalt, CT 06414

World Boxing Magazine
PO Box 48
Rockville Centre, NY 11571

■ **INDIVIDUALS**

Muhammad Ali
55 Fremont Place
Los Angeles, CA 90005

Robert Arum
250 East 63rd Street
New York, NY 10021

Carmen Basillo
PO Box 153
Chittenango, NY 13237

Mark Breland
760 Park Avenue
Brooklyn, NY 11206

Billy Conn
1715 Denniston Street
Pittsburgh, PA 15217

Gerry Cooney
225-01 Linden Boulevard
Cambria Heights, NY

Henry Cooper
36 Brampton Grove
London NW4
England

Angelo Dundee
1700 Washington Avenue
Miami, FL 33143

Roberto Duran
Box 157, Arena Colon
Panama City, Panama

George Foreman
6 West Rivercrest Drive
Houston, TX 77042

Joe Frazier
2917 North Broad Street
Philadelphia, PA 19132

Paul Gonzalez
129 Paseo Los Alisis
Los Angeles, CA 90033

Rocky Graziano
300 East 57th Street
New York, NY 10022

Marvin Hagler
24 Ward Street
Brockton, MA 02403

Thomas Hearns
Emanuel Steward
19600 West McNichol Street
Detroit, MI 48219

Larry Holmes
413 Northampton Street
Easton, PA 18042

Ingemar Johansson
Sven Ekstrom
Rakegaton 9 S-41320
Goteborg, Sweden

Don King
PO Box 121089
Nashville, TN 37212

Jake LaMotta
400 East 57th Street
New York, NY 10022

Sugar Ray Leonard
1505 Brady Court
Mitchellville, MD 20716

Ray Mancini
807 Cambridge Avenue
Youngstown, OH 44502

Archie Moore
3517 East Street
San Diego, CA 92102

Ken Norton
500 Shatto Place #200
Los Angeles, CA 90020

Carlos Palomino
6501 Oxford Drive
Huntington Beach, CA 92647

Floyd Patterson
Springtown Road
Box 336
New Paltz, NY 12561

Sugar Ray Robinson
1060 Crenshaw Boulevard   #101
Los Angeles, CA 90019

Ernie Shavers
Knockout Janitorial Services
Martinsville, VA 24112

Max Schmeling
2115 Hallenstedt
Hamburg , West Germany

Leon Spinks
19300 Britton Drive
Detroit, MI

Michael Spinks
20284 Archdale
Detroit, MI 48235-2143

Teofilo Stevenson
Comite Olimpico
Hotel Habana
Libre, Habana
Cuba

Mike Tyson
c/o Ohlmeyer Communications
625 Madison Avenue
New York, NY 10019

CRICKET

■ **ORGANIZATIONS—U.S. & CANADA**

U.S. Cricket Association
c/o Art Hazelwood
City of Alexandria
Office of Internal Audit
PO Box 178
Alexandria, VA 22314
(703) 838-4918

■ **ORGANIZATIONS— INTERNATIONAL**

AUSTRALIA

Australian Cricket Board
70 Jolimont Street
Jolimont, VIC 3002
(03) 654-3977

UNITED KINGDOM

English Schools Cricket Association
68 Hatherley Road
Winchester, Hants SO22 6RR
England
(0962) 65773

National Cricket Association
Lord's Cricket Ground
London NW8 8QN
England
01-289-1611

Scottish Cricket Union
18 Ainslie Place
Edinburgh 3
Scotland
031-226 3452

CROQUET ━━━━━━━━━━━━━━━

■ ORGANIZATIONS—U.S. & CANADA

U.S. Croquet Association
500 Avenue of Champions
Palm Beach Gardens, FL 33418
(305) 627-4009

■ ORGANIZATIONS—INTERNATIONAL

AUSTRALIA

Australian Croquet Council
95 Westmoreland Road
Leumeah, NSW 2560
Australia
(02) 603 1772

UNITED KINGDOM

The Croquet Association
The Hurlingham Club
Ranleigh Gardens, SW6
London, England

■ INDIVIDUALS

Louis Jordan
1139 Maybrook
Beverly Hills, CA 90210

Jack Osborn
500 Avenue of Champions
Palm Beach, FL 33418

CYCLING ━━━━━━━━━━━━━━━

■ ORGANIZATIONS—U.S. & CANADA

American Bicycle Association
PO Box 718
Chandler, AZ 85244
(602) 961-1903

Bicycle Federation of America
1818 R Street N.W.
Washington, DC 20009
(202) 332-6986

Bicycle Touring Network
PO Box 7559
Ann Arbor, MI 48107

Bicycle USA
6707 Whitestone Road, Suite 209
Baltimore, MD 21207
(301) 944-3399

Bikecentennial Bicycle Travel Association
113 Main
Missoula, MT 59807
(406) 721-1776
Mailing Address:
PO Box 8308
Missoula, MT 59807

Canadian Cycling Association
333 River Road
Vanier, Ontario, Canada
K11 8H9
(613) 748-5629

National Bicycle League, Inc.
555 Metro Center North
Suite 524
PO Box 729
Dublin, OH 43017
(614) 766-1625

National Off-Road Bicycling Association (NORBA)
PO Box 1901
Chandler, AZ 85224
(602) 961-0635

U.S. Cycling Federation
1750 East Boulder Street
Colorado Springs, CO 80909
(303) 578-4581

U.S. Professional Cycling Federation
Route 1, Box 130
New Tripoli, PA 18066
(215) 298-3262

■ ORGANIZATIONS— INTERNATIONAL

Federation Internationale Amateur De Cycling
Via Dei Campi Sportivi, 48
00197 Rome
Italy

International Bicycle Touring Society
2115 Paseo Dorado
La Jolla, CA 92037
(619) 459-8775

International Cycling Union
6, rue Amat
CH-1202 Geneve
Switzerland

International Unicycling Federation
16152 Kinloch
Redford, MI 48240

World Cycling, Ltd.
43 King Street
Port Chester, NY 10573
(914) 937-2909

■ PUBLICATIONS

Bicycle Business Journal
1904 Weneca Street
Fort Worth, TX 76102

Bicycle Guide
711 Boylston Street
Boston, MA 02116

Bicycle Rider
29901 Agoura Road
Agoura, CA 91301

Bicycle USA
6707 Whitestone Road, Suite 209
Baltimore, MD 21207

Bicycling Magazine
33 East Minor Street
Emmaus, PA 18049

BMX Action
3162 Kashiwa Street
Torrance, CA 90505

Cycling USA
1750 East Boulder Street
Colorado Springs, CO 80909

Cyclist
20916 Higgins Court
Torrance, CA 90501

Freestylin'
3162 Kashiwa Street
Torrance, CA 90505

Pro Bike News
1818 R Street N.W.
Washington, DC 20009

Velo-News
Box 1257
Brattleboro, VT 05301

Winning/Bicycle Racing Illustrated
1127 Hamilton Street
Allentown, PA 18102

■ **EVENTS**

Coors International Bicycle Classic
International Classics, Ltd.
1540 Lehigh Street
Boulder, CO 80303
(303) 499-1108

U.S. Pro Cycling Championship
WMAR-TV
6400 York Road
Baltimore, MD 21212

■ **CAMPS**

Kern River Tours
PO Box 3444
Lake Isabella, CA 93240
(619) 379-4616

Dana Hall Summer Journeys
Barbara J. Lynch, Dr.
45 Dana Road
Wellesley, MA 02181

Midwest Cycling Camps
Gerry Fornes
385 Garden Road
Columbus, OH 43214
(614) 268-2325

EQUESTRIAN SPORTS ━━━━

■ **ORGANIZATIONS—U.S. & CANADA**

American Horse Council, Inc.
1700 K Street N.W., Number 300
Washington, DC 20006
(202) 296-4031

American Horse Shows Association
220 East 42nd Street
New York, NY 10017
(212) 972-2472

American Vaulting Association
Sub. of: Amer. Horse Show Assn.
c/o Judith S. Bryer, Exec. Secy.
20066 Glen Brae Drive
Saratoga, CA 95070
(408) 867-0402

Canadian Equestrian Federation
333 River Road
Ottawa, Ontario, Canada
K1L 8H9
(613) 748-5632

Hall of Fame of the Trotter
240 Main Street
Goshen, NY 10924
(914) 294-6330

Kentucky Derby Museum
704 Central Avenue
PO Box 3513
Louisville, KY 40201
(502) 637-1111

National Steeplechase & Hunt Association
PO Box 308
Elmont, NY 11003
(516) 437-6666

North American Harness Racing Association
405 Lexington Avenue
New York, NY 10017
(212) 983-4460

The American Hanover Society
831 Bay Avenue, Suite 2-E
Capitola, CA 95010
(408) 476-4461

U.S. Combined Training Association
292 Bridge Street
South Hamilton, MA 01982-1497
(617) 468-7133

U.S. Dressage Federation, Inc.
1212 "O" Street
Lincoln, NE 68508
(402) 474-7632
Mailing Address:
PO Box 80668
Lincoln, NE 68501

U.S. Equestrian Team
c/o Bill Landsman
Bill Landsman Associates
17 East 45th Street
New York, NY 10017
(212) 370-4160

U.S. Polo Association
120 North Mill Street
Lexington, KY 40507
(606) 255-0593

U.S. Trotting Association
750 Michigan Avenue
Columbus, OH 43215
(614) 224-2291

■ ORGANIZATIONS— INTERNATIONAL

Federation Equestrian Internationale
Schosshaldenstrasse 12
CH-3000 Berne 32
Switzerland

International Arabian Horse Association
PO Box 33696
Denver, CO 80234
(303) 450-4774

■ PUBLICATIONS

Canadian Rider/Canadian Quarter Horse Journal
491 Book Road West
Ancaster, Ontario, Canada L9G 3L1

Equus Magazine
656 Quince Orchard Road
Gaithersburg, MD 20878

Harness Horse
Sub. of: Commonwealth
Communication Services
PO Box 1831
Harrisburg, PA 17105

Horse & Horseman
34249 Camino Capistrano
Capistrano Beach, CA 92624

Horse Illustrated
33171 Paseo Cerveza
San Juan Capistrano, CA 92675

Polo Magazine
656 Quince Orchard Road
Gaithersburg, MD 20878

Practical Horseman
Gum Tree Corner
Unionville, PA 19375

Speedhorse Magazine
PO Box 1000
Norman, OK 73070

The Racing Report
PO Box 1000
Norman, OK 73070

Western Horseman
3850 N. Nevada Ave.
Colorado Springs, CO 80933

■ THOROUGHBRED RACE TRACKS

Ak-Sar-Ben Field
Omaha, NE 68106
(402) 556-2305

Aqueduct
New York Racing Association, Inc.
PO Box 90
Jamaica, NY 11417
(718) 641-4700

Arapahoe Park
PO Box 1004
4100 South Parker Road
Aurora, CO 80014
(303) 699-2900

Arlington Park Race Track
PO Box 7
Arlington Heights, IL 60006
(312) 255-4300

Atlantic City Racing Association, Inc.
PO Box 719
Atlantic City, NJ 08404
(609) 641-2190

Bay Meadows Racing Association
PO Box 5050
San Mateo, CA 94402
(415) 574-RACE

Belmont Park
New York Racing Association, Inc.
PO Box 90
Jamaica, NY 11417
(718) 641-4700
(516) 488-6000

Beulah Park
Capital Racing Club, Inc.
PO Box 6
Grove City, OH 43123
(614) 871-9600

Birmingham Turf Club, Inc.
1000 John Rogers Drive
Birmingham, AL 35210
(205) 836-3100

Calder Race Course
PO Box 1808
Carol City Branch
Opa Locka, FL 33055
(305) 625-1311

Canterbury Cowns
Minnesota Race Track, Inc.
PO Box 508
Shakopee, MN 55379
(612) 445-7223

Churchill Downs
700 Central Avenue
Louisville, KY 40208
(502) 636-3541

Delaware Park
Delaware Racing Association
PO Box 6008
Stanton, DE 19804
(302) 994-2521

Del Mar Thoroughbred Club
PO Box 700
Del Mar, CA 92014
(619) 755-1141

Detroit
Ladbrook Racing Corporation
28001 Schoolcraft
Livonia, MI 48150-2288
(313) 525-7300

Ellis Park
Dade Park Jockey Club, Inc.
PO Box 33
Henderson, KY 45420
(812) 425-1456

Erie Downs Racing Association, Inc.
PO Box 27
Fairview, PA 16415
(814) 474-5584

Exhibition Park
The British Columbia Jockey
Club, Inc.
Exhibition Park
Vancouver, B.C. V5K 3N8
Canada
(604) 254-1631

Finger Lakes Racing Association
PO Box 364
Canandaigua, NY 14424
(716) 924-3232

Fonner Park
Hall County Livestock Improvement
Association, Inc.
PO Box 490
Grand Island, NE 68802
(308) 382-4515

Fort Erie
see listing for
The Ontario Jockey Club

Garden State Race Track
PO Box 4274
Cherry Hill, NJ 08034
(609) 488-8400

Greenwood Race Track
1669 Queen Street
Toronto, Ontario, Canada
(416) 698-3131

Keeneland Association, Inc.
PO Box 1690
Lexington, KY 40592-1690
(606) 254-3512

Longacres Race Course, Inc.
PO Box 60
Renton, WA 98057
(206) 226-3131

Louisiana Downs, Inc.
PO Box 5519
Bossier City, LA 71171-5519
(318) 742-5555

The Meadowlands
East Rutherford, NJ 07073
(201) 935-8500

Monmouth Park
PO Box MP
Ocean Port, NJ 07757
(201) 222-5100

Mountainview Racing Association
Box 100
Grantville, PA 17028
(717) 469-2211

National Steeplechase & Hunt Association
PO Box 308
Elmont, NY 11003
(516) 437-6666

Oaklawn Jockey Club
PO Box 699
Hot Springs, AR 71909
(501) 623-4411

Oak Tree Racing Association
285 West Huntington Drive
Arcadia, CA 91006
(818) 574-7223

The Ontario Jockey Club
PO Box 156
Rexdale, Ontario
Canada M9W 5L2
(416) 675-6110

Penn National Turf Club
Box 100
Grantville, PA 17028
(717) 469-2211

Philadelphia Turf and Racing Club
PO Box 1000
Bensalem, PA 19020-2096
(215) 639-9000

Pimlico Race Course
Maryland Jockey Club
Baltimore, MD 21215
(301) 542-9400

Santa Anita Park
Los Angeles Turf Club
285 West Huntington Drive
Arcadia, CA 91006
(818) 574-7223

Saratoga
PO Box 564
Saratoga Springs, NY 12866
(518) 584-6200
or
New York Racing Association
PO Box 90
Jamaica, NY 11417
(718) 641-4700

Sportsman's Park
3301 Laramie Avenue
Cicero, IL 60650
(312) 242-1121

Tampa Bay Downs
PO Box E
Oldsmar, FL 33557
(813) 855-4401

Thistledown
Box 7050
Cleveland, OH 44128
(216) 662-8600

Timonium
Maryland State Fair
PO Box 188
Timonium, MD 21903
(301) 252-0200

Tropical Park
PO Box 1808
Carol City Branch
Opa-Locka, FL 33055
(305) 625-1311

Turfway Park
PO Box 75007
Cincinnati, OH 45257
(606) 371-0200

Woodbine
see listing for
The Ontario Jockey Club

■ SPECIALTY EVENTS

Greenwich Polo Tournament
c/o Rolex Watch
665 Fifth Avenue
New York, NY 10022
(212) 758-7700

International All-Stars Polo Benefit
656 Quince Orchard Road
Gaithersburg, MD 20878
(301) 977-3900

Killington Mountain Equestrian Festival
PO Box 114
Killington, VT 05751
(802) 773-4181

Radnor Hunt Races
Brandywine Conservancy
PO Box 141
Chadds Ford, PA 19317
(215) 388-7601

Washington, D.C. International Turf Horse Race
Center for Sports Sponsorship
Plainsboro, NJ 08536
(609) 921-8329

■ CAMPS

Equestrian Camp
University of California-Davis
Davis, CA 95616
1-800-752-0881
(916) 752-0880

Equestrian Camp
Ivy Rasco
Riding Director
Oak Grove-Coburn School
Vassalboro, ME 04989
(207) 873-2721

Equestrian Camp
The Selwyn School
3333 University Drive West
Denton, TX 76201
(817) 566-3050

Equestrian Camp
Office of Summer Programs
Southern Sem
Buena Vista, VA 24416
(703) 261-6181
Ext. 222 or 212
(G)

■ POLO

Cornell Summer Sports School
PO Box 729
Cornell University
Ithaca, NY 14851
(607) 255-7333

■ INDIVIDUALS

Angel Cordero
NY Racing Association
PO Box 90
Jamaica, NY 11009

Willie Shoemaker
1900 Avenue of the Stars #2820
Los Angeles, CA 90067

Bill Steinkraus
PO Box 3038
Noroton, CT 06820

Jorge Velasquez
Jockey Club
20 East 46th Street Room 901
New York, NY 10017

FENCING ▬▬▬▬▬▬▬▬▬▬▬▬▬▬▬

■ **ORGANIZATIONS—U.S. & CANADA**

Canadian Fencing Association
333 River Road
Ottawa, Ontario,Canada K1L 8H9
(613) 748-5633

National Intercollegiate Women's Fencing Association
235 McCosh Road
Upper Montclair, NJ 07043
(201) 783-9871

U.S. Fencing Association
1750 East Boulder Street
Colorado Springs, CO 80909
(303) 578-4511

U.S. Fencing Coaches Association
PO Box 274
New York, NY 10159
(212) 532-2557

■ **ORGANIZATIONS— INTERNATIONAL**

Federation Francaise d'Escrime
45 rue de Liege
75008 - Paris
France
(1) 294.91.38

Federation Internationale D'Escrime
Corso Porta Vigentina 54
20122 Milano
Italy

■ **PUBLICATIONS**

American Fencing
1750 East Boulder Street
Colorado Springs, CO 80909

Swordmaster Magazine
279 East Northfield Road
Livingston, NJ 07039

■ **CAMPS**

Fencing Camp
Grimm House
The College at New Paltz
State University of New York
New Paltz, NY 12561
(914) 257-2620

FIELD HOCKEY

■ ORGANIZATIONS—U.S. & CANADA

Canadian Field Hockey Association
333 River Road
Ottawa, Ontario, Canada K1L 8H9
(613) 748-5634

Canadian Women's Field Hockey Association
333 River Road
Ottawa, Ontario, Canada K1L 8H9
(613) 748-5634

Field Hockey Association of America, Inc.
1750 East Boulder Street
Colorado Springs, CO 80909
(303) 578-4587

U.S. Field Hockey Association (Women)
1750 East Boulder Street
Colorado Springs, CO 80909
(303) 578-4567

■ ORGANIZATIONS— INTERNATIONAL

AUSTRALIA

Australian Hockey Association
36 Park Street
Melbourne, VIC 3205
Australia
(03) 690 8944

Australian Women's Hockey Association
95 York Street, 12th Floor
Sydney NSW 2000
Australia
(02) 290 2844

■ PUBLICATIONS

The Eagle
1750 East Boulder Street
Colorado Springs, CO 80909

■ CAMPS

Yale Sports Camps
402A Yale Station
New Haven, CT 06520
(203) 436-4158
(G)

All Star Field Hockey Camp
Dottie Zenaty
Springfield College
Box 1670
Springfield, MA 01109
(413) 788-3167
(413) 783-4225
(G)

Mercersburg Field Hockey Camp
Box 212
Hadley, MA 01035
(413) 584-4914
(G)

Field Hockey Camp
Sauk Valley Sports Center
Irish Hills
Brooklyn, MI 49230
(517) 467-2061
(G)

Field Hockey Camp
Conference Services
Princeton University
3rd Floor Prospect
Princeton, NJ 08544
(609) 452-3369

The Vassar College Field Hockey Camp
PO Box 281
Vassar College
Poughkeepsie, NY 12601
(914) 452-7000, ext. 2562

Penn State Field Hockey Camp
Gretchen Leathers
The Pennsylvania State University
410 Keller Conference Center
University Park, PA 168-2
(814) 863-4563
(G)

White Mountain Sports Camp at Bates College
Box 82
Hampden-Sydney College
Hampden-Sydney, VA 23943
(804) 223-8722

FISHING

■ ORGANIZATIONS—U.S. & CANADA

American Fishing Tackle Manufacturers Association
1250 Grove Avenue, Suite 300
Barrington, IL 60010
(312) 381-9490

Catskill Fly Fishing Center
Roscoe, NY 12776
(607) 498-5500

Izaak Walton League of America
1701 North Fort Meyer Drive
Suite 1100
Arlington, VA 22209

National Fresh Water Fishing Hall of Fame
PO Box 33
One Hall of Fame Drive
Hayward, WI 54843
(715) 634-4440

Sport Fishing Institute
1010 Massachusetts Ave N.W.
Suite 110
Washington, DC 20001
(202) 898-0770

U.S. Bass Fishing Association
2090 South Grand Avenue
Santa Ana, CA 92705
(714) 556-2116

■ ORGANIZATIONS— INTERNATIONAL

International Bass Association
1907 West Highway 62
PO Box 227
Prairie Grove, AR 72753
(501) 846-3739

International Casting Federation
Correspondence:
c/o Chris Korich
3960 Patterson Avenue
Oakland, CA 94619

International Game Fish
Association
3000 East Las Olas Boulevard
Ft. Lauderdale, FL 33316-1616
(305) 467-0161

■ TOURNAMENT AND SPORT
FISHING ORGANIZATIONS
—U.S. & CANADA

ALABAMA

American Bass Association
PO Box 4158
Montgomery, AL 36103

B.A.S.S.
PO Box 17900
Montgomery, AL 36141

ARIZONA

U.S. Bass
PO Box 696
Mesa, AZ 85201

CALIFORNIA

Fishing International
Bob Nauheim
PO Box 2132
Santa Rosa, CA 95405

Pacific Anglers
2044 Federal Avenue
Costa Mesa, CA 92627

CANADA

Ontario Federation of Anglers
& Hunters
PO Box 28
Peterborough, Ontario, Canada
K9J 6Y5

FLORIDA

Cat Cay Club Limited
PO Box 530950
Miami Shores, FL 33153

Florida Sportfishing Assn.
PO Box 1216
Cape Canaveral, FL 32903

Fort Pierce Sportfishing Club
PO Box 4051
Fort Pierce, FL 33448-4051

International Women's Fishing
Association
PO Drawer 3125
Palm Beach, FL 33480

Jockey Club, The
11111 Biscayne Boulevard
Miami, FL 33161

Rod & Reel Club of Greater
Miami
208 South Hibiscus Island
Miami, FL 33139

UM Marine School
BLR
4600 Rickenbacker Causeway
Miami, FL 33149

HAWAII

Hawaii Big Game
Fishing Club
PO Box 22487
Honolulu, HI 96822

Western Sports Tournaments
78-505 Puuiki Road
Kailu-Kona, HI 96740

KENTUCKY

Red Man Operation Bass
Route 2 Box 74B
Gilbertsville, KY 42044

LOUISIANA
Lady Bass Tournaments
810 Stubbs Avenue
Monroe, LA 71201

MARYLAND
Ocean City Sharkers
PO Box 583
Ocean City, MD 21842

MASSACHUSETTS
Boston Big Game Fishing Club
Box 2993
Boston, MA 02101

NORTH CAROLINA
Hatteras Marlin Club
Box 218
Hatteras, NC 27943

TEXAS
Bassing America
PO Box 796908
Dallas, TX 75379

Bass'n Gal
PO Box 13925
Arlington, TX 76013

■ ORGANIZATIONS— INTERNATIONAL

AUSTRALIA
Bermagui Big Game Angler's Club
PO Box 52
Bermagui, NSW 2547

Game Fishing Club of So. Australia
PO Box 95
Stepney, SA 5069

Moreton Bay Game Fish Club
PO Box 105
Brisbane Market
Queensland 4106

Shoalhaven Game Fishing Club
PO Box 5
Greenwell Point 2540
NSW

Sunshine Coast Game Fishing Club
PO Box 97
Mooloolaba, Queensland 4558

Victorian Game Fishing Club
PO Box 240
Cheltenham 3192
Victoria

BAHAMAS
Bimini Big Game Fishing Club
PO Box 523238
Miami, FL 33152
USA

COSTA RICA
Baja Fishing Adventures
2221 Palo Verde Avenue
Suite 1D
Long Beach, CA 90815

JAPAN
Japan Game Fish Assn.
Okada Bldg, Room 003
4-3-5 Shiba Minato-Ku
Tokyo, 108

NEW ZEALAND
Auckland Gamefishing Club
PO Box 6115
Wellesley Street
Auckland

Bay of Islands Swordfish Club
PO Box 31
Russell

Whakatane Big Game Fishing Club
PO Box 105
Whakatane

Whangaroa Big Gamefish Club
R.D. 1
Kaeo, Whangaroa

TAHITI
Haura Club de Tahiti
PO Box 4503
Papeete

■ **PUBLICATIONS**

Field & Stream
1515 Broadway
New York, NY 10036

The Fisherman
PO Box 1994
Sag Harbor, NY 11963

Fishing World Magazine
51 Atlantic Avenue
Floral Park, NY 11001

International Angler
3000 East Las Olas Boulevard
Fort Lauderdale, FL 33316

Rod & Reel
PO Box 42000
Bergenfield, NJ 07621

SFI Bulletin
1010 Massachusetts Avenue N.W.
Suite 100
Washington, DC 20001

Sport Fishing News
1010 Massachusetts Avenue N.W.
Suite 100
Washington, DC 20001

Texas Fisherman Magazine
5314 Bingle Road
Houston, TX 77092

■ **SCHOOLS**

L.L. Bean Fly Fishing School
Freeport, ME 04033
(800) 341-4341 ext. 7100

Orvis Fly Fishing School
Ten River Road
Manchester, VT 05254
(802) 362-3900

FOOTBALL

■ **PROFESSIONAL LEAGUES**

UNITED STATES
National Football League
410 Park Avenue
New York, NY 10022
(212) 758-1500
Comm: Pete Rozelle

Atlanta Falcons
Suwanee Road at I-85
Suwanee, GA 30174
(404) 945-1111
Chmn of Bd: Rankin M. Smith
PR Director: Charlie Dayton

Buffalo Bills
One Bills Drive
Orchard Park, NY 14127
(716) 648-1800
Pres: Ralph C. Wilson Jr.
PR Director: L. Budd Thalman

Chicago Bears
Halas Hall
250 North Washington Road
Lake Forest, IL 60045
(312) 295-6600
Chmn of Bd: Edward W. McCaskey
PR Director: Ken Valdiserri

Cincinnati Bengals
200 Riverfront Stadium
Cincinnati, OH 45202
(513) 621-3550
GM: Paul Brown
PR Director: Allan Heim

Cleveland Browns
Cleveland Stadium
Cleveland, OH 44114
(216) 695-5555
Pres: Arthur Modell
PR Director: Kevin Byrne

Dallas Cowboys
1 Cowboys Parkway
Irving, TX 75063
(214) 556-9900
Gen Partner: H.R. Bright
Pres and GM: Tex Schramm
PR Director: Doug Todd

Denver Broncos
5700 Logan Street
Denver, CO 80216
(303) 296-1982
Pres: Patrick Bowen
PR Director: Jim Saccomano

Detroit Lions
Pontiac Silverdome
1200 Featherstone Road
PO Box 4200
Pontiac, MI 48057
(313) 335-4131
Pres: William Clay Ford
PR Director: George Heddleston

Green Bay Packers
1265 Lombardi Avenue
Green Bay, WI 54303
(414) 494-2351
Pres: Judge Robert Parins
Chmn of Bd: Dominic Olejniczak
PR Director: Lee Remmel

Houston Oilers
6910 Fannin Street
Houston, TX 77030
(713) 797-9111
Pres: K.S. Adams Jr.
Media Relations Dir: Chip Namias

Indianapolis Colts
7001 West 56th Street
PO Box 24100
Indianapolis, IN 46254
(317) 297-2658
Pres: Robert Irsay
PR Director: Bob Eller

Kansas City Chiefs
One Arrowhead Drive
Kansas City, MO 64129
(816) 924-9300
Chmn of Bd: Lamar Hunt
PR Director: Bob Sprenger

Los Angeles Raiders
332 Center Street
El Segundo, CA 90245
(213) 322-3451
Gen Partner: Al Davis
Exec Asst: Al LoCasale

Los Angeles Rams
2327 West Lincoln Avenue
Anaheim, CA 92801
(714) 535-7267
Pres: George Frontiere
PR Director: Pete Donovan

Miami Dolphins
4770 Biscayne Boulevard
Miami, FL 33137
(305) 576-1000
Pres: Joseph Robbie
PR Director: Eddie White

Minnesota Vikings
9520 Viking Drive
Eden Prairie, MN 55344
(612) 828-6500
Pres: Max Winter
PR Director: Merrill Swanson

New England Patriots
Sullivan Stadium
Route 1
Foxboro, MA 02035
(617) 543-7911
Pres: William H. Sullivan Jr.
PR Director: Jim Greenidge

New Orleans Saints
6928 Saints Avenue
Metairie, LA 70003
(504) 733-6147
Managing Gen Partner: Tom
Benson Jr.
PR Director: Greg Suit

New York Giants
Giants Stadium
East Rutherford, NJ 07073
(201) 935-8111
Pres: Wellington T. Mara
Dir of Media Services: Ed Croke

New York Jets
598 Madison Avenue
New York, NY 10022
(212) 421-6600
Chmn of Bd: Leon Hess
Pres: James L. Kensil
PR Director: Frank Ramos

Philadelphia Eagles
Veterans Stadium
Broad Street & Pattison
Philadelphia, PA 19148
(215) 463-2500
Owner: Norman Braman
Dir of Comm: Ed Wisneski

Pittsburgh Steelers
Three Rivers Stadium
300 Stadium Circle
Pittsburgh, PA 15212
(412) 323-1200
Chmn of Board: Art Rooney
PR Director: Joe Gordon

St. Louis Cardinals
Busch Stadium, Box 888
St. Louis, MO 63188
(314) 421-0777
Pres: William V. Bidwill
PR Director: Bob Rose

San Diego Chargers
Jack Murphy Stadium
PO Box 20666
San Diego, CA 92120
(619) 280-2111
Pres: Alex Spanos
PR Director: Rick Smith

San Francisco 49ers
711 Nevada Street
Redwood City, CA 94061
(415) 365-3420
Pres: Edward J. Bartolo Jr.
PR Director: Jerry Walker

Seattle Seahawks
11220 N.E. 53rd Street
Kirkland, WA 98033
(206) 827-9777
Managing Gen Partner: John
Nordstrom
PR Director: Gary Wright

Tampa Bay Buccaneers
One Buccaneer Plaza
Tampa, FL 33607
(813) 870-2700
Pres: Hugh F. Culverhouse
PR Director: Rick Odioso

Washington Redskins
Redskin Park
PO Box 17247
Dulles International Airport
Washington, DC 20041
(703) 471-9100
Chmn of Brd: Jack Kent Cooke
PR Director: Charles M. Taylor

CANADA

Canadian Football League
1200 Bay Street, 12th Floor
Toronto, Ontario, Canada M5R 2A5
(416) 928-1200
Commissioner: Doug Mitchell
Dir of Media/PR: John Iaboni

Argonaut Football Club (E)
Exhibition Stadium
Exhibition Place
Toronto, Ontario, Canada
M6K 3C3
(414) 595-9600

B.C. Lions Football Club (W)
10605 135th Street
Surrey,
British Columbia V3T 4C8
(604) 588-5466

Edmonton Eskimo Football Club (W)
9023-111 Avenue
Edmonton, Alberta, Canada
T5B 0X3
(403) 429-2821

Hamilton Tiger-Cat Football Club (E)
75 Balsam Avenue North
PO Box 172
Hamilton, Ontario, Canada
L8N 3A2
(416) 547-2418

Montreal Alouettes Football Club (E)
P Box 100
Station M
Montreal, Quebec, Canada
H1V 3L6
(514) 253-8088

Ottawa Football Club Limited (E)
Lansdowne Park
Ottawa, Ontario, Canada
K1S 3W7
(613) 563-4551

Saskatchewan Roughrider Football Club (W)
2940 10th Avenue
PO Box 1277
Regina, Saskatchewan, Canada
S4P 3B8
(306) 569-2323

Stampeder Football Club Ltd. (W)
McMahon Stadium
1827 Crowchild Trail Northwest
Calgary, Alberta, Canada
T2M 4T6
(403) 289-0205

Winnipeg Blue Bomber Football Club (W)
1465 Maroons Road
Winnipeg, Manitoba, Canada
R3G 0L6
(204) 775-9751

■ ORGANIZATIONS—U.S. & CANADA

American Football Coaches Association
7758 Wallace Road, Suite 1
Orlando, FL 32819
(305) 351-6113

Arena Football
2250 East Devon Avenue
Suite 337
Des Plains, IL 60018
(312) 390-8660

Blue Gray All Star Football Classic
Box 94
Montgomery, AL 36101
(205) 265-1266

Canadian Amateur Football Association
333 River Road
Vanier, Ontario, Canada K1L 8H9
(613) 748-5636

Canadian Football Hall of Fame and Museum
58 Jackson Street West
Hamilton, Ontario, Canada L8P 1L4
(416) 528-7566

Canadian Football League Players Association
1919 Scarth Street
Regina, Saskatchewan, Canada
S4P 2H1
(306) 525-2158

College Football Association
6688 Gunpark Drive, Suite 201
Boulder, CO 80301-3339
(303) 530-5566

Collegiate Kickoff Classic
c/o New Jersey Sports and
Exposition Authority
Byrne Meadowlands Arena
East Rutherford, NJ 07073
(201) 460-4367

Football Writers Association of America
Box 1022
Edmond, OK 73083
(405) 341-4731

Green Bay Packer Hall of Fame
1901 South Oneida
PO Box 10567
Green Bay, WI 54307-0567
(414) 499-4281

Indiana Football Hall of Fame
PO Box 1035
Richmond, IN 47374
(317) 966-2235

National Association of Division 1-A (NCAA Football) Independents
Director of Athletics
c/o Cecil W. Ingram, Dr.
Florida State University
Tallahassee, FL 32316
(904) 644-1060

National Collegiate Football Association
Div of: National Club Sports
Association
15 Tulipwood Drive
Commack, NY 11725
(516) 543-0730

National Football Foundation and Hall of Fame, Inc., The
1865 Palmer Avenue
Larchmont, NY 10538
(914) 834-0478
Hall of Fame Location:
King's Island, OH 45034
(513) 241-5600

National Football League Alumni
2866 E. Oakland Park Boulevard
Ft. Lauderdale, FL 33306
(305) 564-6118

National Football League Official's Association
609 Brainerd Place
Exton, PA 19341
(215) 363-1733

National Football League Players' Association
1300 Connecticut Avenue N.W.
Suite 407
Washington, DC 20036
(202) 463-2200

National Football League Properties, Inc.
410 Park Avenue
New York, NY 10022
(212) 838-0660

National Football Scouting
4821 South Sheridan Road
Fountain Plaza, Suite 104
Tulsa, OK 74145

Pop Warner Football
1315 Walnut Street Building
Suite 606
Philadelphia, PA 19107
(215) 735-1450

Pro Football Hall of Fame
2121 George Halas Drive N.W.
Canton, OH 44708
(216) 456-8207

Pro Legends, Inc.
2866 East Oakland Park Boulevard
Ft. Lauderdale, FL 33306
(305) 561-9445

Professional Football Researchers Association
12870 Route 30
North Huntington, PA 15642

Professional Football Writers of America
c/o Howard Balzer, Secy
The Sporting News
1212 North Lindbergh
St. Louis, MO 63132
(314) 997-7111

United States Flag Football League
5834 Pine Tree Drive
Sanibel, FL 33957
(813) 472-0544

■ **INTERNATIONAL FOOTBALL LEAGUES AND ORGANIZATIONS**

AUSTRALIA

National Football League of Australia, LtD
120 Jolimont Road, 2nd Floor
Jolimont, VIC 3002
Australia
(03) 63 4977

BRITAIN

Budweiser League
30-35 Drury Lane
London WC2 B5RH
England
011-44-1-379-3480

■ BOWL GAMES

All American Bowl
(Formerly: Hall of Fame Bowl)
PO Box 11304
Birmingham, AL 35202

Aloha Bowl
1000 Lower Campus Road
Honolulu, HI 96822

Bluebonnet Bowl
3300 Main, Third Floor
Houston, TX 77002

California Bowl
1341 Bulldog Lane, Suite C
Fresno, CA 93710

Cherry Bowl
PO Box 27488
Lansing, MI 48909

Cotton Bowl Athletic Assoc.
Box 47420
Dallas, TX 75247-0420

Fiesta Bowl
5144 East Camelback Road
Phoenix, AZ 85018

Florida Citrus Bowl
250 North Orange Avenue
Suite 300
Orlando, FL 32801

Gator Bowl Association
1801 Art Museum Drive
Jacksonville, FL 32207

Holiday Bowl
9449 Friars Road, Gate P
San Diego, CA 92108

Hula Bowl
1000 Lower Campus Road
Honolulu, HI 96822

Independence Bowl
PO Box 1723
Shreveport, LA 71166

Liberty Bowl
4735 Spottswood, No. 102
Memphis, TN 38117

Orange Bowl
PO Box 350748
Miami, FL 33135

Peach Bowl
PO Box 1336
Atlanta, GA 30301

Rose Bowl
391 South Orange Grove Blvd
Pasadena, CA 91184

Senior Bowl
63 South Royal St, Suite 107
Mobile, AL 36602

Sugar Bowl
Louisiana Superdome
1500 Sugar Bowl Drive
New Orleans, LA 70112

Sun Bowl
PO Box 95
El Paso, TX 79941

■ **FANTASY FOOTBALL GAMES AND SERVICES**

ACFL Kit
PO Box 112
Auburndale, MA 02166

APBA Pro League Football Game
1001-10F Millersville Road
PO Box 4547
Lancaster, PA 17604-4547

BCD Enterprises
2220 Westcreek #88E
Houston, TX 77027

Cascade Leisure Services
PO Box 99
Milltown, NJ 08850

Fantasy Sports Inc.
1533 University Avenue
St. Paul, MN 55104
(800) 233-9809
(612) 647-1380

Simulated Sports Services
Box 2871
Boston, MA 02101
(800) TEAM-SSS
(617) 864-6060

Software City Computer Services
PO Box 109
Le Sueur , MN 56058
(612) 665-6241

Strat-o-matic Pro Football
46 Railroad Plaza
Department 1110
Glen Head, NY 11545
(800) 645-3455

TGIFG
PO Box 2203
La Jolla, CA 92038

■ **PUBLICATIONS**

All-Pro
15723 Vanowen, Suite 145
Van Nuys, CA 91406

Arkansas Football
PO Box 47420
Dallas, TX 75247
(214) 631-1160

Athlon's Inside Saturday
3814 Cleghorn Avenue
Nashville, TN 37215
(615) 297-7581

Bear Report
112 Market Street
Sun Prairie, WI 53590

Browns News Illustrated
PO Box 799
Berea, OH 44017

California Football
1801 South Catalina Avenue
Redondo Beach, CA 9027
(213) 373-3630

Chargers Football Weekly
PO Box 90729
San Diego, CA 92109

Coffin Corner
12870 Route 30
North Huntington, PA 15642
(412) 863-6345

Dallas Cowboys Official Weekly
One Cowboys Parkway
Irving, TX 75063
(800) 4-Center
(800) 5-Cowboy

Dolphin Digest
PO Box 6600
Miami, FL 33152
(800) 334-4378
(800) 334-4005

The Football Clinic
117 Cuttermill Road
Great Neck, NY 11021
(516) 466-9300

Football News
17820 East Warren Avenue
Detroit, MI 48224
(800) 521-8808

49ers Report
PO Box 3269
Redwood City, CA 94064

The Giants Newsweekly
PO Box 816
Red Bank, NJ 07701
(800) 843-0215

Inside Football
1133 Pleasantville Road
Briarcliff Manor, NY 10510

Inside the Seahawks
PO Box 3449
Kirkland, WA 98083-3449
(206) 828-6538

Packer Report
112 Market Street
Sun Prairie, WI 53590

Pro Football Weekly
666 Dundee Road, Suite 1101
Northbrook, IL 60062
(312) 272-1237

Street & Smith's Pro Football
350 Madison Avenue
New York, NY 10017
(212) 880-8800

Texas Football
PO Box 47420
Dallas, TX 75247
(214) 631-1160

■ CAMPS

The Pat Dye Football Camp
PO Box 351
Auburn, AL 36831-0351
(205) 826-4750
(B)

Razorback Sports Camp
University of Arkansas
Fayetteville, AR 72701
(501) 575-5552
(B)

Football Camp
Athletic Department
Stanford University
Stanford, CA 94305
(415) 723-4511
(B)

*Offense-Defense
P.O. Box 317
Trumbull, CT 06611
(800) 243-4296
(B)

Bulldog Football Camp
University of Georgia
Athens, GA 30613
(404) 542-1515
(B)

The University of Iowa Sports Camps
E216 Field House
Iowa City, IA 52242
(319) 353-3149
(B)

Eddie Robinson Football Camp
GSU Athletic Department
Box 868
Grambling, LA 71245
(318) 274-2216
(B)

Football Camp
Howard Vandersea
Bowdoin College
Brunswick, ME 04011
(B)

"Contact" Football Camp
14000 North Gate Drive
Silver Spring, MD 20906
(301) 871-6676
(B)

Michigan Camps of Champions
1000 South State Street
Ann Arbor, MI 48109
(313) 763-6767
(313) 763-4422
(313) 663-2411
(B)

Ole Miss Football Camp
University of Mississippi
Division of Continuing Education
University, MS 38677
(601) 232-7282
(B)

Professional Kicking Services, Inc.
PO Box 2747
Sparks, NE 89431
(702) 359-5973
(B)

Football Camp
Dick Sheridan, Director
North Carolina State University
Football Office
Box 8502
Raleigh, NC 27695-8502
(919) 737-2114
(B)

Camp America
Box 47
Oxford, OH 45056
(513) 798-2794
(513) 523-2958
(B)

Penn State Kicking Camp
Kathy Kurchner
The Pennsylvania State University
410 Keller Conference Center
University Park, PA 16802
(814) 865-7557
(B)

Penn State Football Camps
Ron Avillion
The Pennsylvania State University
Faculty Building
University Park, PA 16802
(814) 865-7557
(B)

Clemson Tiger Football Camp
P.O. Box 552
Clemson, SC 29631
(803) 656-2214
(B)

Johnny Majors Tennessee Volunteer Football Camp
P.O. Box 47
Knoxville, TN 37901
(615) 974-1247
(B)

Husky Football Camp
Graves Building GC-20
University of Washington
Seattle, WA 98195
(B)

Sports Camps, Inc.
RR1, Box 213
River Falls, WI 54022
(715) 425-3135
(B)

■ **INDIVIDUALS**

Marcus Allen
332 Center Street
El Segundo, CA 90245

Dick Bass
506 Montana Street
Santa Monica, CA 90403

Sammy Baugh
Rotan, TX 79546

Maxie Baughan
c/o Athletic Dept.
Cornell University
Ithaca, NY 14350

Chuck Bednarick
1812 Canterbury Road
Abington, PA 19001

Ricky Bell
4259 Enoro Drive
Los Angeles, CA 90008

Joe Bellino
45 Hayden Lane
Bedford, MA 01730

Jay Berwanger
1245 Warren Avenue
Downers Grove, IL 60126

Felix "Doc" Blanchard
307 Stonewood
San Antonio, TX 78284

George Blanda
78001 Lago Drive
La Quinta, CA 92253

Rocky Bleier
1055 Edgewood Road
New Kensington, PA 15068-5352

Mel Blount
M. Blount Youth Home
108 Market Street
Pittsburgh, PA 15222

Brian Bosworth
c/o The Seattle Seahawks
11220 N.E. 53rd Street
Kirkland, WA 98033

Terry Bradshaw
Community National Bank Building
Suite 102
Shreveport, LA 71101

Dick Butkus
119 San Vincente Boulevard #203
BH, CA 90211

Earl Campbell
1209 Baylor Street
Austin, TX 78703

Billy Cannon
1640 Sherwood Forest
Baton Rouge, LA 70815

Bernie Casey
10100 Santa Monica Boulevard
Los Angeles, CA 90067

Todd Christensen
2327 W. Lincoln Avenue
Anaheim, CA 92801

Larry Csonka
1940 S.W. 56th
Plantation, FL 33314

Glenn Davis
4428 Agnes Avenue
North Hollywood, CA 91067

Peter Dawkins
c/o Shearson Lehman Bros.
American Express Tower
World Financial Center
New York, NY 10258

Edward J. De Bartolo
Edward J. De Bartolo Corp.
7620 Market Street
Youngstown, OH 44512

Eric Dickerson
2327 West Lincoln Avenue
Anaheim, CA 92801

Lynn Dickey
8100 Parkhill
Lenexia, KS 66215

Mike Ditka
233 West Ontario
Chicago, IL 60616

Art Donovan
1517 Jeffers Road
Towson, MD 21204

Vincent Dooley
Univ. of Georgia Athletic Dept.
PO Box 1472
Athens, GA 30613

Tony Dorsett
6116 North Central Expressway
Dallas, TX 75206

John Elway
5700 Logan Street
Denver, CO 80216

Dan Fouts
9449 Friars Road
San Diego, CA 92120

Georgia Frontiere
10410 Bellagio Road
Los Angeles, CA 90077

Mark Gastineau
598 Madison Avenue
New York, NY 10022

Willie Gault
250 North Washington Road
Lake Forest, IL 60045

Frank Gifford
355 Taconic Road
Greenwich, CT 06830

Otto Graham
41 Heritage Road
East Lyme, CT 06333

Red Grange
12 North Amarylis Drive
Lake Wales, FL 33855

Roosevelt Grier
c/o "Are You Committed"
3005 South Grand Avenue
Los Angeles, CA 90007

Bob Griese
3250 Mary Street
Miami, FL 33133

Archie Griffin
2389 Brookwood
Columbus, OH 45209

Steve Grogan
17 Laurel Road
Sharon, MA 02067

John Hannah
c/o L.F. Rothschild, Unterberg,
Towbin
One Post Office Square
Boston, MA 02109

Tom Harmon
320 North Gunston Drive
Los Angeles, CA 90049

Franco Harris
996 Greentree Road
Pittsburgh, PA 15220

Leon Hart
1155 Puritan
Birmingham, MI 48009

Bob Hayes
c/o The Staubach Company
6750 LBJ Freeway
Dallas, TX 75230

Don Henrich
19701 Via Escula
Saratoga, CA 95070

Clark Hinkle
720 North 7th Street
Steubenville, OH 43952

Louis Holtz
Athletic Department
Notre Dame University
South Bend, IN 46556

Paul Hornung
5800 Creighton Hill Road
Louisville, KY 40207

Bo Jackson
PO Box 2517
Auburn, AL 36831-2517

Vic Janowicz
1966 Jervis Road
Columbus, OH 43221

Lee Roy Jordan
6536 Ivy Glen
Dallas, TX 75238

Sonny Jurgensen
PO Box 53
Mount Vernon, VA 22121

Alex Karras
7943 Woodrow Wilson Drive
Los Angeles, CA 90046

Jack Kemp
111 West Huron Street #1101
Buffalo, NY 14202

Chuck Knox
5305 Lake Washington Boulevard
Kirkland, WA 98033

Jack Lambert
222 Highland Drive
Carmel, CA 93921

Tom Landry
6116 North Central Expressway
Dallas, TX 75206

Dick Lane
18100 Meyers
Detroit, MI 48233

Yale Lary
Mid Cities National Bank
500 Grapevine Highway
PO Box 1588
Hurst, TX 76053

Edward LeBaron
I-85 at Suwanee Road
Suwanee, GA 30174

Sid Luckman
5303 St. Charles Road
Bellwood, IL 60104

Johnny Lujack
2612 E. Locust Street
Davenport, IA 52801

John Majors
Beechwood Road, Route 23
Knoxville, TN 37920

Ollie Matson
1319 South Hudson Street
Los Angeles, CA 90019

George McAfee
4011 Bristol Road
Durham, NC 27707

Hugh McElhenny
4023 171st Avenue, SE
Bellevue, WA 98008

John McKay
1 Buccaneer Road
Tampa, FL 33607

Jim McMullen
515 Mount Holyoke Avenue
Pacific Palisade, CA 90272

Don Meredith
2222 LTV Tower
Dallas, TX 75201

Dickie Moegle
4047 Aberdeen Way
Houston, TX 77025

Joe Montana
711 Nevada Street
Redwood City, CA 94061

Earl Morrell
Arrowhead Country Club
8201 S.W. 24th Street
Ft. Lauderdale, FL 33324

Marion Motley
5560 Dressler Road
Canton, OH 44720

Bronko Nagurski
Box 191
International Falls, MN

Joe Namath
906 Hillcrest Road
Beverly Hills, CA 90210

Ray Nitschke
410 Peppermint Court
Oneida, WI 54155

Merlin Olsen
1080 Lorain Road
San Marino, CA 91108

Jim Parker
5488 Wingborne Court
Columbia, MD 21045

Ara Parseghian
1326 East Washington Street
South Bend, IN 46601

Joseph Paterno
Pennsylvania State University
Department of Athletics
University Park, PA 16802

Ray Perkins
PO Box K 2nd Floor
University, AL 35486

Richard Phelps
University of Notre Dame
Department of Athletics
Notre Dame, IN 46556

Dail "Bum" Phillips
1500 Poydras Street
New Orleans, LA 70112

Jim Plunkett
332 Center Street
El Segundo, CA 90245

Eddie Robinson
Grambling State University
Football Department
Grambling, LA 71245

Andy Robustelli
74 Wedgemore Road
Stamford, CT. 06905

Kyle Rote
1175 York Avenue
New York, NY 10021

Pete Rozelle
410 Park Avenue
New York, NY 10022

Gale Sayers
624 Buch Road
Northbrook, IL 60062

Bo Schembechler
870 Arlington Boulevard
Ann Arbor, MI 48106

Glenn Schembechler
Department of Athletics
University of Michigan
Ann Arbor, MI 48109

Joe Schmidt
29600 Northwestern Highway
Box 2210
Southfield, MI 48037

Howard Schnellenberger
9825 Willowbrook Circle
Louisville, KY 40223

Jackie Sherrill
Texas A & M University
Athletic Department
College Station, TX 77843

Don Shula
16220 W. Prestwick Place
Miami Lakes, FL 33014

Phil Simms
1775 Broadway #700
New York, NY 10019

O.J. Simpson
360 Rockingham Avenue
Los Angeles, CA 90049

Bubba Smith
8816 Burton Way
Beverly Hills, CA 90211

Steve Spurrier
c/o Duke University
Durham, NC 27706

Kenny Stabler
Box 382
Selma, AL 36701

Bart Starr
1339 Summer Rounge
DePere, WI 54115

Roger Staubach
c/o The Staubach Company
6750 LBJ Freeway
Dallas, TX 75230

Lynn Swann
1230l Wilshire Boulevard #203
Los Angeles, CA 90025

Barry Switzer
University of Oklahoma
Athletic Department
Norman, OK 73019

Fran Tarkenton
3340 Peachtree Road, N.E.
Atlanta, GA 30326

Jim Taylor
8069 Summa Avenue, #A
Baton Rouge, LA 70809

Joe Theismann
5912 Leesburg Pike
Baileys Crossroads, VA 22041

Y.A. Tittle
611 Burleson Street
Marshall, TX 75670

Richard Todd
598 Madison Avenue
New York, NY 10022

Charlie Trippi
125 Riverhiol Court
Athens, GA 30601

Johnny Unitas
603 West Timonium Road
Lutherville, MD 21093

Mark Van Eghen
1600 Fleet Bank Building
Providence, RI 02903

Hershell Walker
3 Empire Boulevard
South Hackensack, NJ 07606

Bill Walsh
Redwood City, CA 94061

Alex Webster
16 Shady Lane
TeQuesta, FL 33458

Alex Wojciechowicz
1106 Skiffway Drive
Forked River, NJ 0873

FRISBEE DISC

■ ORGANIZATIONS—
INTERNATIONAL

**International Frisbee Disc
Association**
PO Box 970
San Gabriel, CA 91776
(213) 287-2257

■ PUBLICATIONS

Disc Sports News
PO Box 419
Fair Haven, VT 05743

GOLF

■ ORGANIZATIONS—U.S. &
CANADA

American Golf Sponsors, Inc.
Box 41
Golf, IL 60029
(312) 724-4600

**American Junior Golf
Association**
2415 Steeplechase Lane
Roswell, GA 30076
(404) 998-4653

**American Society of Golf
Course Architects**
221 North LaSalle Street
Chicago, IL 60601
(312) 372-7090

**Canadian Ladies' Golf
Association**
333 River Road
Ottawa, Ontario, Canada K1L 8H9
(613) 748-5642

**Canadian Professional Golfers'
Association**
333 River Road
Ottawa, Ontario, Canada K1L 8H9

**Golf Coaches Association of
America**
Athletic Department
USAF Academy
USAF Academy, CO 80840
(303) 472-2280

Golf Collectors' Society
PO Box 5483
Akron, OH 44313

**Golf Course Superintendents
Association of America**
1617 St. Andrews Drive
Lawrence, KS 66046
(913) 841-2240

**Golf Writers Association of
America**
PO Box 37324
Cincinnati, OH 45222
(513) 631-4400

**Group Fore-Women's
Professional Golf Tour**
1137 San Antonio Road, Suite E
Palo Alto, CA 94303

Ladies Professional Golf Association
4675 Sweetwater Boulevard
Sugar Land, TX 77479
(713) 980-5742

National Advertising Golf Association
5520 Park Avenue
Trumbull, CT 06611-0395
(203) 373-7000

National Association of Left-Handed Golfers
10149 Hammerly, No. 714
Houston, TX 77080
(713) 464-8683

National Golf Foundation
1150 South U.S. Highway One
Jupiter, FL 33477
(305) 744-6006

PGA Tour
Sawgrass
Ponte Vedra Beach, FL 32082
(904) 285-3700

Pro Golfers' Association Hall of Fame
PO Box 12458
100 Avenue of the Champions
Palm Beach Gardens, FL 33410
(305) 626-3600

Professional Golfers' Association of America
100 Avenue of the Champions
PO Box 12458
Palm Beach, FL 33410
(305) 626-3600

Professional Putters Association (Miniature Golf)
PO Box 35237
Fayetville, NC 28303
(919) 485-7131

Royal Canadian Golf Association
Golf House
R.R. No. 2
Oakville, Ontario, Canada
L6J 4Z3
(416) 844-1800

U.S. Golf Association
Liberty Corner Road
Far Hills, NJ 07931
(201) 234-2300

U.S. Golf Association Hall of Fame
Golf House
Far Hills, NJ 07931
(201) 234-2300

Western Golf Association
1 Briar Road
Golf, IL 60029
(312) 724-4600

World Golf Hall of Fame
PO Box 1908
Gerald Ford Boulevard
Pinehurst, NC 28364
(919) 295-6651

■ **ORGANIZATIONS— INTERNATIONAL**

International Golf Association
625 Madison Avenue
New York, NY 10022
(212) 872-9500

Australian Golf Union
3 Bowen Crescent
Melbourne, VIC 3004
Australia
(03) 2675422

Professional Golfers Association of Australia
113 Queen Street
North Strathfield, NSW 2137
Australia
(02) 2 73 2999

FRANCE
Federation Francaise de Golf
69 avenue Victor Hugo
75116 - Paris
France
(1) 500.62.20

GERMANY, FEDERAL REPUBLIC OF
Deutscher Golf-Verband
Leberberg 25, Postfach 2106
6200 Wiesbaden
Germany
06121/526041-43

JAPAN
Japan Golf Association
Palace Building
1-1 Marunouchi 1-chome
Chiyoda-ku
Japan
215-003

UNITED KINGDOM
English Golf Union
12A Denmark Street
Wokingham, Berks RG11 2BE
England
(0734) 781952

Ladies Golf Union
12 The Lionks
St. Andrews, Fife KY16 9JB
England
(0334) 75811

Professional Golfers' Association
Apollo House
The Belfry, Sutton Coldfield
West Midlands B76 9PT
England
(0675) 70333

Royal and Ancient Golf Club
St. Andrew's, Fife KY16 9JD
England

Scottish Golf Union
54 Shandwick Place
Edinburgh EH2 4RT
Scotland
031-226 6711

Welsh Golfing Union
2 Isfryn, Burry Port
Dyfed SA16 OBY
Wales
(05546) 2595

■ PGA TOURNAMENTS

Anheuser-Busch Golf Classic
Orion Burkhardt
328 McLaws Circle
Williamsburg, VA 23185
(804) 253-3985

AT&T Pebble Beach National Pro-Am
Louis Russo
Monterey Peninsula Golf Foundation
PO Box 869
Monterey, CA 93942
(408) 649-1533Bank of Boston Classic
Edward Mingolla
PO Box 596
Millbury, MA 01527
(617) 865-4441

B.C. Open
Alex Alexander
Broome Country Community Charities, Inc.
PO Box 571
Union Station
Endicott, NY 13760
(607) 754-2482
(607) 785-1086 (home)

Beatrice Western Open
Marshall Dann
One Briar Road
Golf, IL 60029
(312) 724-4600

Big "I" Houston Open
Duke Butler
Houston Golf Association
1830 South Millbend Drive
The Woodland, TX 77380
(713) 367-7999

Bob Hope Chrysler Classic
Walter Probst
75-855 Topaz Lane
Indian Wells, CA 92210
(619) 328-2141

British Open
Royal & Ancient Golf Club
St. Andrews
Fife, Scotland KY16-9-JD
011-44-334-72112

Buick Open
Tom Pond
902 East Hamilton Avenue
Flint, MI 48550
(313) 236-5844

Byron Nelson Golf Classic
Jack I. McJunkin
Centre Development Co., Inc.
PO Box 802087
Dallas, TX 75380-2087
(214) 980-8060

Canadian Open
Richard H. Grimm
Royal Canadian Golf Association
Golf House, R.R. #2
Oakville, Ontario, Canada
L6J 4Z3
(416) 844-1800

Centel Classic
Mac Cairns
2077 Ox Bottom Road
Tallahassee, FL 32312
(904) 222-0921

Chrysler Team Championship
Mike LaMedica
13198 Forest Hill Boulevard
West Palm Beach, FL 33414
(305) 790-1900

Colonial National Invitational
Dr. H. Wallace Schmuck
603 College Avenue
Fort Worth, TX 76104
(817) 332-7975

Deposit Guaranty Golf Classic
Robert Morgan
PO Box 15369
Hattiesburg, MS 39402-5369
(601) 268-9584

Doral Ryder Open
Sheri Oliver
PO Box 522927
Miami, FL 33152
(305) 477-GOLF

Federal Express St. Jude Classic
H. H. "Dutch" Akers
2736 Countrywood Parkway
Cordova, TN 38018
(901) 388-5370

Georgia-Pacific Atlanta Golf Classic
David Kaplan
6065 Roswell Road, NE
Atlanta, GA 30328
(404) 255-0790

Greater Greensboro Open
J. Michael Solomon
332 South Green Street
Box 900
Greensboro, NC 27402
(919) 379-1570

Greater Milwaukee Open
Gordon Kress
4724 West Forest Home Avenue
Milwaukee, WI 53219
(414) 545-6820

Hardee's Golf Classic
Jim Epperley
534 West 1ˢᵗ Avenue
Milan, IL 61264
(309) 787-4663

Hawaiian Open
Art Campbell
The Hawaiian Open Office
PO Box 31267
Honolulu, HI 96820
(808) 836-0060

Hertz Bay Hill Classic
James J. Bell
9000 Bay Hill Boulevard
Orlando, FL 32819
(305) 876-2888

The Honda Classic
Cliff Danely
Tournament Management Board
TPC at Eagle Trace
(305) 755-4220

The International
Larry Thiel
1000 Hummingbird Drive
Castle Rock, CO 80104
(303) 688-6000

Isuzu Kapalua International
Mark Rolfing
Rolfing Productions, Inc.
1000 Kapalua Drive
Kapalua, Maui, HI 96761
(808) 669-4844

JC Penny Classic
Bob Gorham
7998 Boardmoor Boulevard
Largo, FL 33543
(813) 398-5566

Kemper Open
Benjamin Brundred, Jr.
10000 Oaklyn Drive
Potomac, MD 20854
(301) 469-3737

Los Angeles Open
Kevin McCloskey
Los Angeles Junior Chamber of
Commerce
404 South Bixel Street
Los Angeles, CA 90017
(213) 482-1311

Manufacturers Hanover Westchester Classic
John F. McGillicuddy
Manufacturers Hanover Trust
Grand Central Station
PO Box 2702
New York, NY 10163
(212) 286-5381

The Masters Tournament
Colonel David L. Daivs
Augusta National Golf Club
PO Box 2086
August, GA 30913
(404) 738-7761

MCI Heritage Classic
Michael D. Stevens
PO Box 7000
Hilton Head Island, SC 29938
(803) 686-4800

Memorial Tournament
John G. Hines
Muirfield Village GC
PO Box 396
Dublin, OH 43017
(614) 889-6700

Mony Tournament of Champions
Allard Roen
La Costa Country Club
Costa del Mar Road
Carlsbad, CA 92008
(619) 438-9111 ext. 4212/4213

Nabisco Championships of Golf
Jim Wiggins
San Antonio Golf Association
10715 Gulfdale, Suite 265
San Antonio, TX 78216
(512) 341-0823

NEC World Series of Golf
Jim Cook
Firestone Country Club
South Course
452 East Warner Road
Akron, OH 44319
(216) 644-2299

Panasonic Las Vegas Invitational
Jim Cook
801 South Rancho Drive
Suite C-3
Las Vegas, NV 89106
(702) 382-6616

Pensacola Open
Jerry Stephens
Pensacola Sports Association
Civic Center (SE Corner)
PO Box 32582
Pensacola, FL 32506
(904) 434-2800

PGA Championship
John Montgomery
Executive Sports
PGA National Golf Club
1000 Avenue of the Champions
Palm Beach Gardens, FL 33410
(305) 694-1987

Phoenix Open
Pete Ladigo
The Thunderbirds
100 West Clarendon #1812
Phoenix, AZ 85013
(602) 222-5050

Provident Classic
Bob Gary
Provident Life & Accident Insurance
Company
Fountain Square
Chattanooga, TN 37402
(615) 755-1991

Seiko Tucson Open
Bill Reeves
Tucson Conquistadores Inc.
10 North Norton
Tucson, AZ 85719
(602) 792-4501

Shearson Lehman Brothers Andy Williams Open
Tom Morgan
Century Club of San Diego
San Diego Jack Murphy Stadium
9449 Friars Road
San Diego, CA 92108-1771
(619 281-4653

Skins Game
55955 PGA Boulevard
La Quinta, CA 92253
(619) 564-7429

Southern Open
Robert D. Berry
PO Box 2056
Columbus, GA 31902
(404) 324-0411

Southwest Golf Classic
Hal McGlothlin
34 Fairway Oaks Boulevard
Abilene, TX 79606
(915) 698-8800

Tournament Players Championship
John Tucker
TPC Charities, Inc.
TPC Headquarters
PO Box 829
Ponte Vedra Beach, FL 32082
(904) 285-3301

USF&G Classic
925 Common Street Building
Suite 1050
New Orleans, LA 70112
(504) 529-3343

U.S. Open
Bob Murphy
U.S. Open Tournament Office
524 Post Street
San Francisco, CA 94102
(415) 587-0240

Walt Disney World/Oldsmobile Golf Classic
Eric Fredricksen
One Magnolia-Palm Drive
Lake Buena Vista, FL 32830
(305) 824-2250

World Championships of Golf
PGA Tour
Sawgrass
Ponte Vedra Beach, FL 32082
(904) 285-3700

■ LPGA TOURNAMENTS

Atlantic City LPGA Classic
Marriott Seaview Country Club &
Resort
Route 9 and Jimmy Leeds Road
Absecon, NJ 08201
(609) 652-1800

Boston Five Classic
Sheraton Tara Hotel at Ferncroft
Village
Ferncroft Road
Danvers, MA 01923
(617) 777-2500

**Cellular One-Ping Golf
Championship**
Columbia-Edgewater Country Club
2220 N.E. Marine Drive
Portland, OR 97211
(503) 285-3676

Chrysler-Plymouth Classic
Navesink Country Club
PO Box 100
Navesink River Road
Middletown, NJ 07748
(201) 842-3111

Circle K Tucson Open
Randolph North Golf Course
600 South Alverton
Tucson, AZ 85716
(602) 325-2811

du Maurier Classic
Islesmere Golf Club
1199 Bord de l' Eau
Laval, Quebec
Canada H7Y 1A9
(514) 689-4130

GNA/Glendale Federal Classic
Oakmont Country Club
3100 Country Club Drive
Glendale, CA 91208
(818) 242-3106

Henredon Classic
Willow Creek Golf Classic
c/o Emerywood Country Club
800 Country Club Drive
High Point, NC 27262
(919) 889-0818

Jamie Farr Toledo Classic
Glengarry Country Club
Hill Avenue and Crissy Roads
Holland, OH 43528
(419) 865-5831

JC Penney Classic
Bardmoor Country Club
7998 Bardmoor Boulevard
Largo, FL 33543
(813) 398-5566

Konica San Jose Classic
Almaden Golf & Country Club
6663 Hampton Drive
San Jose, CA 95120
(408) 268-4653

Kyocera Inamori Golf Classic
Bernardo Heights Country Club
16066 Bernardo Heights Parkway
San Diego, CA 92128
(619) 487-4022

Lady Keystone Open
Hershey Country Club
Derry Road
Hershey, PA 17033
(717) 533-2360

LPGA Corning Classic
Corning Country Club
East Corning Road
Corning, NY 14830
(607) 936-3711

LPGA National Pro-Am
Lone Tree Country Club
9808 Sunningdale Boulevard
Littleton, CO 80124
(303) 799-4043

**Mastercard International
Pro-Am**
Westchester Hills Golf Club
Ridgeway
White Plains, NY 10605
(914) 948-5020

Mayflower Classic
Country Club of Indianapolis
2801 Country Club Road
Indianapolis, IN 46234
(317) 291-9770

Mazda Champions
Tryall Golf and Beach Club
PO Box 1
Tryall Sandy Bay
Hanover
Jamaica, West Indies
(809) 952-5110

Mazda Classic
Stonebridge Golf & Country Club
17501 No. State Road 7
Boca Raton, FL 33434
(305) 488-0811

Mazda Japan Classic
Musashigaoka Golf Club
665 Nakayama, Hanno City
Saitama Prefecture, Japan
04297-3-333

Mazda LPGA Championship
Jack Nicklaus Sports Center
3565 Kings Mills Road
Kings Island, OH 45034
(513) 241-5200

McDonald's Championship
Du Pont Country Club
Rockland & Black Gates Roads
Wilmington, DE 19898
(302) 654-4435

Nabisco Dinah Shore
Mission Hills Country Club
34-600 Mission Hills Drive
Rancho Mirage, CA 92270
(619) 321-8484

Nestle World Championship
Stouffer Pine Isle Resort
Lake Lanier Island
Holiday Road
Buford, GA 30518
(404) 945-8921

Nichirei Ladies Cup
Tsukuba Country Club
Ohaza Takaoka, Ina-Machi,
Tksukuba-Gun
Ibaragi- ken, 300-23, Japan
02975-1515

Rail Charity Classic
Rail Golf Club
RR 5, Route 124 N
Springfield, IL 62701
(217) 525-0365

Rochester International
Locust Hill Country Club
2000 Jefferson Road
Pittsford, NY 14534
(716) 427-7010

Safeco Classic
Meridian Valley Country Club
24830 135th Avenue SE
Kent, WA 98042
(206) 631-3131

S&H Golf Classic
Pasadena Yacht and Country Club
1600 Royal Palm Drive
St. Petersburg, FL 33707
(813) 345-2646

Santa Barbara Open
Sandpiper Golf Club
7925 Hollister Avenue
Golleta, CA 93117
(805) 968-1541

Sarasota Classic
Bent Tree Country Club
4700 Bent Tree Boulevard
Sarasota, FL 34241
(813) 371-5854

Standard Register Turquoise Classic
Moon Valley Country Club
151 West Moon Valley Drive
Phoenix, AZ 85023
(602) 942-1278

Tsumura Hawaiian Ladies Open
Turtle Bay Country Club
57-091 Kam Highway
Kahuku, Oahu, HI 96731
(808) 293-8811

U.S. Women's Open
Plainfield Country Club
Woodland and Maple Avenues
PO Box 311
Plainfield, NJ 07061
(201) 753-1987

United Virginia Bank Golf Classic
Portsmouth Sleepy Hole
Golf Course
4700 Sleepy Hole Road
PO Box 5130
Suffolk, VA 23435
(804) 393-5050

Women's Kemper Open
Princeville Makai Golf Course
Ka Haku Road, PO Box 3040
Princeville, Kauai, HI 96722
(808) 826-3510

■ SENIOR TOURNAMENTS

American Seniors Golf Association
PO Box 6645
Clearwater, FL 33518
(813) 799-3105

Belleair Invitational Seniors Tournament
25 Belleview Boulevard
Clearwater, FL 33516
(813) 442-6171

Bermuda Seniors Stroke Championship
PO Box HM-433
Hamilton 5
Bermuda
(809) 298-1367

Breakers Seniors Golf Championship
1775 Broadway
New York, NY 10019
(212) 265-7800

British Seniors
The Royal & Ancient Golf Club
St. Andres
Fife KY16 9JD
Scotland

Canadian Senior
R.R. #2
Oakville, Ontario, Canada
L6J 4Z3
(416) 844-1800

Canadian Ladies' Senior
333 River Road
Ottawa, Ontario, Canada
K1L 8H9
(613) 748-5642

Curtis Person Senior Invitational
445 Colonial Road
Memphis, TN 38117
(901) 683-2666

Doherty Challenge Cup
Corla Ridge Country Club
PO Box 24099
Ft. Lauderdale, FL 33307
(305) 564-1271

Giddings Cup
La Quinta Hotel Golf Club
PO Box 29
La Quinta, CA 92253
(619) 564-3672

Great Lakes Seniors
2635 Noble Road
Cleveland Heights, OH 44121
(216) 381-0124

Illinois Senior Women's Invitational
2116 Gunn Drive
Champaign, Il 61821
(217) 356-0311

International Seniors Amateur Mid-Winter Tournament
1775 Broadway
New York, NY 10019
(212) 265-7800

NSSA Tournaments
National Senior Sports Association, Inc.
317 Cameron Street
Alexandria, VA 22314-3269
(703) 549-6711

North Carolina Senior Golf Association
PO Box 488
Wilson, NC 27894

North Carolina Senior Womens' Golf Association
114 Beechwood Drive
Rt. 3
Pine Knoll Shores
Moorehead, NC 28557
(919) 247-4400

North & South Senior Invitational
Pinehurst Country Club
PO Box 4000
Pinehurst, NC 28374
(919) 295-6811

Palmetto Dunes Senior Women's Invitational
4 Tomotley Court
Hilton Head Island, NC 29928
(803) 785-2216

PNGA Seniors
Pacific Northwest Golf Association
10303 Meridian Avenue North
Suite 101
Seattle, WA 98133-9436
(206) 526-1238

**Puerto Rico International
Seniors**
GPO Box 3862
San Juan, PR 00936
(809) 781-2070

Retired Military Seniors
PO Box 7293
Laguna Niguel, CA 92677 ·
(714) 831-3703

**Senior Golf Championship of
Canada**
Golf House, R.R. #2
Oakville, Ontario, Canada
L6J 4Z3
(416) 844-1800

Senior Masters
1749 Port Hemley Circle
Newport Beach, CA 92660
(714) 640-2710

Society of Seniors
5523 Lincoln Street
Bethesda, MD 20817
(301) 530-4315

Southwestern Golf Tournament
Colorado Golf Association
1805 South Bellaire, Suite 100
Denver, CO 80222
(303) 759-9502

SSGA Tournaments
PO Box 1629
Winter Park, FL 32790
(305) 644-2747
(M/W)

**Tarheel Seniors Golf
Association**
PO Box 2223
Charlotte, NC 28211
(704) 542-9161

United States Senior
Governors Division
5 Holly Berry Woods
Lake Wylie, SC 29710
(803) 831-7414

United States Senior
Grand Masters Division
5 Holly Berry Woods
Lake Wylie, SC 29710
(803) 831-7414

USGA Events
Golf House
Far Hills, NJ 07931
(201) 234-2300

USSWGA Championship
United States Senior Women's Golf
Association
Mid Pines Club
1010 Midland Road
Southern Pines, NC 28387

Western Seniors Golf Association and Western Seniors Four-Ball
APRIL-OCTOBER:
4335 Black Oak Drive
Indianapolis, IN 46208
(317) 299-4762
NOVEMBER-APRIL:
1123 Magellan Drive
Sarasota, FL 33580
(813) 756-2615

Wild Dunes Senior Invitational
PO Box 388
or
5757 Palm Boulevard
Isle of Palm, SC 29451
(800) 845-8880

Willow Creek Hall of Fame Championship
Willow Creek Golf Club
PO Box 5046
High Point, NC 27262
(919) 889-0878

Women's North & South Seniors Tournament
326 Jeffrey Lane
Northfield, IL 60093
(312) 446-3766

World Senior
Broadmoor Golf Club
Box 1439
Colorado Springs, CO 80901
(303) 577-5790
(303) 634-7711

■ **PUBLICATIONS**

Florida Golfweek
226 West Central Avenue
PO Box 1458
Winter Haven, FL 33882

Golf Digest
Box 395
Trumbull, CT 06611-0395

Golf Journal
Far Hills, NJ 07931

Golf Traveler
1137 East 2100 South
Salt Lake City, UT 84106

Golf World Magazine
Box 2000
Southern Pines, NC 28387

Green Section Record
USGA Green Section
Golf House
Far Hills, NJ 07931

Gulf Coast Golfer
9182 Old Katy Road, Ste 212
Houston, TX 77055

The Michigan Golfer
7990 West Grand River, Suite C
Brighton, MI 48116

North Texas Golfer
PO Box 162097
Irving, TX 75016

On the Green
PO Box 1463
North Myrtle Beach, SC 29582

PGA Magazine
PO Box 109601
Palm Beach Gardens, FL 33410-9601

Senior Golfer
PO Box 4718
Clearwater, FL 33518

Tour
380 Madison Avenue
New York, NY 10017

■ CAMPS

Conrad Rehling Golf Academy
Box 3355
Tuscaloosa, AL 35404
(205) 348-7041
(J)

John Jacobs Practical Golf Schools
7127 East Suaharo, Suite 101
Scottsdale, AZ 85254
(800) 472-5007
(A/J)

Billy Casper Hall of Fame Golf Camp
5764 Paradise Drive
Suite 7
Corte Madera, CA 94925
(415) 924-8725
In Calif: (800) 542-6005
(J)

Jack Guio Academy of Golf
600 Tabor Drive
Scotts Valley, CA 95066
(J)

LaQuinta Hotel Golf & Tennis Resort
49499 Eisenhower Drive
PO Box 69
LaQuinta, CA 92253
(619) 564-4111
(A)

Northern California PGA Jr. School
Haggin Oaks Golf Club
3645 Fulton Avenue
Sacramento, CA 95820
(J)

Craft-Zavichas Golf School
600 Dittmer
Pueblo, CO 81005
(303) 564-4449
(A)

Golf Digest Instruction Schools
Box 395
Trumbull, CT 06611
(800) 243-6121
(A/J)

FCA Junior Golf Camp
2020 Oak Hammock Drive
Ponte Vedra Beach, FL 32082
(J)

Gator Golf Camp
2800 S.W. 2nd Avenue
Gainesville, FL 32604
(J)

National Academy of Golf
490 Fourth Avenue, North
Naples, FL 33940
(800 642-4340
(A/J)

PGA National Golf Club
1000 Avenue of the Champions
Palm Beach Gardens, FL 33410
(305) 627-2000
(A)

Georgia Junior Golf Foundation Junior Golf Academy
1640 Powers Ferry Road
Building 2
Manetta, GA 30067
(404) 952-4742
(J)

Georgia Southern Golf Camp
Box 8082
Statesboro, GA 30460
(J)

Cyclone Country Golf Camp
PO Box 1995
Ames, IA 50010
(515) 232-3999
(J)

Jayhawks Golf Camp
2104 Inverness Drive
Lawrence, KS 66046
(913) 842-1907
(J)

Murray State University Golf School
c/o Summer Youth Program
Murray State University
Murray, KY 42071
(502) 762-2186
(J)

Tiger Golf Camp
PO Box 16362
Baton Rouge, LA 70893
(J)

Ronnie Scales Golf Camp
University of Maryland Golf Course
College Park, MD 20740
(J)

Chase Golf Camp
Box 1446
Manchester, MA 01944
(617) 526-7514
(J)

Katke Golf Camp
Ferris State College
Big Rapids, MI 49307
(616) 796-0461
(J)

Michigan State University
Summer Sports School
221 Jenison Fieldhouse
E. Lansing, MI 48224
(517) 355-5264
(J)

University of Michigan Summer Camps
1000 South State Street
Ann Arbor, MI 48109
(303) 763-6870
(J)

Minnesota PGA Junior Golf Academy
7101 York Avenue South
Suite 370
Edina, MN 55435
(612) 541-7104
(J)

Rob Hary Golf School
6300 Auto Club Road
Bloomington, MN 55437
(J)

Ole Miss Golf Camp
Division of Continuing Education
University of Mississippi
University, MS 38677
(601) 232-7282, 7241
(J)

Sun Country Section PGA Golf Academy
10035 Country Club Lane, N.W.
Albuquerque, NM 87114
(505) 897-0864
(J)

Campbell University Golf School
Box 10
Blue Creek, NC 27506
(919) 893-4111
(J)

Ben Sutton Golf School
PO Box 9199
Canton, OH 44711
(800) 225-6923
(A)

Duke University Youth Golf School
Duke University Golf Course
Durham, NC 27706
(919) 684-2817
(J)

Elon College Golf School
Box 2197
Elon College, NC 27244
(919) 584-2248
(J)

Jesse Haddock Golf, Inc.
Wake Forest University
Box 6696
Winston-Salem, NC 27109
(919) 761-5619
(J)

Paul Bertholy Golf School
Foxfire Village, NC 27281
(919) 281-3093
(A/J)

Pinehurst Golf Advantage School
Pinehurst Hotel & Country Club
Box 4000
Pinehurst, NC 28374
(919) 295-6811
(A/J)

Pine Needles Camp
Box 88
Southern Pines, NC 28387
(919) 692-7111
(A/J)

University of North Carolina
Junior Golf School
Box 2675
Chapel Hill, NC 27514
(919) 962-2041
(J)

Vince Heafner Golf School
Box 3
Cory, NC 27511
(J)

Whispering Pines Golf School
Whispering Pines, NC 28327
(A/J)

■ INDIVIDUALS

Amy Alcott
c/o Little Woman Enterprises
PO Box 956
Pacific Palisades, CA 90272

Bruce Crampton
7107 Spanky Branch Drive
Dallas, TX 75248

Ben Crenshaw
U.S. Golf Association
Liberty Corners Road
Far Hills, NJ 07931

Lee Elder
1725 K Street NW, Suite 1201
Washington, DC 20006

Dow Finsterwald
c/o Broadmoor Golf Club
Colorado Springs, CO 80906

Joanne Garner
1250 Shoreline Drive
Sugar Land, TX 77478

Hubert Green
PO Box 71
Bay Point
Panama City, FL 32407

Ben Hogan
1917 Centerbury Drive
Fort Worth, TX 76107

Gene Littler
PO Box 1949
Rancho Santa Fe, CA 92067

Nancy Lopez
3203 Country Club Boulevard
Stafford, TX 77477

Bill McIntosh
600 Windsor
Glenview, IL 60025

Dr. Cary Middlecoff
c/o Early Maxwell Association
139 South Main Street
Memphis, TN 38103

Johnny Miller
Silverada Country Club
Napa, CA 94558

Byron Nelson
Route #2 Fairway Ranch
Roanoke, TX 76262

Jack Nicklaus
1208 U.S. Highway #1
North Palm Beach, FL 33408

Arnold Palmer
Box 616
Latrobe, PA 15650

Sandra Palmer
399 West Camino Gardens
Boca Raton, FL 33432

Jerry Pate
PO Box 1790
Pensacola, FL 32598

Calvin Peete
2050 Collier Avenue
Fort Myers, FL 33901

Gary Player
1 Erieview Plaza
Cleveland, OH 44114

Judy Rankin
Kingsmill on the James
Williamsburg, VA 23185

Doug Sanders
8828 Sandrigham Road
Houston, TX 77024

Gene Sarazen
Emerald Beach Box 677
Marco, FL 33937

Sam Snead
Box 777
Hot Springs, VA 24445

Hollis Stacy
c/o LPGA
437 North Sycamore
Los Angeles, CA 90030

Craig Stadler
PO Box 3504
Rancho Santa Fe, CA 92067

Jan Stephenson
6300 Ridglea #1118
Fort Worth, TX 76116

David Stockton
32373 Tres Lagos
Mentone, CA 92359

Lee Trevino
14901 Quorum Drive, Suite 170
Dallas, TX 75240

Ken Venturi
1320 Calle de Maria
Palm Springs, CA 92262

Tom Watson
1726 Commerce Towers
Kansas City, KS 64105

Tom Weiskopf
5412 East Morrison Lane
Paradise Valley, AZ 85253

GYMNASTICS

■ **ORGANIZATIONS—U.S. & CANADA**

Canadian Gymnastics Federation
333 River Road
Ottawa,Ontario,Canada
K1L 8H9
(613) 748-5654

Canadian Rhythmic Sportive Gymnastic Federation
333 River Road
Vanier,Ontario,Canada
K1L 8H9
(613) 748-5654

National Association of Collegiate Gymnastic Coaches (Men)
University of Pittsburgh
PO Box 7436
Pittsburgh, PA 15213
(412) 648-8204

National Gymnastics Judges Association
1150 Morehead Drive
Ann Arbor, MI 48103
(313) 662-4472

U.S. Gymnastics Federation
1099 N. Meridian, Suite 380
Indianapolis, IN 46204
(317) 638-8743

U.S. Gymnastics Safety Association
Washington Office
PO Box 465
Vienna, VA 22180
(703) 476-6660

U.S. Sports Acrobatics Federation
Secretary Address:
725 Piikoi Street, No. 801
Honolulu, HI 96814

President's Address:
5538 South Marine Drive
Tempe, AZ 85283

■ ORGANIZATIONS— INTERNATIONAL

Federation Internationale De Gymnastique
Case Postale 16
CH-3250 Lyss
Switzerland

Internationale Federation of Sports Acrobatics
Boul."Tolboukhine" 18
1000 Sofia
Bulgaria

International Professional Gymnastics Association, Inc.
6825 E. Tennessee, Suite 240
Denver, CO 80224
(303) 695-3850

Trampoline Federation International De
Otzbergstrasse 10
6000 Frankfort am Main 71
R.F.A.
Germany

AUSTRALIA
Australian Gymnastics Federation
27 Levanswell Road
Moorabbin, Vic 3189
Australia
(03) 553-1447

FRANCE
Federation Francaise de Gymnastique
15 rue Taitbout
75009 - Paris
France
(1) 246.39.11

UNITED KINGDOM
British Amateur Gymnastics Association
2 Buckingham Avenue East
Slough SLl 3EA
England
(0753) 32763

Scottish Amateur Gymnastics Association
18 Ainslie Place
Edinburgh EH #6AU
Scotland
031-226 4401

■ PUBLICATIONS

Gymnastics Today
2006 Pine Street
Philadelphia, PA 19103

International Gymnast Magazine
225 Brooks
P.O. Box G
Oceanside, CA 92054

■ CAMPS

Gymnastics Camp
Athletic Department
Stanford University
Stanford, CA 94305
(415) 725-0734
(415) 723-4591
(G)

Gymnastics Camp
University of Denver
Dan G. Garcia
University of Denver Ice Arena
University Park Campus
Denver, CO 80208-0321
(303) 871-3904
(G)

Fighting Illini Summer Camps
113 Assembly Hall
180 South First Street
Champaign, Il 61820
(217) 333-1102

Summer Camps Program
Room 41 Boyden Building
University of Massachusetts
Amherst, MA 01003
(413) 545-3522

Gymnastics Camp
Office of Continuing and Graduate
Education
Attn. Cortland Summer Sports
School
SUNY/Cortland
PO Box 2000
Cortland, NY 13045
(607) 753-5715
(607) 753-4955
(G)

Summer Sports Camps
Charlie McSpiritt, Asst. Dir.
BGSU Athletic Department
Bowling Green, OH 43403
(419) 372-2401
(G)

Coordinator, Summer Sports Camps
Memorial Field House
Indiana University of Pennsylvania
Indiana, PA 15705
(G)

Gymnastics Camp of America
c/o Steve Waples, Camp Director
219 Springwood Lane
San Antonio, TX 78216
(512) 341-3666 (gymnasium)
(512) 680-0944 (gymnasium)
(512) 826-8845 (secretary)
(G)

Sports Camps
University of Wisconsin-Oshkosh
Oshkosh, WI 54901
(414) 424-3212
(G)

■ INDIVIDUALS

Nadia Comaneci
Deva
Romania

Bart Conner
2325 Westwood Drive
Norman, OK 73069

Mitch Gaylord
13441 Delano Street
Van Nuys, CA 91401

Bela Karolyi
17203 Bamwood
Houston, TX 77090

Cathy Rigby McCoy
PO Box 387
Blue Jay, CA 92317

Mary Lou Retton
1637 Beverly Road
Fairmont, WV. 26554

Kurt Thomas
8431 North 75th Street
Scottsdale, AZ 85258

HIGHLAND GAMES

Chicago Highland Games
Pipefest USA, Inc.
230 West Willow
Chicago, IL 60614
(312) 644-8152

Scottish Country Fair
Macalester College
1600 Grand Avenue
Saint Paul, MN 55105
(612) 696-6239

HOCKEY

■ **PROFESSIONAL LEAGUES**

MAJOR LEAGUE

National Hockey League
500 Fifth Avenue
34th Floor
New York, NY 10110
(212) 398-1100
Montreal Address:
1155 Metcalfe, Suite 960
Montreal, Quebec H3B 2W2
(514) 871-9220
President: John A. Ziegler, Jr.

Boston Bruins
Boston Garden
150 Causeway Street
Boston, MA 02114
(617) 227-3209
GM: Harry Sinden
PR Director: Nate Greenberg

Buffalo Sabres
Memorial Auditorium
140 Main Street
Buffalo, NY 14202
(716) 856-7300
GM: Gerry Meehan
PR Director: John Gurtler

Calgary Flames
Olympic Saddledome
PO Box 1540, Station M
Calgary, AL T2P 3B9
(403) 261-0475
GM: Cliff Fletcher
PR Director: Rick Skaggs

Chicago Black Hawks
Chicago Stadium
1800 West Madison
Chicago, IL 60612
(312) 733-5300
GM: Bob Pulford
PR Director: Jim DeMaria

Detroit Red Wings
Joe Louis Arena
600 Civic Center Drive
Detroit, MI 48226
(313) 567-7333
GM: Jim Devellano
PR Director: Bill Jamieson

Edmonton Oilers
Northlands Coliseum
7424-118 Avenue
Edmonton, Alberta, Canada
T5B 4M9
(403) 474-8561
GM: Glen Sather
PR Director: Bill Tuele

Hartford Whalers
One Civic Center Plaza
Hartford, CT 06103
(203) 728-3366
GM: Emile Francis
PR Director: Phil Langan

Los Angeles Kings
The Forum
PO Box 10
Inglewood, CA 90306
(213) 674-6000
GM: Rogie Vachon
PR Director: David Courtney

Minnesota North Stars
Met Center
7901 Cedar Avenue South
Bloomington, MN 55420
(612) 853-9377
GM: Lou Nanne
PR Director: Dick Dillman

Montreal Canadiens
1414 Lambert-Closse Street
Montreal, Quebec, Canada
H3H 1N2
(514) 932-2582
GM: Serge Sevard
PR Director: Michele Lapointe

New Jersey Devils
Byrne Meadowlands Arena
East Rutherford, NJ 07073
(201) 935-6050
GM: Max McNab
PR Director: Dave Freed

New York Islanders
Nassau Vet Memorial Coliseum
Hempstead Turnpike
Uniondale, NY 11553
(516) 794-4100
GM: Bill Torrey
PR Director: Greg Bouris

New York Rangers
Madison Square Garden
4 Penn Plaza
New York, NY 10001
(212) 563-8036
GM: Phil Esposito
PR Director: John Halligan

Philadelphia Flyers
The Spectrum-Pattison Place
Philadelphia, PA 19148
(215) 465-4500
GM: Bob Clarke
PR Director: Roger Gottlileb

Pittsburgh Penguins
Gate No. 7 Civic Arena
Pittsburgh, PA 15219
(412) 642-1894
GM: Ed Johnston
PR Director: Cindy Himes

Quebec Nordiques
Colisee de Quebec
2205 Avenue du Colisee
Quebec, Quebec, Canada
GlL 4W7
(418) 529-8441
GM: Quebec Nordiques
PR Director: Marius Fortier

St. Louis Blues
The Arena
5700 Oakland Avenue
St. Louis, MO 63110
(314) 781-5300
GM: Ron Caron
PR Director: Susie Mathieu

Toronto Maple Leafs
Maple Leaf Gardens
60 Carlton Street
Toronto, Ontario, Canada
M5B ILI
(416) 977-1641
GM: Gerry McNamara
PR Director: Bob Stellick

Vancouver Canucks
Pacific Coliseum
100 North Renfrew Street
Vancouver, B.C., Canada
V5K 3N7
(604) 254-5141
GM: Jack Gordon
PR Director: Norm Jewison

Washington Capitals
Capital Center
Landover, MD 20786
(301) 967-5880
GM: David Poile
PR Director: Lou Corletto

Winnipeg Jets
Winnipeg Arena
15-1430 Maroons Road
Winnipeg Manitoba Can
R3G 0L5
(204) 772-9491
GM: John Ferguson
PR Director: Murray Harding

MINOR LEAGUES

American Hockey League
218 Memorial Avenue
West Springfield, MA 01089
(413) 781-2030

Adirondack Red Wings
1 Civic Center Plaza
Glen Falls, NY 12801
(518) 798-0366

Baltimore Skipjacks
Civic Center, Suite 412
201 West Baltimore Street
Baltimore, MD 21201
(301) 727-0703

Binghamton Whalers
Broome County Arena
Binghamton, NY 13901
(607) 723-8937

Fredericton Express
Aitken Centre, U of NB
Fredericton, NB E3B 5G4
(506) 455-0861

Hershey Bears
Hersheypark Arena
PO Box 866
Hershey, PA 17033
(717) 534-3380

Maine Mariners
1 Civic Center Plaza
Portland, ME 04101
(207) 775-3411

Moncton Golden Flames
PO Box 967
Moncton, N.B., ElC 8N8
(506) 857-4000

New Haven Nighthawks
PO Box 1444
New Haven, CT 06506
(203) 787-0101

Newmarket Saints
PO Box 116
Newmarket Ont Can L3Y 4W3
(416) 895-7078

Nova Scotia Oilers
5284 Duke Street
Halifax, NS B3J 3L2
(902) 429-7600

Rochester Americans
War Memorial Aud
100 Exchange Street
Rochester, NY 14614
(716) 454-5335

Sherbrooke Canadians
360 Parc Street
Sherbrooke Quebec Canada J1E 2J9
(819) 566-2114

Springfield Indians
58 Dwight Street
Springfield, MA 01103
(413) 736-4546

International Hockey League
8650 Commerce Park Place
Suite D
Indianapolis, IN 46268
(317) 872-1524

Flint Spirits Hockey Club
IMA Sports Arena
3501 Lapeer Road
Flint, MI 48503
(313) 743-1780

Kalamazoo Wings
Wings Stadium
3629 Van Rick Drive
Kalamazoo, MI 49002
(616) 349-9772

Muskegon Lumberjacks Hockey Club
L.C. Walker Sports Arena
470 West Western Avenue
Muskegon, MI 49440
(616) 726-5058

Saginaw Generals
118 North Washington
Saginaw, MI 48607
(517) 754-3940

Toledo Goldiggers Hockey Club
Sports Arena
One Main Street
Toledo, OH 43605
(419) 698-1800

Fort Wayne Komets Hockey Club
Allen County Memorial Coliseum
PO Box 5419
(219) 484-2581

Indianapolis Checkers
54 Monument Circle, Suite 800
Indianapolis, IN 46204
(317) 637-8425

Milwaukee Admirals Hockey Club
320 East Michigan
Milwaukee, WI 53202
(414) 278-7711

Peoria Riverman Hockey Club
201 South West Jefferson
Peoria, IL 61602
(309) 673-0562

Salt Lake Golden Eagles
Salt Palace
100 Southwest Temple Street
Salt Lake City, UT 84101
(801) 521-6120

Western Hockey League
616-5920 Macleod Trail South
Calgary Alb Can T2H OK2
(403) 253-8113

Brandon Wheat Kings
Box 832
Brandon, Manitoba
Canada R7A 5Y6
(204) 728-0182

Calgary Wranglers
Box 1060
Calgary, Alberta
Canada T2P 2K8
(403) 262-2100

Kamloops Blazers
737 Victoria Street
Kamloops, B.C.
Canada V2C 2B5
(604) 828-1144

Medicine Hat Tigers
Box 507
Medicine Hat, Alberta
Canada T1A 7G2
(403) 526-2666

Moose Jaw Warriors
Box 74
Moose Jaw, Saskatchewan
Canada S6H 4N7
(306) 694-5711

New Westminster Bruins
Box 2167
New Westminster, B.C.
Canada V3L 5A5
(604) 520-6336

Portland Winter Hawks
Box 3009
Portland, OR 97208
(503) 238-6366

Prince Albert Raiders
Box 351
Prince Albert, Saskatchewan
Canada S6V 5R7
(306) 764-5348

Regina Pats
Box 104
Regina, Saskatchewan
Canada S4P 2Z5
(306) 522-5604

Saskatoon Blades
No. 202-374-3rd Avenue
Saskatoon, Saskatchewan
Canada S7K 1M5
(306) 652-7611

Seattle Thunderbirds
Box 19391
Seattle, WA 98119
(206) 728-9121

Spokane Chiefs
Box 5371
Spokane, WA 99205
(509) 328-0450

Swift Current Broncos
Box 2345
Swift Current, Saskatchewan
Canada S9H 4X6

Victoria Cougars
107-1961 Douglas Street
Victoria, B.C.
Canada V8T 4K7
(604) 385-5611

■ ORGANIZATIONS—U.S. & CANADA

Amateur Hockey Association of the United States
2997 Broadmoor Valley Road
Colorado Springs, CO 80906
(303) 576-4990

American Hockey Coaches Association
c/o Herb Hammond, Secy/Treas
Brown University
Athletic Office, Box 1847
Providence, RI
(401) 863-2236

Canadian Amateur Hockey Association
333 Silver Road
Vanier, Ontario, Canada K1L 8H9
(613) 748-5617

Canadian Oldtimer's Hockey Association
333 River Road
Ottawa, Ontario, Canada K1L 8H9
(613) 748-5646

Central Collegiate Hockey Association
BGSU Ice Arena
Bowling Green, OH 43403
(419) 372-2365

Hockey Canada
333 River Road
Ottawa, Ontario, Canada K1L 8H9
(613) 746-3153

Hockey Hall of Fame and Museum
Exhibition Place
Toronto, Ontario, Canada M6K 3C3
(416) 595-1345

International Hockey Hall of Fame and Museum
York & Alfred Streets, Box 82
Kingston, Ontario, Canada K7L 4V6
(613) 544-2355

National Hockey League Players Association
65 Queen Street West
Suite 210
Toronto, Ontario, Canada M5H 2M5
(416) 868-6574

National Hockey League Services, Inc.
500 Fifth Avenue, 34th Floor
New York, NY 10110
(212) 398-1100

Professional Hockey Writers' Association
c/o Fran Rosa, President
135 Morrisey Boulevard
Boston, MA 02107
(617) 929-2853

U.S. Hockey Hall of Fame
Hat Trick Avenue
PO Box 657
Eveleth, MN 55734
(218) 744-5167

■ ORGANIZATIONS— INTERNATIONAL

Federation Internationale De Hockey
1 Avenue des Arts (Boite 5)
B-1040 Bruxelles, Belgium
+32+2/2194537

International Ice Hockey Federation
Bellevue Str. No. 8
1190 Vienna, Austria
+43+222/325252

AUSTRALIA

Victorian Ice Hockey Association
2a Robe Street
St. Kilda, VIC 3182
Australia
(03) 534 7008

GERMANY, FEDERAL REPUBLIC OF

Deutscher Hockey-Bund
Guts-Muths-Weg 1
5000 Koln 41
Germany
0221/488584

UNITED KINGDOM

British Ice Hockey Association
48 Barmouth Road
Shirley, Croydon CRO 5EQ
England
01-654 6851

USSR

State Committee for Sports
Soviet Ice Hockey Team
USSR - Moscow

■ PUBLICATIONS

American Hockey Magazine
2997 Broadmoor Valley Road
Colorado Springs, CO 80906

Let's Play Hockey
10620 Johnson Road
Bloomington, MN 55437

Michigan Hockey Weekly
25042 W. Warren Road
Dearborn Heights, MI 48127

■ CAMPS

UNITED STATES

Vic's Hockey School Alaska
3343 Vassar Drive
Anchorage, AK 99508
(604) 936-VICS
(907) 274-0046

Hockey Camp
Dobson Ice Arena
Attn: V. Garnsey
321 East Lionshead Circle
Vail, CO 81657
(303) 476-1560
(B)

Summer Camp Program
University of Denver Ice Arena
University Park Campus
Denver, CO 80208-0321
(303) 871-3904
(B)

SVS Hockey School
PO Box 5014
Hamden, CT 06518
(203) 288-0462

Canadian Professional Hockey Schools
1019 West Lake Street
Peoria, IL 61614
(309) 682-2020
(B)

Chicagoland Goaltenders School
c/o Downers Grove Ice Arena
5501 Walnut Avenue
Downers Grove, IL 60515
(312) 971-3780
(B)

Hockey Clinic Registration
Memorial Gymnasium
University of Maine at Orono
Orono, ME 04469-0143
(207) 581-1073

Hockey Camp
Gerholz Institute for Lifelong Learning
Ferris State College
Big Rapids, MI 49307
(616) 796-0461, ext. 3180
(B)

*Michigan Camps of Champions
1000 South State Street
Ann Arbor, MI 48109
(313) 763-5215
(B)

Hockey Camp
Michigan Tech Hockey Development Center
Michigan Technological University
Houghton, MI 49931
(906) 487-2715
(B)

Bemidji International Hockey Camp
Bemidji State University
Bemidji, MN 56601
(218) 751-8403
(B)

Detroit Lakes International Hockey School
PO Box 1299
Detroit Lakes, MN 56501
(218) 847-1970
(B)

Steve Jensen Hockey Schools
8108 Tierneys Woods Road
Bloomington, MN 55438
(612) 941-2132
(612) 424-3637
(218) 534-3298

Ice Time Hockey Schools, Inc.
PO Box 24024
Minneapolis, MN 55424
(612) 920-2620
(B)

Minnesota Hockey Schools
12890 Dory Avenue
Apple Valley, MN 55124
(612) 423-2447

Hockey Camp
Brian Mason
Alumni Gym
Dartmouth College
Hanover, NH 03755
(603) 646-2469

Exeter Hockey School
Phillips Exeter Academy
Exeter, NH 03833
(603) 772-4311, Ext. 323
(B)

Sport-O-Rama
Hockey Camp
18 College Road
Monsey, NY 10952
(B)

Summer Hockey School
St. Lawrence University
Augsbury Physical Education Center
St. Lawrence University
Canton, NY 13617
(315) 379-5696
(B)

*Miami Summer Sports School
Miami University
220 Millett Hall
Oxford, OH 45056
(513) 529-3924
(513) 529-3343
(B)

Penn State Collegiate Prep Ice Hockey Camp
William Curley
The Pennsylvania State University
410 Keller Conference Center
University Park, PA 16802
(814) 865-9173
(B)

CANADA

Hockey Camp
Site 8
Box 9, RR 1
Belcarra, Port Moody
British Columbia V3H 3C8
Canada
(604) 936-VICS

Canadian Professional Hockey Schools
Box 2283
Winnipeg, Manitoba R3C 4A6
(204) 222-2335

Can/Am Hockey Group
Guelph Camp
PO Box 510
Peterborough, Ontario
K9J 6Z6
Canada
(705) 745-2338

Haliburton Hockey Haven
Sept.–June:
Box 631
Thornhill, Ontario L3T 4A5
Canada
(416) 731-6116
July–August:
Box 508
Haliburton, Ontario K0M 1S0
Canada
(705) 457-2392

Hockey Opportunity Camp
Lance Barrs
PO Box 448
Sunridge, Ontario POA 1ZO
Canada
(705) 386-7701
(B)

Huron Hockey School
Paul O'Dacre or Debbie Raymond
Office of Administration
PO Box 203
Cornwall, Ontario K6H 5S7
Canada
(613) 933-2582

Can/Am Hockey Group
PO Box 510
Peterborough, Ontario
K9J 6Z6
Canada
(705) 745-2338
(B)

Paul Torkoff Hockey Schools
162 Glen Springs Drive
Scarborough, Ontario M1W 1X8
Canada
(B)

Trinity Hockey School
Mrs. Diana Sheeler
Port Hope, Ontario L1A 3W2
Canada
(416) 885-4565
(416) 885-2828
(B)

Canadian Professional Hockey Schools
199 Georgian Way
Sherwood Park, Alberta
T8A 2W9 Canada
(403) 467-4404
(B)

Okanagan Hockey School
PO Box 201
Penticton, British Columbia
V2A 6K3 Canada
(604) 493-1408
(B)

International Goaltenders School
PO Box 1605
Yorkton, Saskatchewan
S3N 3L2 Canada
(306) 782-2062
(B)

■ INDIVIDUALS

Syl Apps
241 Alwington Place
Northboro, Massachusetts 01532

Don Awrey
261 Main Street
Northboro, Massachusetts 01532

Doug Barkley
c/o Calgary Flames
PO Box 1540, Station M
Calgary, Alta. Canada T2P 3Bp

Andrew Bathgate
43 Brentwood Drive
Bramalea, Ontario
Canada

Frank Brimsek
1017 13th Street North
Virginia, Minnesota 55792

Lorne B. Carr
2528 66 Avenue SW
Calgary, Alberta
Canada

William Chadwick
22 Rugby Road
Westbury, New York 11590

Bobby Clarke
c/o Philadelphia Flyers
The Spectrum
Pattison Place
Philadelphia, PA 19148

Arthur Coulter
10600 SW 128th Street
Miami, Florida 33176

Bill Cowley
75 Sunnyside
Ottawa, Ontario
Canada

Jim Craig
36 North Main Street
North Easton, MA 02156

Clarence Day
RR 7
St. Thomas, Ontario
Canada

Jacques Demers
5700 Oakland Avenue
St. Louis, MO 63110

Marcel Dionne
30 Empty Saddle
Rolling Hills, CA 90274

Gary Doak
106 Union Wharf
Boston, Massachusetts 02109

Ron Duguay
150 East 58th Street #2610
New York, NY 10010

Woody Dumart
36 Old Farm Road
Needham, Massachusetts 02192

Mervyn Dutton
Balwin Crescent
Calgary, Alberta
Canada

Tony Esposito
16 Masion Court
Elmhurst, IL 60126

Don Gallinger
c/o Mansfield Shirt Co. Ltd.
152 Victoria Street
Kitchener, Ont. Canada N2G 2B5

Rod Gilbert
4 Adams Place
Harrison, New York 10528

Wayne Gretzky
7424 118th Avenue
Edmonton, Alb. Canada T5B 4M9

William D. "Red" Hay
246 Gilmore Trail SW
Calgary, Alberta
Canada

Foster Hewitt
205 Lytton
Toronto, Ontario
Canada

Charlie Hodge
15-1430 Maroons Road
Winnipeg, Manitoba Canada R3G
0L5

Gordie Howe
32 Plank Avenue
Glastonbury, CT 06033

Bobby Hull
14-430 Maroons Road
Winnipeg, Man.,Canada R3G 0L5

Dennis Hull
3300 South Federal Street
Chicago, IL 60616

Tommy Ivan
1800 West Madison Street
Chicago, IL 60612

Forbes Kennedy
178 Kensington Road
Charlottetown, Prince Edward
Island
Canada

Theodore Kennedy
290 Russel Hill Road
Toronto, Ontario
Canada

Guy LaFleur
2313 West St. Catherine Street
Montreal, PQ H3H 1N2
Canada

Guy LaPointe
2313 West St. Catherine Street
Montreal PQ H3H 1N2
Canada

Edgar Laprede
12 Shuniah Street
Thunder Bay, Ontario
Canada

Doug Mohns
c/o New England Rehabilitation
Hospital
Rehabilitation Way
Woburn, MA 01801

Hartland Molson
21 Rosemount
Westmount, Quebec
Canada

Richard Moore
76 Chatillon Drive
Dollard des Ormeaux, Quebec
Canada

William Mosienko
889 Cathedral
Winnipeg, Manitoba
Canada

Lou Nanne
5801 Hidden Lane
Minneapolis, MN 55436

Bruce Norris
11111 Biscayne Boulevard
North Miami, Florida 33161

Willie O'Ree
c/o Strategic Securities Services,
Inc.
2425 Camino Del Rio Street
San Diego, CA 92108

Bobby Orr
1800 West Madison Street
Chicago, IL 60612

Jacques Plante
Mont-Noble, 22
Sierre, Valais 3960
Switzerland

Dennis Potvin
David Cogan Management Co.
330 W. 42nd Street
New York, NY 10036

Qalter Pratt
420 7th Street
New Westminster, British Columbia
Canada

Hubert Quackenbush
18 Washington Street
Rocky Hill, New Jersey 08553

Chuck Rayner
120 Mellick Avenue
Kenora, Ontario
Canada

Leo Reise
c/o Willpak Industries Ltd.
2030 Speers
Oakville, Ontario, Canada L6L 2X8

Maurice Richard
2313 St. Catherine West
Montreal 108 Quebec
Canada

Elwin Romnes
Eastlake Boulevard
Colorado Springs, CO 80910

Jim Rutherford
c/o Windsor Spitfires Hockey Club
334 Wyandotte East
Windsor, Ontario Canada N9A
5W9

David Shrine
3217 Upland Place NW
Calgary, Alberta
Canada

Eddie Shack
71 Fairway Heights Drive
Thornhill, Ontario
Canada

Fred Shero
c/o New Jersey Devils
Meadowlands Arena
PO Box 504
East Rutherford, NJ 07073

J. Cooper Smeaton
1009 Laird
Montreal, Quebec
Canada

William Tutt
2621 Spring Grove Terrace
Box 64
Colorado Springs, Colorado 80906

Norm Ullman
19 Averdon Crescent
Don Mills, Ontario
Canada

Benny Woit
228 Ray Boulevard
Thunder Bay, Ontario
Canada

HORSESHOES

■ ORGANIZATIONS—U.S. & CANADA

Horseshoe Palladium Sports Enterprises, Inc.
34 Munroe Falls, OH 44262
(216) 688-0882

National Horseshoe Pitchers Association
PO Box 278
Munroe Falls, OH 44212
(216) 688-6522

■ PUBLICATIONS

Horseshoe Pitcher's News Digest
PO Box 1606
Aurora, IL 60507

HUNTING & SHOOTING

■ ORGANIZATIONS—U.S. & CANADA

Amateur Trapshooting Association
601 West National Road
Vandalia, OH 45377
(513) 898-4638

Ducks Unlimited, Inc.
1 Waterfowl Way
Ling Grove, IL 60047
(312) 438-4300

National Association of Federally Licensed Firearms Dealers
2801 East Oakland Park Boulevard
Fort Lauderdale, FL 33306
(305) 561-3505

National Rifle Association
1600 Rhode Island Avenue, N.W.
Washington, DC 20036
(202) 828-6255

National Shooting Sports Foundation
1075 Post Road
Riverside, CT 06878
(203) 637-3618

National Skeet Shooting Association
FM 47 at Roft Road
San Antonio, TX 78253
(512) 688-3371

Shooting Federation of Canada
333 River Road
Ottawa, Ontario, Canada K1L 8H9
(613) 748-5659

■ ORGANIZATIONS— INTERNATIONAL

Union Internationale Shooting
Bavariaring No. 21
D-8000 Munchen 2, R.F.A.
Germany
49-89/531-012

■ PUBLICATIONS

Field & Stream
1515 Broadway
New York, NY 10036

The Fisherman
P.O. Box 1994
Sag Harbor, NY 11963

Fishing World Magazine
51 Atlantic Avenue
Floral Park, NY 11001

International Angler
3000 East Las Olas Boulevard
Fort Lauderdale, FL 33316

Rod & Reel
PO Box 42000
Bergenfield, NJ 07621

SFI Bulletin
1010 Massachusetts Avenue, N.W.
Suite 100
Washington, DC 20001

Sport Fishing News
1010 Massachusetts Avenue, N.W.
Suite 100
Washington, DC 20001

Texas Fisherman Magazine
5314 Bingle Road
Houston, TX 77092

■ SCHOOLS

L.L. Bean Hunting School
Freeport, ME 04033
(800) 341-4341 ext. 7100

JAI-ALAI

■ FRONTONS—U.S. & CANADA

Bridgeport Jai-Alai
255 Kossuth Street
Bridgeport, CT 06608
(203) 576-1976

Maimi Jai-Alai
3500 N.W. 37th Avenue
Miami, FL 33142
(305) 633-6400

Milford Jai-Alai
311 Old Gate Lane
Milford, CT 06460
(203) 877-4242

Tampa Jai-Alai
5124 South Dale Mabry Highway
Tampa, FL 33611
(813) 831-1411

Newport Jai-Alai
150 Admiral Kalbfus Road
Newport, RI 02840
(401) 849-5000

■ ORGANIZATIONS— INTERNATIONAL

Federacion Internacional De Pelota Vaca
Sede Central
Aldamar, 5-1 Dcha.
20003 San Sebastian, Espagne

KORFBALL

■ ORGANIZATIONS— INTERNATIONAL

International Korfball Federation
PO Box 1000
3700 BA ZEIST
The Netherlands

LACROSSE

■ ORGANIZATIONS—U.S. & CANADA

Canadian Lacrosse Association
333 River Road
Vanier, Ontario, Canada
K1L 8H9
(613) 748-5641

Canadian Lacrosse Hall of Fame
41–7th Avenue
New Westminster, B.C. V3L 1V9
(604) 521-4740

Eagle League Pro Box Lacrosse
8880 Ward Parkway, Suite 150
PO Box 33088
Kansas City, MO 64114
(816) 926-0060

Intercollegiate Women's Lacrosse Coaches Association
c/o Fefie Barnhill, Pres
College of William & Mary
Williamsburg, VA 23185
(804) 253-4015

The Lacrosse Foundation, Inc.
Newton H. White Athletic Center
Baltimore, MD 21218
(301) 235-6882

Lacrosse Hall of Fame and Museum
Newton H. White Athletic Center
Baltimore, MD 21218
(301) 235-6882

New England Intercollegiate Lacrosse Association
c/o Jim Grube, Pres
Middlebury College
Memorial Field House
Middlebury, VT 05753
(802) 388-3711, Ext. 5263

United States Club Lacrosse Association, Inc.
c/o Harvey Cohen
Murtagh, Cohen & Byrne
1122 Franklin Avenue
Garden City, NY 11530
(516) 747-1000

U.S. Intecollegiate Lacrosse Association
c/o Edward Athey, Secy
Washington College
Chestertown, MD 21620
(301) 778-2800

U.S. Lacrosse Coaches Association
c/o Fran McCall, Secy
Three Roman Lane
West Islip, NY 11795
(516) 587-1748

U.S. Women's Lacrosse Association
c/o Women's Athletic Director
West Chester University
West Chester, PA 19383
(215) 436-2743

■ PUBLICATIONS

Lacrosse Magazine
Newton H. White Athletic Center
Homewood
Baltimore, MD 21218

■ CAMPS

SDSU Lacrosse Camp
San Diego State University
5300 Campanile Drive
San Diego, CA 92182
(619) 265-6871
(B)

Lacrosse Camp
Doug Locker
Whittier College
Whittier, CA 90608
(213) 693-0771, ext. 238
(B)

Lacrosse Camp
Artie Wachter
29885 Roan Drive
Evergreen, CO 80439
(303) 674-7763

Notre Dame Summer Lacrosse Camp
Athletic and Convocation Center
University of Notre Dame
Notre Dame, IN 46556
(219) 239-7724
(B)

The Retriever Lacrosse Camp
Dick Watts
University of Maryland
Baltimore County
5401 Wilkins Avenue
Baltimore, MD 21228
(301) 455-2206
(B)

Lacrosse Camp
Don Zimmerman
Athletic Department
Johns Hopkins University
Baltimore, MD 21218
(301) 338-7479
(B)

Lacrosse Camp
Bob Scalise
Harvard University
Cambridge, MA 02138

Summer Camps Program
Room 41, Boyden Building
University of Massachusetts
Amherst, MA 01003
(413) 545-3522
(B)

New Hampshire Lacrosse Clinic
Ted Garber
Athletic Department
University of New Hampshire
Durham, NH 03824
(203) 488-0221
(B)

All-American Lacrosse Camp
Walt Munze, Director
Box 375
Manlius, NY 13104
(315) 682-2997
(B)

Cornell Summer Sports School
P.O. Box 729
Cornell University
Ithaca, NY 14851
(607) 255-7333
(B)

Lacrosse Camp
David L. Labe
Director of Summer Programs
Hobart and William Smith Colleges
Geneva, NY 14456
(315) 789-5500, ext. 535
(B)

Duke Lacrosse Camp
Tony Cullen
Cameron Indoor Stadium
Duke University
Durham, NC 27706
(919) 684-4427
(B)

Lacrosse Camp
Mr. H. Wayne Curtis
Summer Program Director
The Hill School
Pottstown, PA 19464
(215) 326-1000, ext. 241
(B)

Penn State Lacrosse Camp
The Pennsylvania State University
410 Keller Conference Center
University Park, PA 16802
(814) 863-4563
(G)

Lacrosse Camp
Jim Adams
Box 122
Ivy, VA 22945
(804) 924-3635
(804) 295-7802
(B)

MARTIAL ARTS

■ **ORGANIZATIONS—U.S. & CANADA**

American Amateur Karate Federation
1930 Wilshire Boulevard
Suite 1208
Los Angeles, CA 90057
(213) 283-8261

American Taekwondo Association
6210 Baseline Road
Little Rock, AR 72209

Judo Canada
333 River Road
Ottawa, Ontario, Canada
K1L 8H9
(613) 748-5640

Professional Karate Association
2930 Hutton Drive
Beverly Hills, CA 90210
(213) 550-8831

U.S. Judo, Inc.
PO Box 10013
El Paso, TX 79991
(915) 565-8754

■ ORGANIZATIONS— INTERNATIONAL

Internationale Aikido Federation
Correspondence Address:
Dr. Peter Goldsbury
5-1 Yoshijima Higashi
2-Chome, Naku-ku
Hiroshima City 733
Japan

International Judo Federation
Correspondence:
Matsumae International Judo Institute
Kasumigaseki Building. 33F
3-2-5, Kasumigaseki.
Chiyoda-ku, Tokyo, Japan

World Taekwondo Federation
635 Yoksamdong
Kangnam - ku
Seoul, Korea (135)

World Union of Karatedo Organizations
Senpaku Shinko Building
1-15-16 Toranomon
Minato- ku
Tokyo, 105 Japan

■ PUBLICATIONS

American Karate
351 West 54th Street
New York, NY 10019

ATA Magazine/Martial Arts and Fitness
4180 Elvis Presley Blvd
PO Box 240835
Memphis, TN 381104

Black Belt
1813 Victory Place
Burbank, CA 91504

Fighting Stars-Ninja
1813 Victory Place
Burbank, CA 91504

Inside Kung-Fu
4201 Vanowen Place
Burbank, CA 91505

Karate Illustrated
1813 Victory Place
Burbank, CA 91504

■ CAMPS

KARATE
Shotokan Karate of America, Inc.
Marion Taylor
Hampshire College
Amherst, MA 01002

MARTIAL ARTS
Martial Arts Camp
John Lally
174 Brush Hill Avenue
West Springfield, MA 01089
(413) 676-9391

Martial Arts Camp
Sauk Valley Sports Centre
Irish Hills
Brooklyn, MI 49230
(517) 467-2061

MOTOR SPORTS ━━━━━━

■ **ORGANIZATIAONS—U.S. & CANADA**

American Auto Racing Writers and Broadcasters Association
c/o Dusty Brandel
922 North Pass Avenue
Burbank, CA 91505
(818) 842-7005

Automobile Racing Club of America
PO Box 5217
Toledo, OH 43611
(313) 847-6726

Canadian Racing Drivers Association
11 Yorkkille Avenue, Suite 404
Toronto, Ontario, Canada
M4W 1L2
(416) 924-0533

Championship Auto Racing Teams
2655 Woodward Avenue, Suite 274
Bloomfield Hills, MI 48013
(313) 334-8500

Formula One Spectators Association
8033 Sunset Boulevard, No. 60
Los Angeles, CA 90046
(213) 658-5884

Indianapolis Motor Speedway
Hall of Fame and Museum
4790 West 16th Street
Indianapolis, IN 46222
(317) 248-6747

National American Motors Drivers and Racers Association
923 Plainfield Road
Countryside, IL 60525
(312) 352-8815

National Association for Stock Car Auto Racing
1801 Volusia Avenue
Daytona Beach, FL 32015
(904) 253-0611

National Association of Auto Racing Memorabilia Collectors
214 Meadow Street, Suite 3
Naugatuck, CT 06770
(203) 729-7874

National Hot Rod Association
PO Box 5555
Glendora, CA 91740
(818) 914-4761

National Motorsports Hall of Fame
20 Division Street
Coldwater, MI 49036
(517) 278-7223

National Motorsports Press Association
PO Box 500
Darlington, SC 29532
(803) 393-5931

Sports Car Club of America
6750 South Emporia Street
PO Box 3278
Englewood, CO 80112
(303) 790-1044

United Drag Racers Association
PO Box 4372
Rockford, IL 61110
(815) 877-8041

United Racing Club
PO Box 62
Woodbury Heights, NJ 08097
(609) 468-0825

United States Auto Club
4910 West 16th Street
Indianapolis, IN 46224
(317) 247-5151

World of Outlaws
1750 Alma Road, Suite 112
Richardson, TX 75081
(214) 644-8888

■ ORGANIZATIONS— INTERNATIONAL

International Motor Sports Association
PO Box 3465
Bridgeport, CT 06605
(203) 336-2116

International Hot Rod Association
PO Box 3029
Bristol, TN 37625
(615) 764-1164

World Karting Association
10184 Cleveland Avenue
PO Box 2548
North Canton, OH 44720
(216) 499-0454

AUSTRALIA
Australian Automobile Racing Clubs
PO Box 311
Kings Cross, NSW 2011
(02) 331-7920

FRANCE
Federation Francaise de Sport Automobile
136 rue de Longchamp
75116-Paris
France
(1) 727.97.39

GERMANY, FEDERAL REPUBLIC OF
Automobilclub von Deutschland
Lyoner Strasse 16, Postfach 710166
6000 Frankfurt 71
West Germany
069-6606-0

UNITED KINGDOM
British Automobile Racing Clubs
Thruxton Circuit
Andover, Hants
England
02-6477 2607

British Drag Racing Association
29 West Drive, Highfields
Caldecote, Cambs CB3 7NY
England
(0954) 2110028

**British Stock Car Drivers
Association**
101 Mountain Road
Dewsbury, W Yorks WF12 0BS
England
(0924) 463695

Scottish Motor Racing Club Ltd.
PO Box 5
Duns TD11 3EQ
Scotland
(0361) 82370

■ **INDY CAR TEAMS**

Alex Foods Racing
140 North Roena Street
Indianapolis, IN 46222
Driver: Johnny Rutheford

All American Racers
2334 South Broadway, Box 2186
Santa Ana, CA 92707
Driver: Jan Lammers

Arciero Racing
950 N. Tustin Avenue
Anaheim, CA 92807
Driver: Fabrizio Barbazza

Dale Coyne Racing
19 Lake Drive
Plainfield, IL 60544
Driver: Dale Coyne

Dick Simon Racing
3205 N. Tansel Road
Clermont, IN 46234
Drivers: Ludwig Heimrath, Jr.
         Dick Simon

Domino's Pizza/Team Shierson
4650 West US 223, Box 177
Adrian, MI 49221
Driver: Al Unser, Jr.

Galles Racing
2725 'C' Broadbent Parkway NE
Albuquerque, NM 87107
Drivers: Geoff Brabham
         Jeff MacPherson

Gilmore/Foyt Racing
6415 Toledo Street
Houston, TX 77008
Driver: A. J. Foyt

Gohr Racing
11441 West Rockville Road
Indianapolis, IN 46234
Drivers: Gary Bettenhausen
         Rocky Moran

Hemelgarm Racing
8225 Country Club Place
Indianapolis, IN 46224
Driver: Arie Luyendyk

Kraco Racing
505 East Euclid Avenue
Compton, CA 90224
Driver: Michael Andretti

Leader Cards Racing
8135 West Crawfordsville Road
Indianapolis, IN 46224
Driver: TBA

Machinists Union Racing
Al Unser's Industrial Park
11717 West Rockville Road
Indianapolis, IN 46234
Driver: Josele Garza

M-Group Racing
2265 South Kalamath
Denver, CO 80223
Driver: Rick Miaskiewicz

Mike Curb Motorsports
948 Tourmaline Drive
Newbury Park, CA 91320
Driver: Tom Sneva

Newman-Haas Racing
425 Tower Parkway
Lincolnshire, IL 60015
Driver: Mario Andretti

Patrick Racing
3821 Industrial Drive
Indianapolis, IN 46254
Drivers: Emerson Fittipaldi
        Kevin Cogan

Penske Racing
366 Penske Plaza
Reading, PA 19603
Drivers: Rick Mears
        Danny Sullivan

Raynor Motorsports
East River Road
Dixon, IL 61021
Driver: Dennis Firestone

Truesports
4601 Lyman Drive
Hilliard, OH 43026
Driver: Bobby Rahal

Vince Granatelli Racing
130 North Roena Street
Indianapolis, IN 46222
Driver: Robert Guerrero

■ CART TRACKS

ARIZONA
Phoenix International Raceway
PO Box 13088
Phoenix, AZ 85002
(602) 252-3833

CALIFORNIA
Grand Prix Association of Long Beach
110 West Ocean Boulevard
Suite 22
Long Beach, CA 90802
(213) 437-0341

Laguna Seca Raceway
1025 Monterey Highway 68
Salinas, CA 93908
Mailing Address:
PO Box SCRAMP
Monterey, CA 93940
(408) 373-1811

CANADA
Molson Indy Exhibition Stadium
Gate 9, 4th Floor
Toronto Ontario Canada
M6K 3C3
(416) 869-8538

FLORIDA
Miami Motorsports
7254 SW 48th Street
Miami, FL 33155
(305) 662-5660

INDIANA
Indianapolis Motor Speedway
4790 West 16th Street
Speedway, IN 46224
(317) 241-2501

MICHIGAN

Michigan International Speedway
12626 U.S. 12
Brooklyn, MI 49230

NEW JERSEY

New Jersey Sports & Exposition Authority
Meadowlands Arena
East Rutherford, NJ 07073
(201) 460-4367

OHIO

Indy Car Grand Prix
Burke Lakefront Airport
Cleveland, OH 44114
(216) 781-3500

Mid-Ohio Sports Car Course
Steam Corners Road
PO Box 3108
Lexington, OH 44904
(419) 884-2295

OREGON

Portland Rose Festival
220 NW Second Avenue
Portland, OR 97209
(503) 227-8200

PENNSYLVANIA

Pennsylvania International Raceway
PO Drawer F
Highway 191
Nazareth, PA 18064
(215) 759-8000

Pocono International Raceway
PO Box 500
Long Pond, PA 18334
(717) 646-2300

WISCONSIN

Go Racing
5941 West Bluemound Road
Milwaukee, WI 53213
(414) 453-5514

Road America
81 Lake Street
Elkhart Lake, WI 53020
(414) 876-3366

■ USAC RACING EVENTS

ARIZONA

Manzanita Park Speedway
(602) 276-9401
(602) 276-7575
Race Organizer:
Keith Hall
3417 West Broadway
Phoenix, AZ 85041
(602) 276-9401

Phoenix International Raceway
(602) 246-7777
Race Organizer:
Buddy Jobe & Patrick T. Johnson
PO Box 11388
Phoenix, AZ 85061
(602) 246-7777

ARKANSAS

Riverside Speedway
(501) 735-8071
Race Organizer:
Gust Mirestes
3710 Summer Avenue
Memphis, TN 38122
(901) 372-7734
(901) 353-0870

CALIFORNIA
Ascot Park
(213) 323-1142
Race Organizer:
Cary Agajanian
PO Box 98
Gardena, CA 90247
(213) 321-5323

Garden State Raceway
(415) 373-9300
Race Organizer:
John Williams
PO Box 3300
Livemore, CA 94550
(415) 373-9300

Madera Speedway
(209) 673-7223
Race Organizer:
Ron Banks
PO Box 837
Madera, CA 93639
(209) 674-8511

Mesa Marin Raceway
(805) 366-5711
Race Organizer:
Marion Collins
PO Box 9518
Bakersfield, CA 93389
(805) 366-5711

Santa Maria Speedway
(805) 922-2233
Race Organizer:
Doug Fort
PO Box 1270
Morro Bay, CA 93442

Shasta Speedway
(916) 241-5027
Race Organizer:
Gary Cressey
PO Box 524
Redding, CA 96099
(916) 241-4932

Spinners Airport Raceway Park
Race Organizer:
Jess Land
PO Box 1843
Porterville, CA 93258
(209) 784-6301

Ventura Raceway
(805) 985-5433
Race Organizer:
Jim Naylor
2810 West Wooley Road
Oxnard, CA 93030
(805) 985-5433

CANADA
Western Speedway
(604) 474-2151
Race Organizer:
Reg Midgely
PO Box 4190
Station A
Victoria, B.C. Canada
V8X 3X8
(604) 381-7223

ILLINOIS
DuQuoin State Fairgrounds
(618) 542-5484
Race Organizer:
Merle Miller
DuQuoin State Fair
PO Box 191
DuQuoin, IL 62832

Illinois State Fairgrounds

(217) 782-1977
(217) 782-1978
Race Organizer:
Merle Miller
Illinois State Fairgrounds
PO Box 576
Springfield, IL 62705
(217) 782-6661

Prairie Capital Convention Center

(217) 788-8800
Race Organizer:
Pat Fitzgerald
No. 1 Convention Center Plaza
Springfield, IL 62701
(217) 788-8800

Santa Fe Park Speedway

(312) 839-1050
Race Organizer:
Howard Tiedt
91st and Wolf Road
Hinsdale, Illlinois 60521
(312) 839-1051

Springfield Speedway

(217) 522-3522
Race Organizer:
Joe Shaheen
3200 East Clear Lake Avenue
Springfield, IL 62702
(217) 522-3522

Tri-City Speedway

(618) 797-6579
Race Organizer:
Dave Reidt
8877 Highway 70 (Suite 14)
St. Charles, MO 63303
(314) 447-3158

Vermilion County Fair & Expo Speedway

(217) 443-6588
Race Organizer:
Wayne Etzel
R.R. #2, Box 412
Kankakee, IL 60901
(815) 932-2518

INDIANA

Action Track Speedway

(812) 232-9627
Race Organizer:
James Bogetto
Route 2
Clinton, IN 47842
(812) 234-2615

Anderson Speedway

(317) 642-0206
Race Organizer:
Trackside Associates, Inc.
2900 Mock Avenue
Muncie, IN 47302
(317) 288-4587

Bloomington Speedway

(812) 824-7400
Race Organizers:
Dennis Richardson
Mike Miles
351 Church Lane
Bloomington, IN 47401
(812) 824-7862

Hoosier Dome

(317) 632-8165
Race Organizer:
Entertainment & Sports Promotions, Inc.
5567 Hollister Drive
Speedway, IN 46224
(317) 293-4963

Indianapolis Motor Speedway

(317) 241-2501
Race Organizer:
Joseph R. Cloutier
4790 West 16th Street
Speedway, IN 46224
(317) 241-2501

Indianapolis Raceway Park

(317) 291-4090
Race Organizer:
Bob Daniels
9700 Crawfordsville Road
PO Box 34377
Indianapolis, IN 46234
(317) 291-4090

Indianapolis Speedrome

(317) 353-9301
Race Organizer:
John Stiles
American Productions, Inc.
PO Box 301
Greenwood, IN 46142
(317) 888-7265

Indiana State Fairgrounds

(317) 923-3431
Race Organizer:
Bruce Walkup
558 South Section
Sullivan, IN 47882
(812) 268-4393

Kokomo Speedway

(317) 459-3877
Race Organizer:
Bill Lipkey
Box 448
Kokomo, IN 46901
(317) 452-5527

Lawrenceburg Speedway

(812) 537-3599
Race Organizers:
Mel Johnson & Bill Hummel
Box 111
Lawrenceburg, IN 47025
(812) 537-4793
(812) 926-3599

Lincoln Park Speedway

(317) 653-3485
Race Organizers:
Mike & Venola Farrar
4830 Industrial Parkway
Indianapolis, IN 46226
(317) 545-7157
(317) 359-8168

Memorial Coliseum

(219) 482-9502
Race Organizer:
Bill Lipkey
Memorial Coliseum
4000 Parnell Avenue
Fort Wayne, IN 46805
(219) 489-1016

Paragon Motor Speedway

(317) 537-2366
Race Organizers:
Mike & Sue Johnson
2240 State Road 252
Martinsville, IN 46151
(317) 342-3018

Sportsdome Speedway

(812) 282-7551
Race Organizer:
Paul Gibson
PO Box 607
Jeffersonville, IN 47130
(502) 267-7362

KANSAS

81 Speedway
(316) 755-1781
Race Organizer:
C. Ray Hall
4761 Krueger
Wichita, KS 67220
(316) 744-1322

KENTUCKY

Barren County Speedway
(502) 678-5418
Race Organizers:
Ricky Pollock & Dennis Bull
Rt. #1, Box 180
Glasgow, KY 42141
(502) 678-3391

MARYLAND

Hagerstown Speedway
(301) 796-0252
Race Organizer:
Con Meyer
140 Bond Street
Westminster, MD 21157
(301) 461-2736
(301) 796-9746

MASSACHUSETTS

Seekonk Speedway
(617) 336-8488
Race Organizer:
D. Anthony Venditti
1782 Fall River Avenue
Seekonk, MA 02771
(617) 336-8488

MISSOURI

St. Charles Speedway
(314) 838-7277
Race Organizers:
Bobby Wente
1001 Autumn Leaf
St. Charles, MO 63303
(314) 441-7287

NEVADA

Las Vegas International Speedrome
(702) 644-1482
Race Organizer
Alex Rodriguez
6445 Alta Drive
Las Vegas, NE 89107
(702) 870-4541

NEW HAMPSHIRE

Lee, USA Speedway
(603) 659-2719
Race Organizer:
Russ Conway
693 Salem Street
Groveland, MA 01834
(617) 373-3589

NEW JERSEY

Flemington Fairgrounds Speedway
(201) 782-2413
Race Organizer:
Paul Kuhl
PO Box 293
Flemington, NJ 08822
(201) 782-2034

NEW YORK
Dundee Raceway Park
(315) 243-8686
Race Organizer:
Steve Wetmore
109 Burns Terrace
Penn Yan, NY 14527
(315) 536-4608

Five Mile Point Speedway
(607) 775-2376
Race Organizer
Jim Randall
RD #2, Box 396
Windsor, NY 13865
(605) 655-2243

OHIO
Eldora Speedway
(513) 338-8511
Race Organizer:
Earl Baltes
Eldora Speedway
Rossburg, OH 45362
(513) 338-3815

Southern Ohio Raceway
(614) 776-7896
Race Organizer:
Benny Christian
7901 Gallia Street
Wheelsburg, OH 45694
(614) 574-8759

OKLAHOMA
Lawton Speedway
(405) 355-6417
Race Organizer:
Lanny Edwards
328 North 40th Street
Lawton, OK 73501
(405) 355-0907

Oklahoma City Fairgrounds Speedway
(405) 946-1122
Race Organizer:
Larry Hill
PO Box 10774
Midwest City, OK 73140
(405) 947-6864

OREGON
Coos Bay Speedway
(503) 267-7045
Race Organizers:
Phil & Mary Kuykendall
590 Adams Street
Coos Bay, OR 97420
(503) 267-7045

Portland International Raceway
(503) 285-2883
Race Organizer:
Dennis Huth
PO Box 1146
Medford, OR 97501
(503) 285-2881
(503) 285-2883

Roseburg Speedway
(503) 440-4505
Race Organizer:
Roy Harvey
PO Box 278
Roseburg, OR 97470
(503) 679-4849

PENNSYLVANIA
Williams Grove Speedway
(717) 766-4778
Race Organizer:
Nick Turo
Williams Grove Speedway
1 Speedway Drive
Mechanicsburg, PA 17055
(717) 766-4778

TEXAS

Devil's Bowl Speedway

(214) 222-2421
Race Organizer:
Lanny Edwards
328 North 40th Street
Lawton, OK 73501
(405) 355-0907

UTAH

Bonneville Raceway Park

(801) 250-2600
Race Organizer:
Robert Ipson
6555 West 2100 South
Salt Lake City, UT 84120
(801) 250-2600

WASHINGTON

Ephrata Speedway

(509) 754-2192
Race Organizer:
Lawrence Borck
PO Box 453
Ephrata, WA 98823
(509) 754-3983

Evergreen Speedway

(206) 794-7711
Race Organizer
International Promotions
7012 220th SW
Mount Lake Terrace, WA 98043
(206) 776-2802

Spanaway Speedway

(206) 537-7551
Race Organizer:
Dick Boness
Route #3, Box 395-D
Eatonville, WA 98328
(206) 832-3126

Tri-City Raceway

(509) 967-3851
Race Organizer
Wayne Walden
3301 South Cascade
Kennewick, WA 99336
(509) 582-5694

WEST VIRGINIA

West Virginia Motor Speedway

(304) 489-9125
Race Organizer:
Jim Weigle
c/o Holiday Inn
U.S. 50 and I-77
Parkersburg, WV 26101
(304) 485-6200

WISCONSIN

Hales Corners Speedway

(414) 425-4700
Race Organizers:
John Kaishian and Jim Engel
Midwest Speedways, Inc.
6646 West Fairview Avenue
Milwaukee, WI 53213
(414) 774-4748

Wisconsin State Fair Park Speedway

Race Organizer:
GO Racing (Grant King & Frank Giuffre)
King: 8155 Crawfordsville Road
Indianapolis, IN 46234
(317) 297-1209
Giuffre: 9770 S. Ridgeview Drive
Oak Creek, WI 53154
(414) 761-2300

■ SCHOOLS

*Skip Barber Racing School, Inc.
Ashley Fall Road
North Canaan, CT 06018
(203) 824-0771

Bob Bondurant School of High Performance Driving
Sears Point International Raceway
Highways 37 and 121
Sonoma, CA 95476
(707) 938-4741

*Jim Russel British School of Motor Racing
PO Box 119 Ac-6
Mt. Tremblant
Quebec JOT 1Z0
Canada
(800) 821-8755

Bertil Roos School of High Performance Driving
PO Box 221A
Blakeslee, PA 18610
(717) 646-7227

■ INDIVIDUALS

Bobby Allison
140 Church Street
Hueytown, AL 35020

Mario Andretti
53 Victory Lane
Nazareth, PA 18064

A. J. Foyt
6415 Toledo
Houston, TX 77008

Andrew Furman
Latonia Race Course
PO Box 75007
Cincinnati, OH 45275

Andy Granatelli
24615 West Park Mirimar
Calabasas, CA 91302

Dan Gurney
2334 South Broadway
Santa Anna, CA 92707-0186

Janet Guthrie
343 East 30th Street #312N
New York, NY 10016

Gordon Johncock
PO Box 546
Pima, AZ 85543

Rick Mears
12101 Cattle King Drive
Bakersfield, CA 93307

Sterling Moss
46 Shepherd Street, Mayfair
London W1Y 8JN
England

Shirley Muldowney
16755 Parthenia Street #4
Sepulveda, CA 91343

Paul Newman
59 Coleytown Road
Westport, CT 06880

Richard Petty
Route #3, Box 631
Randleman, NC 27317

Tom Sneva
3001 E. Valley Vista
Paradise, AZ 85253

Jackie Stewart
24 Rte. de Divonne
1260 Lyon
Switzerland

Danny Sullivan
100000 Santa Monica Boulevard
#400
Los Angeles, CA 90067-7007

Al Unser
7625 Central, N.W.
Albuquerque, NM 87105

Bobby Unser
7700 Central, S.W.
Albuquerque, NM 87105

Cale Yarborough
c/o National Association of Stock
Car Auto Racers
1811 Volusia Avenue
Daytona Beach, FL 32015

MOTORCYCLING

■ ORGANIZATIONS

**American Motorcyclist
Association**
33 Collegeview Avenue
Westerville, OH 43081
(614) 891-2425
(800) AMA-JOIN
Mailing Address:
PO Box 6114
Westerville, OH 43081-6114

■ PUBLICATIONS

*American Motorcyclist
Magazine*
PO Box 6114
Westerville, OH 43081-6114

Cycle Magazine
3807 Wilshire Boulevard
Los Angeles, CA 90010

Cycle News Inc.
PO Box 498
Long Beach, CA 90801

Cycle World Magazine
1499 Monrovia Avenue
Newport Beach, CA 92663

Dirt Bike Magazine
Dirt Wheels Magazine
Motocross Action Magazine
10600 Sepulveda Boulevard
Mission Hills, CA 91345

Harley Women Magazine
P O Box 864
Addison IL 60101

■ INDIVIDUALS

Evel Knievel
9960 York Alpha Drive
North Royalton, OH 44133

NETBALL

■ ORGANIZATIONS—
INTERNATIONAL

**International Federation of
Netball Associations**
Miss Moira Ord, Pres
9 Belhaven Terrace
Kelvinside
Glasgow G12 OTG
Scotland

ORIENTEERING

■ ORGANIZATIONS—U.S. &
CANADA

**Canadian Orienteering
Federation**
333 River Road
Ottawa, Ontario, Canada
K1L 8H9
(613) 748-5649

U.S. Orienteering Federation
PO Box 1444
Forest Park, GA 30051
(404) 363-2110

■ ORGANIZATIONS—
INTERNATIONAL

**International Orienteering
Federation**
c/o Mrs. Sue Harvey, Secy/Genl
Mile End, Maint Street
Doune
Scotland GB-FK16 6BJ

PENTATHLON

■ ORGANIZATIONS—U.S. &
CANADA

**U.S. Modern Pentathlon
Association**
PO Box 8178
San Antonio, TX 78208
(512) 228-0007

PETANQUE

■ ORGANIZATIONS—U.S. & CANADA

American Petanque Association USA, Inc.
PO Box 19234
Washington, DC 20036
(301) 839-3721

■ ORGANIZATIONS— INTERNATIONAL

Federation International De Petanque
12, Cours Joseph-Thierry
F-13001 Marseille
France

RACQUET SPORTS

■ ORGANIZATIONS—U.S. & CANADA

American Amateur Racquetball Association
815 North Weber
Colorado Springs, CO 80903
(303) 635-5396

American Collegiate Racquetball Association
110 1/2 North Michigan Avenue
Big Rapids, MI 49307
(616) 796-9291

American Platform Tennis Association
Box 901
Upper Montclair, NJ 07043
(201) 732-5325-6

American Professional Racquetball Organization
5089 North Granite Reef Road
Scottsdale, AZ 85253
(602) 945-0143

Canadian Badminton Association
333 River Road
Ottawa, Ontario, Canada K1L 8H9
(613) 748-5605

Canadian Racquetball Association
333 River Road
Ottawa, Ontario, Canada K1L 8H9
(613) 748-5653

Canadian Squash Racquets Association
333 River Road
Ottawa, Ontario, Canada K1L 8H9
(613) 748-5672

Canadian Table Tennis Association
333 River Road
Ottawa, Ontario, Canada K1L 8H9
(613) 748-5675

National Intercollegiate Squash Racquets Association
c/o Ken Torrey, Pres
Columbia University
Dodge Fitness Center
119th & Broadway
New York, NY 10027
(212) 280-4001

National Left-Handers Racquet Sports Association
2701 Sterlington Road
Box 252
Monroe, LA 71203

National Paddleball Association
PO Box 712
Flint, MI 48501

National Squash Tennis Association
50 Vanderbilt Avenue
New York, NY 10017
(212) 661-2070

National Table Tennis League
1218 Third Avenue North
Seattle, WA 98109
(206) 282-6449

U.S. Badminton Association
501 West Sixth Street
Papillion, NE 68046
(402) 592-7309

U.S. Handball Association
930 North Benton Avenue
Tuscon, AZ 85711
(602) 795-0434

U.S. Paddle Tennis Association
189 Seeley Street
Brooklyn, NY 11218
(718) 788-2094
West Coast Office:
Box 30
Culver City, CA 90232
(213) 625-1511

U.S. Squash Racquets Association
211 Ford Road
Bala-Cynwyd, PA 19004
(215) 667-4006

U.S. Table Tennis Association
Olympic Complex
1750 East Boulder Street
Colorado Springs, CO 80909
(303) 578-4583

Women's Professional Racquetball Association
PO Box 95563
Atlanta, GA 30347
(404) 636-7575

World Professional Squash Association
12 Sheppard Street, Suite 500
Toronto Ontario Canada M5H 3A1
(416) 869-3499

■ **INTERNATIONAL**

International Amateur Racquetball Federation
Laan van N.O. Indie 287
2593 BS DEN HAAG
Holland
+31+70/838300

International Badminton Federation
24 Winchcombe House
Winchcombe Street
Cheltenham, Glos
England
+4+242/34904

International Racquet Sports Association
132 Brookline Avenue
Boston, MA 02215
(617) 236-1500

International Squash Racquets Association

National Sports Centre
Sophia Gardens
Cardiff, Wales, CF1 9SW
+44+222/374771

International Table Tennis Federation

53, London Road
St. Leonards-on-Sea
East Sussex
TN37 6AY England
+44+424/430971

■ PUBLICATIONS

Indiana Racquet Sports
207 South Main
PO Box 216
Frankfort, IN 46041

National Racquetball

416 Douglas Avenue
Dunedin, FL 33528

Racquet

32 West 39th Street
New York, NY 10018

Squash News

Arcadia Road, Box 52
Hope Valley, RI 02832

■ CAMPS

Squash Camp
Dave Fish
Director, A.R.C. Inc.
c/o Harvard Department of Athletics
60 J.F.K. Street
Cambridge, MA 02138
(617) 449-2499

RODEO ━━━━━━━━━

■ ORGANIZATIONS—U.S. & CANADA

International Pro Rodeo Association, Inc.
PO Box 615
Pauls Valley, OK 73075
(405) 238-6488

Longhorn World Championship Rodeo, Inc.
3679 Knight Road
Whites Creek, TN 37189
(615) 876-1016
Mailing Address:
PO Box 8160
Nashville, TN 37207

National High School Rodeo Association, Inc.
118 North Third Street
Douglas, WY 82633
(307) 358-4391

National Intercollegiate Rodeo Association
Walla Walla Community College
500 Tausick Way
Walla Walla, WA 99362
(509) 527-4321

National Little Britches Rodeo Association
411 Lakewood Circle, Suite C205
Colorado Springs, CO 80910
(303) 597-0451

Professional Rodeo Cowboys Association, Inc.
101 Pro Rodeo Drive
Colorado Springs, CO 80919
(303) 593-8840

■ **EVENTS**

American Royal Livestock, Horse Show and Rodeo
1701 American Royal Court
Kansas City, MO 64102
(816) 221-9800

Calgary Exhibition and Stampede
Box 1060
Stampede Park
Calgary, AB T2P 2K8
Canada
(403) 261-0101

Grand National Livestock, Expo, Rodeo and Horse Show
Cow Palace
PO Box 34206
San Francisco, CA 94134
(415) 469-6000

Houston Livestock Show and Rodeo
PO Box 20070
Houston, TX 77225
(713) 791-9000

Payson Rodeo and Parade
Chamber of Commerce
Drawer A
Payson, AZ 85541
(602) 474-4515

Pendleton Round-Up
Box 609
Pendleton, OR 97801
(503) 276-2553

■ **PUBLICATIONS**

Prorodeo Sports News
101 Pro Rodeo Drive
Colorado Springs, CO 80919

Rodeo News
PO Box 587
Pauls Valley, OK 73075

ROLLERSKATING

■ **ORGANIZATIONS—U.S. & CANADA**

Roller Skating Rink Operators Association
7700 A Street
Lincoln, NE 68501
(402) 483-7551

U.S. Amateur Confederation of Roller Skating
7700 A Street
PO Box 83067
Lincoln, NE 68501
(402) 483-7551

■ **ORGANIZATIONS—
INTERNATIONAL**

**Federation Internationale De
Roller Skating**
PO Box 83067
Lincoln, NE 68501
(402) 483-7551

■ **PUBLICATIONS**

Roller Skating Business
Box 81846
Lincoln, NE 68501

Skate Magazine
PO Box 81846
Lincoln, NE 68501

RUGBY

■ **ORGANIZATIONS—U.S. &
CANADA**

**Canadian Rugby Union/
Federation Canadience De
Rugby**
333 River Road
Vanier, Ontario, Canada K1L 8H9
(613) 748-5657

**Cape Fear Rugby Sevens
Tournament**
Box 5351 Station 1
Wilmington, NC 28403
(919) 256-4658

**Eastern Rugby Union of
America, Inc.**
226 Lauriston Street
Philadelphia, PA 19128
(215) 483-1399

Midwest Rugby Football Union
PO Box 51
Milwaukee, WI 53201
(414) 771-8895

**Pacific Coast Rugby Football
Union**
PO Box 15157
San Francisco, CA 94115
(415) 531-9161

**U.S. of America Rugby Football
Union, Ltd.**
625 Broadway
San Diego, CA 92101
(619) 239-3094

**Western Rugby Football Union
of the U.S.**
Office of the Chancellor
University of Kansas
Lawrence, KS 66045
(913) 864-3134

■ **ORGANIZATIONS—
INTERNATIONAL**

AUSTRALIA

**Australian Rugby Football
League**
8-18 Bent Street, 19th Floor
Sydney, NSW 2000
Australia
(02) 231 4488

**Australian Rugby Football
Union**
Rugby Union House
Crane Place
Sydney, NSW 2000
Australia
(02) 27 7777

Australian Rugby Football School's Union
St. Edmunds College, Canberra Avenue
Manuka, ACT 2603
(062) 95 3598

FRANCE
Federation Francaise de Rugby
7 cité d'Antin
75009 - Paris
France
(1) 874.84.75

IRELAND
Irish Rugby Football Union
62 Lansdowne Road
Dublin 4
Ireland
684601

UNITED KINGDOM
Rugby Football League
180 Chapeltown Road
Leeds LS7 4HT
England
(0532) 624637

Rugby Football Schools Union
Whitton Road
Twickenham TW2 7RQ
England
01-892 8161

Scottish Rugby Union
Marrayfield
Edinburgh EH12 5PJ
031-337 2346

Welsh Rugby Union
PO Box 22
Cardiff CF1 1JL
(0222) 390111

■ **PUBLICATIONS**

In Touch
1106 Oregon
Joliet, IL 60435

Rugby
2414 Broadway
New York, NY 10024

RUNNING

■ **ORGANIZATIONS—U.S., CANADA & INTERNATIONAL**

American Medical Joggers Association
PO Box 4704
North Hollywood, CA 91607
(818) 989-3432

American Running & Fitness Association
2001 S Street N.W., Suite 540
Washington, DC 20009
(202) 667-4150

Association of Road Racing Athletes
1081 Paulsen Building
Spokane, WA 99201
(509) 838-8784

Los Angeles Marathon, Inc.
9911 W. Pico Blvd. No. 630
Los Angeles, CA 90035
(213) 879-1987

National Running Data Center, Inc.
PO Box 42888
Tucson, AZ 85733
(602) 326-6416

New York Road Runners Club
9 East 89th Street
New York, NY 10028
(212) 860-4455

Road Runners Club of America
1224 Orchard Village Lane
Manchester, MO 63011
(314) 391-6712

Walker's Club of America
PO Box M
Livingston Manor, NY 12758
(914) 439-5155

■ **MARATHONS**

U.S. & CANADA

Pepsi Vulcan Marathon
Rick Melanson
2704 Vistaviz Forest Terrace
Birmingham, AL 35216

Rocket City Marathon
HTC
c/o Harold Tinsley
8811 Edgehill Drive
Huntsville, AL 35802

Equinox Marathon
Marathon Director, UAF
410 Tanana Drive
105 Patty Gym
Fairbanks, AK 99775

Mayor's Midnight Sun Marathon
Municipality of Anchorage, Parks and Recreation
Attn: Jim Mayo
Box 196650
Anchorage, AK 99519-6650

Mica Mountain Marathon
Bob Deeran
9551 East Palm Tree
Tucson, AZ 85748

Mule Mountain Marathon
Army Emergency Relief
USAG
Attn: ASH-PCA-PSR
Fort Huachuca, AZ 85613-6000

Phoenix City Marathon
Marathon Classics, Inc.
PO Box 15432
Phoenix, AZ 85060

Whiskey Row Marathon
Prescott Trailblazers
1955 Thumb Butte
Prescott, AZ 86301

Hogeye Marathon
Dr. George C. Moore
HPER Building, Room 309
University of Arkansas
Fayetteville, AR 72701

Audi-San Francisco Pamakid Runners
San Francisco Marathon
PO Box 27557
San Francisco, CA 94127

Avenue of the Giants Marathon
Six Rivers Running Club
PO Box 214
Arcata, CA 95521

Bidwell Classic
1043 Hobart Street
Chico, CA 95926

Big Sur International
William Burleigh
Box 222620
Carmel, CA 93922

California International Marathon
Sacramento Long Distance Runners
Association
PO Box 161149
Sacramento, CA 95816

David Marathon
Fleet Feet of Davis
132 East Street
Davis, CA 95616

Fresno Marathon
Graham Partlett
846 North Harrison
Fresno, CA 93728

Heart of San Diego Marathon
American Heart Association
3640 Fifth Avenue
San Diego, CA 92103

Hemisphere Marathon
Jack Nakanishi
4117 Overland Avenue
Culver City, CA 90230

Humboldt Redwoods Marathon
Six Rivers Running Club
PO Box 214
Arcata, CA 95521

International Friendship Marathon
End of the Line Race Consulting
PO Box 1049
Coronado, CA 92118

Long Beach Marathon
1827 Redondo Avenue
Long Beach, CA 90804

Los Angeles Marathon
PO Box 67750
Los Angeles, CA 90067

Mission Bay Marathon
11315 Cascada Way
San Diego, CA 92124

Modesto Marathon
Joann Amundson
PO Box 3605
Modesto, CA 95352

Napa Valley Marathon
Kaye or Chuck Hall
4516 Dry Creek Road
Napa, CA 94558

Orange Grove Marathon
Lyle Deem
PO Box 495
Loma Linda, CA 92354

Palos Verdes Marathon
George Owens
PO Box 153
Palos Verdes Estates, CA 90274

Point Reyes Marathon
TRS
c/o Rich Boas
278 Marin Avenue
Mill Valley, CA 94941

Redding Marathon
Steve Davidson
PO Box 3564
Redding, CA 96049

Russian River Run
PO Box 204
Ukiah, CA 95482

Sacramento Marathon
Ron Sturgeon
PO Box 995
Dixon, CA 95620

Santa Monica Sports and Arts Marathon
Santa Monica Recreation and Parks Department
1685 Main Street
Santa Monica, CA 90401

Sri Chinmoy/Foster City Marathon
Sri Chinmoy Marathon Team
2438 16th Avenue
San Francisco, CA 94116

Sri Chinmoy/Santa Barbara Marathon
Sri Chinmoy Marathon Team
200 Entrance Road #3
Goleta, CA 93114

Summit Marathon
Runner's Factory
51 University Avenue
Los Gatos, CA 95030

Valley of the Flowers Marathon
PO Box 694
Lompoc, CA 93438

National Capital Marathon
Andrea Acheson
PO Box 426
STN. A
Ottawa, KIN 8V5
Canada

Wild Wild West Marathon
Lone Pine Chamber of Commerce
PO Box 749
Long Pine, CA 93545

Leadville Marathon
Colorado Mountain College
Leadville, CO 80461

Mayor's Cup Marathon
Bill Michaels & Co.
PO Box 18938
Denver, CO 80218

Pikes Peak Marathon
Nancy Hobbs
PO Box 26250
Colorado Springs, CO 80936

Pueblo River Trail Marathon
Cecil Townsend
Southern Colorado Runners
YMCA
7th and Albany
Pueblo, CO 81003

John W. English Marathon
Middletown Park and Recreation Department
245 DeKoven Drive
Middletown, CT 06457

Nipmuck Trail Marathon
David Raczkowski
PO Box 191
Willington, CT 06279

Stamford Marathon
Stamford Athletic Association
880 Canal Street
Stamford, CT 06902

Billy Gordon, Jr. Memorial Marathon
Box Pringle
28 Charleston Square
Ormond Beach, FL 32074

Blue Angel Marathon
Mr. James Currie, Athletic Director
NAS Pensacola
Pensacola, FL 32508-5000

Jacksonville Marathon
Jacksonville Marathon Association
3853 Baymeadows Road
Jacksonville, FL 32217

Space Coast Marathon
H. Tucker
4200 South A-1-A Hwy
Melbourne Beach, FL 32951

Infantry Marathon
Community Recreation Division
Building 241
Attn: Infantry Marathon
Fort Benning, GA 31905-5226

Big Island Marathon
PO Box 1381
Hilo, HI 96721

Honolulu Marathon
Honolulu Marathon Association
3435 Waiahe Street #208
Honolulu, HI 96816

Kilauea Volcano Wilderness Marathon
PO Box 189
HVNP, HI 96718

Maui Marathon
Valley Isle Road Runners
PO Box 888
Kihea, Maui, HI 96753

Windward Marathon
Carl Ellsworth
502A Kawailua Road
Kailua, HI 96734

Coeur d'Alene Marathon
PO Box 2393
Coeur d'Alene, ID 83814

Salmon River Summer Marathon
Pat Hauf
PO Box 790
Salmon, ID 83407

America's/Chicago Marathon
Pete Kozura
214 West Erie Street
Chicago, IL 60610

Lake County Marathon
636 Ridge Road
Highland Park, IL 60035

Muncie Marathon
Muncie Family YMCA
500 South Mulberry
Muncie, IN   47305
(317) 288-4448

Sunburst Marathon
South Bend Tribune Sunburst Marathon
223 West Colfax Avenue
South Bend, IN 46626

Sioux City Marathon
Dick Benton
2600 Solyn
Sioux City, IA 51106-3911

University of Okoboji Marathon
Paul Williams
Box 3077
Spencer, IA 51301

Derby City Marathon
Gill Clark
Metro Parks Track Club
PO Box 36452
Louisville, KY 40233

KAKE-TV Wichita Marathon
Clark Ensz
121 North River Boulevard
Wichita, KS 67203

Kansas Relays Marathon
Kansas Relays Road Races
Allen Field House
Room 143
Lawrence, KS 66045

Baton Rouge Marathon
Len Bahr, Race Director
2352 Ferndale
Baton Rouge, LA 70808

Red River Marathon
Gary Stroud
122 Southwood
Bossier City, LA 71111

Casco Bay Marathon
PO Box 3172
Department RT787
Portland, ME 04104

Maine Coast Marathon
Susan or Dick Roberge
110 Union Avenue
Old Orchard Beach, ME 04064

Maryland Marathon
PO Box 11394
Baltimore, MD 21239

Washington's Birthday Marathon
Larry Noel
105 Northway Road
Greenbelt, MD 20770

Boston Marathon
17 Main Street
Hopkinton, MA 01748

Cape Cod Marathon
PO Box 699
West Falmouth, MA 02574

Hyannis Marathon
Jack Glennon
PO Box 1678
Hyannis, MA 02601

Bayshore Marathon
Terry McHoskey
4319 Deerwood
Traverse City, MI 49684

Detroit Free Press International Marathon
321 West Lafayette
Detroit, MI 48231

Greater Grand Rapids Marathon
Bob Wilson
652 Crosswell
Grand Rapids, MI 49506

Twin Cities Marathon
Box 24193
Minneapolis, MN 55424

Heart of America Marathon
Joe Duncan
2980 Maple Bluff Drive
Columbia, MO 65201

St. Louis Marathon
St. Louis Track Club
6611 Clayton Road
Suite 200
St. Louis, MO 63117

Third Olympiad Memorial Marathon
c/o Marathon Sports
13453 Chesterfield Plaza
Chesterfield, MO 63017

Governor's Cup Marathon
PO Box 451
Helena, MT 59624

Lincoln Marathon
Thomas Kay
2809 Jackson Drive
Lincoln, NE 68502

Omaha Riverfront Marathon
John Thomas
502 North 40th Street
Omaha, NE 68131

Las Vegas Marathon
Al Boka
PO Box 81262
Las Vegas, NV 81282

Dartmouth-Hitchcock Medical Center Marathon
Dartmouth-Hitchcock Medical Center
HB 7500
Hanover, NH 03756

New Jersey Waterfront Marathon
Tim McLoone
One Path Plaza
Jersey City, NJ 07306

Bandelier Marathon
Aaron Goldman
4723 Sandia Drive
Los Alamos, NM 87544

Duke City Marathon
PO Box 14903
Albuquerque, NM 87191

Shiprock Marathon
Bill Burke
Box 1020
Farmington, NM 87499

Taos Marathon
Bruce Gomez
PO Box 2245
Taos, NM 87571

Atlantic City Marathon
Pete Giunta
215 Partridge Street
Albany, NY 12202

Champlain Valley
Plattsburgh & Clinton County Chamber of Commerce, Inc.
PO Box 310
Plattsburgh, NY 12901

Dutchess County Classic
Pete SanFilippo
8 Carmine Drive
Wappingers Falls, NY 12590

Lake Ontario Marathon
Tim McAvinney
79 Merrick Street
Rochester, NY 14615

Newsday Long Island Marathon
Sports Unit
Eisenhower Park
East Meadow, NY 11554

New York City Marathon
NY Road Runners Club
9 East 89th Street
New York, NY 10128

Taylor Wineglass Marathon
Laura
PO Box 98
Corning, NY 14830

Athens Marathon
James L. Mason
13 North May
Athens, OH 45701

Columbus Marathon
Corporate Processing Department
6290 Busch Boulevard, Suite 20
Columbus, OH 43271-0980

Revco-Cleveland
Reno Starnomi
PO Box 46604
Bedford, OH 44146

Andy Payne Marathon
United National Indian Tribal
Youth, Inc.
PO Box 25042
Oklahoma City, OK 73125

Gage Roadrunner Marathon
Virginia Mann
PO Box 238
Gage, OK 73843

ORRC Portland Marathon
PO Box 4040
Beaverton, OR 97076

Trail's End Marathon
Seaside Chamber of Commerce
PO Box 7
Seaside, OR 97138

Crater Lake Rim Run
Bob Reirich
5830 Mack Avenue
Klamath Falls, OR 97603

God's Country
Potter County Recreation, Inc.
PO Box 245
Coudersport, PA 16915

Jim Thorpe Marathon
Deemer Durham
PO Box 1011
Carlisle, PA 17013

Johnstown YMCA Marathon
100 Haynes Street
Johnstown, PA 15901

Philadelphia Independence Marathon
Memorial Hall
Philadelphia, PA 19131

Pittsburgh Marathon
Pittsburgh Marathon, Inc.
638 USX Building
Pittsburgh, PA 15230

Ocean State Marathon
Kevin Pilkington
591 Angell Street
Providence, RI 02906

Carolina Marathon
Russ Pate
PO Box 5092
Columbia, SC 29250

Black Hills Marathon
Box 9243
Rapid City, SD 55709

Sioux Falls Marathon
Rick Hanson
PO Drawer A
Sioux Falls, SD 57101

Chickamauga Battlefield
The Front Runner
5425 Highway 153
Hickson, TN 37343

Austin Marathon
The Austin Marathon, Inc.
9442 North Capitol of Texas
Highway
Building 1, Suite 625
Austin, TX 78759

Courthouse to Cove Marathon
2829 Main Avenue
Copperas Cove, TX 76522

Dallas White Rock Marathon
PO Box 743335
Dallas, TX 75374-3335

Daybreak Marathon
Wills Point Run
PO Box 44
Wills Point, TX 75169

The Desert Marathon
Half Fast Track Club
PO Box 31218
El Paso, TX 79931

Funfest Marathon
Funfest Races
1700 Polk Street
Amarillo, TX 79102

Galveston Marathon
1920 Black Bay Drive
Galveston, TX 77551

Houston-Tenneco Marathon
PO Box 56682
Houston, TX 77027

Marathon of the Great Southwest
Abilene YMCA
Po Box 3137
Abilene, TX 79604

Prude Ranch Marathon
Prude Ranch
Attn: Fun Run Day
Box 1431
Fort Davis, TX 79734

The Woodlands Marathon
Doug Earl
South County YMCA
PO Box 7152
The Woodlands, TX 77387

St. George Marathon
City of St. George
Leisure Services Department
86 South Main Street
St. George, UT 84770

Marine Corps Marathon
PO Box 188
Quantico, VA 22134

Richmond Newspapers Marathon
333 East Grace Street
Richmond, VA 23219

Shamrock Marathon
Jerry Bocrie
2308 Maple Street
Virginia Beach, VA 23451

Skagit Flats Marathon
1048 Gardner Road
Burlington, WA 98233

Capital City Marathon
Capital City Marathon Association
Box 1681
Olympia, WA 98507

Emerald City Marathon
Kimberly Brown
157 Yesler Way #208
Seattle, WA 98104

Run for Jesus
Yakima Foursquare Church
3414 Tieton Drive
Yakima, WA 98902

Seattle Marathon
Seattle Marathon Association
2464 33rd Avenue #131
Seattle, WA 98199

Paavo Nurmi Marathon
Marja Dashner
Executive Director
Hurley Chamber of Commerce
110A 2nd Ave.
So. Hurley, WI 54534

INTERNATIONAL

Bermuda Marathon
Marathon Tours, Inc.
108 Main Street
Charlestown District
Boston, MA 02129

Catalunya-Barcelona Marathon
Comissio Marathon Catalunya
Jomqueras, no. 16 9e. C. 08003
Barcelona, Spain

Fletcher Challenge
D. H. Kenny
44 Hillcrest Avenue
Roturua, N.Z.

Jamaica International Marathon
Sunburst Holidays
4779 Broadway
New York, NY 10034

London Marathon
Keith Prouse, Inc.
234 West 44th Street
New York, NY 10036

Olympia City Marathon
Marathon Munchen
PO Box 33 06 65
D-8000
Munich 33
West Germany

Paris Marathon
Marathon Tours
108 Main Street
Charlestown District
Boston, MA 02129

Shanghai Cup
Marathon Tours
108 Main Street
Charlestown District
Boston, MA 02129

Stockholm Marathon
Marathon Tours
108 Main Street
Charlestown District
Boston, MA 02129

World Veterans Championships
Sports Travel International, Ltd.
PO Box 7823
San Diego, CA 92107

■ PUBLICATIONS

BAA Boston Marathon Magazine
100 Massachusetts Avenue
Boston, MA 02115

Boston Running News
237 Main Street
Waltham, MA 02154

The Indiana Runner
7990 South Grand River
Brighton, MI 48116

The Michigan Runner
7990 West Grand River
Brighton, MI 48116

New England Running
PO Box 658
Brattleboro, VT 05301

New York Running News
9 East 89th Street
New York, NY 10128

Road Race Management
507 2nd Street, NE
Washington, DC 20002

Runner's World
33 East Minor Street
Emmaus, PA 18049

Running & Fitness
2001 S Street N.W. Suite 540
Washington, DC 20009

Running Through Texas
PO Box 470467
Dallas, TX 75247

■ CAMPS

Running Camp
Coach Jim Hunt
2500 Gold Course Road
Bayside, CA 95524
(707) 826-3731

Nike Mount Elbert Distance Camp
Frank Mencin, Camp Director
PO Box 1276
Leadville, CO 80461
(303) 486-2460
(303) 486-0756

Georgia Tech/Mike Spino Running School
Georgia Tech Athletic Association
150 Third Street N.W.
Atlanta, GA 30332
(404) 894-5433

Jayhawk Track Camps
Steve Kueffer
143 Allen Field House
University of Kansas
Lawrence, KS 66045
(913) 864-3486
(913) 842-1705

Summer Camps Program
Room 41 Boyden Building
University of Massachusetts
Amherst, MA 01003
(413) 545-3522

Vermont Distance Running School
c/o Summer College
Johnson State College
Johnson, VT 05656
(802) 635-2356, ext. 312

Mountaineer Track Camp
PO Box 877
Morgantown, WV 26507
(304) 293-2300

SHOOTING

■ **ORGANIZATIONS—U.S. &
CANADA**

**Amateur Trapshooting
Association**
601 West National Road
Vandalia, OH 45377
(513) 898-4638

**National Association of
Federally Licensed Firearms
Dealers**
2801 East Oakland Park Blvd
Fort Lauderdale, FL 33306
(305) 561-3505

National Rifle Association
1600 Rhode Island Avenue, N.W.
Washington, DC 20036
(202) 828-6255

**National Shooting Sports
Foundation**
1075 Post Road
Riverside, CT 06878
(203) 637-3618

**National Skeet Shooting
Association**
SM 471 at Roft Road
San Antonio, TX 78253
(512) 688-3371
(800) 531-7928
Mailing Address:
PO Box 680007
San Antonio, TX 78268-0007

**Non-Powder Gun Products
Association**
200 Castlewood Drive
North Palm Beach, FL 33408
(305) 842-4100

Shooting Federation of Canada
333 River Road
Ottawa, Ontario, Canada   K1L 8H9
(613) 748-5659

■ **ORGANIZATIONS—
INTERNATIONAL**

Union Internationale Shooting
c/o M. Horst Schreiber, Secy Genl
Bavararing No. 21

SHUFFLEBOARD

■ **ORGANIZATIONS**

**International Shuffleboard
Association, Inc.**
40 South Independence
Pharr, TX 78577
(512) 787-5751

SLED DOG RACING

The Iditarod Visitors Bureau
PO Box 251
Nome, AK 99762
(907) 443-5535

International Sled Dog Association
PO Box 446
Nordman, ID 83848
(208) 443-3153

SOCCER

■ PROFESSIONAL LEAGUES

American Indoor Soccer Association
1200 Boston Post Road
Guilford, CT 06437
(203) 453-9089

Major Indoor Soccer League
757 Third Avenue, Suite 2305
New York, NY 10017
(212) 486-7070

Baltimore Blast
Civic Center
201 West Baltimore Street
Baltimore, MD 21201
(301) 528-0100

Chicago Sting
425 North Michigan Avenue,
Suite 777
Chicago, IL 60611
(312) 245-5444

Cleveland Force
34555 Chagrin Boulevard
Moreland Hills, OH 44022
(216) 247-4740

Dallas Sidekicks
777 Sports Street
Dallas, TX 75207
(214) 760-7330

Kansas City Comets
Kemper Arena
1800 Genesse Street
Kansas City, MO 64102
(816) 421-7770

Los Angeles Lazers
PO Box 10
Inglewood, CA 90306
(213) 419-3179

Minnesota Strikers
8100 Cedar Avenue South,
Suite 115
Minneapolis, MN 55420
(612) 854-3616

St. Louis Steamers
212 North Kirkwood
St. Louis, MO 63122
(314) 821-1111

San Diego Shockers
3500 Sports Arena Boulevard
San Diego, CA 92110
(619) 224-4625

Tacoma Stars
CS 2267 1121 A Street
Tacoma, WA 98401
(206) 627-8474

Wichita Wings
114 South Broadway
Wichita, KS 67202
(316) 262-3545

■ **ORGANIZATIONS—U.S. & CANADA**

American Soccer Industry Council
200 Castlewood Drive
North Palm Beach, FL 33408
(305) 842-4100

American Youth Soccer Organization
5403 West 138th Street
Hawthorne, CA 90250
(213) 643-6455

Canadian Soccer Association
333 River Road
Ottawa,Ontario,Canada K1L 8H9
(613) 746-5667

Intercollegiate Soccer Association of America
c/o John Reeves, Pres.
University of Rochester
Department of Sports and Recreation
Rochester, NY 14627
(716) 275-4301

National Intercollegiate Soccer Officials Association
131 Moffit Boulevard
Islip, NY 11751
(516) 277-3878
(516) 589-6100 Ext. 313

National Soccer Coaches Association of America
PO Box 5074
Stroudsburg, PA 18630
(717) 421-8720

National Soccer Hall of Fame
58 Market Street
Oneonta, NY 13820
(607) 432-3351

Professional Soccer Reporters' Association
c/o John Leptich, Pres.
1922 Williamsburg Drive
Streamwood, IL 60107
(312) 222-3475 (W)
(312) 885-7127 (H)

S.A.Y.-Soccer-U.S.A.
(Soccer Association for Youth)
5945 Ridge Avenue
Cincinnati, OH 45213
(513) 351-7291

U.S. Soccer Federation
1750 East Boulder Street
Colorado Springs, CO 80909
(303) 632-5551

U.S. Youth Soccer Association
PO Box 18406
Memphis, TN 38181-0406
(901) 363-0010

Western Soccer Alliance
2815 Second Avenue, Suite 430
Seattle, WA 98121
(206) 441-3390

■ **ORGANIZATIONS— INTERNATIONAL**

Federation Internationale De Football Association
Case Postale 85
CH-8030 Zurich
Switzerland

ARGENTINA
Asociacion del Futbol Argentina
Viamonte 1366/76
1053 Buenos Aires, Argentina

AUSTRALIA
Australian Soccer Federation
36-38 Clarence Street, 1st Floor
Sydney, NSW 2000
Australia
(02) 29 7025

Australian Women's Soccer Association
1/7 McGhee Avenue
Mitcham, VIC 3132
Australia
(03) 467 3063

BRAZIL
Confederacao Brasilleiria de Desportos
Rua de Alfandega 70
PO Box 1078
Rio de Janeiro, Brazil

CHINA, PEOPLE'S REPUBLIC OF
Football Association of the People's Republic of China
9 Tiyuguan Road
Beijing, China

DENMARK
Dansk Boldspil-Union
P.H. Lings Alle 4
2100 Copenhagen, Denmark

FRANCE
Federation Francaise de Football
60 bis, avenue d'Iena
75783 Paris Cedex 16
France
(1) 720.65.40

GERMANY, FEDERAL REPUBLIC OF
Otto-Fleck-Schneise 6
Postschliessfach 710405
6 Frankfurt (Main) - 71, Germany

IRELAND
Football Association of Ireland
80 Meerion Square
Dublin 2
Ireland
766864

ISRAEL
Israel Football Association
12 Carlebach Street
PO Box 20188
Tel-Aviv, Israel

ITALY
Federazione Italiana Giuoco Calcio
Via Gergorio Allegri, 14
C.P. 2450
00198 - Roma, Italy

JAPAN
The Football Association of Japan
1-1-1 Jinnan, Shibuya-Ku
Tokyo, Japan

MEXICO
Federacion Mexicana de Futbol Asociacion
Abraham Gonzales, 74, Colonia Juarez
Mexico, D.F. Z.P. 6

New Zealand Football Association, Aukland
111 Apirana Avenue
PO Box 18296
Glen Innes, Aukland, New Zealand

SPAIN

Real Federacion Espanola de Futbol
Calle Alberto Bosch, 13
Apartado postal 347
Madrid 14, Spain

UNITED KINGDOM

Association of Football Badge Collectors
46 Ellington Drive
Gershwyn Road
Brighton Hill Rise
Basingstoke, Hants RG 22 4EZ
England

Football Association, LTD
16 Lancaster Gate
London W2 3LW
England
261110

Football Association of Scotland
6 Park Gardens
Glasgow G3 7YF
Scotland
041-332 6372/3

Football Association of Wales, LTD
3 Fairy Road
Wrexham, Clwyd LL13 7PS
England
(0978) 262172

Football League LTD
319 Clifton Drive Suth
Lytham St. Annes, Lancs FY 8 1JG
England

Professional Footballers Association
124 Corn Exchange Buildings
Manchester M4 3BN
England

Scottish Football League
188 West Regent Street
Glasgow G2 4RY
Scotland
041-248 3844/6

USSR

USSR Football Federation
Luzhnetskaya Naberezhnaja, 8
119270 Moscow, USSSR

VENEZUELA

Federacion Venezolana de Futbol
Av. Este Estadio - Quinta Claret 28,
El Paraiso
Abdo. Posto 14160 Candelaria
Caracas, Venezuela

■ PUBLICATIONS

Kick
350 Fifth Avenue
New York, NY 10118

Soccer America
PO Box 23704
Oakland, CA 94623

Soccer Digest
1020 Church Street
Evanston, IL 60201

Soccer-Mania
3686 Clarke Road
Memphis, TN 38115

Soccer Match
PO Box 39A27
Los Angeles, CA 90039

■ CAMPS

*Golden West Sports, Inc.
Box 8454
Fountain Valley, CA 92728
(714) 549-9556

*Team Challenge Soccer Camps
1618 Locust Street
Walnut Creek, CA 94596
(415) 943-1041

Soccer Center, Inc.
8534 East Acampo Road
Acampo, CA 95220
(209) 333-1658

Soccer Camp
Athletic Department
Stanford University
Stanford, CA 94305
(415) 723-9375
(415) 725-0757

Summer Sports Camps-Soccer
Horst Richardson
The Colorado College
Colorado Springs, CO 80903
(303) 473-2233

Soccer Camp
Artie Wachter
29885 Roan Drive
Evergreen, CO 80439
(303) 674-7763

*No. 1 Goalkeeper's Camp
1200 Boston Post Road
Guilford, CT 06437
(203) 453-0059

Goalkeeper Camp
Dan Gaspar
40 Oakwood Drive
Glastonbury, CT 06033
(203) 633-5161

Select Soccer Academy, Inc.
Rick Darella, Director
PO Box 683
Glastonbury, CT 06033
(203) 633-3689
(203) 646-3177

Indiana Soccer Camp
2108 Grovesnor Place
Bloomington, IN 47401
(812) 339-8974

Friends School Soccer Camp
5114 North Charles Street
Baltimore, MD 21210
(301) 435-2800

Soccer Academy
John Ellis
Western Maryland College
Westminister, MD

Tamarack Soccer Camp
Mike or Louisa Kenney
Easton Road
Franconia, NH 03580
(603) 823-8880

Drew Soccer School
Tom Leanos
Drew University
Madison, NJ 07940
(201) 377-3000, Ext. 573

Soccer Camp
Bob Reasso
Rutgers Athletic Center
PO Box 1149
Piscataway, NJ 08854
(201) 932-4206

All-Pro Goalkeepers School
Soccer Office
Monmouth College
West Long Branch, NJ 07764

Colgate University
Soccer Camp
George Herrick
365 First Avenue
Vestal, NY 13850
(607) 754-2818
or
Mike Doherty
Cogate University
Hamilton, NY 13346
(315) 824-1000, ext. 574

*Soccer Camps of America
G. Peppe Pinton
PO Box 97
Tappan, NY 10983
(201) 666-4549

Soccer Camp
David L. Labe
Director of Summer Programs
Hobart and William Smith Colleges
Geneva, NY 14456
(315) 789-5500, ext. 535
(B)

Soccer Camp
Grimm House
The College at New Paltz
State University of New York
New Paltz, NY 12561
(914) 257-2620

Duke Soccer Camp
PO Box 22176
Duke Stadium
Durham, NC 27706
(919) 933-6039

All-Star Camps
Ray S. Alley, Director
PO Box 19445
Greensboro, NC 27419
(919) 282-5414

Soccer Camp
Mr. H. Wayne Curtis
Summer Program Director
The Hill School
Pottstown, PA 19464
(215) 326-1000, Ext. 241
(B)

Post-to-Post Striker's Camp
1054 Anna Knapp Blvd.-20
Mt. Pleasant, SC 29464
(803) 884-9437

Clemson Tiger Soccer Camp
Coach I. M. Ibrahim
PO Box 1469
Clemson, SC 29633
(803) 654-1736
(B)

Virginia Soccer Camp
PO Box 267
Earlysville, VA 22936
(804) 973-4088
(804) 924-3480
(B)

Village Camps
David Fowler
1296 Coppet, Switzerland
4122 7620 59
London: 01 995 5134
(B)

■ INDIVIDUALS

Craig Allen
c/o Cleveland Force
34555 Chagrin Boulevard
Moreland Hills, OH 44022

Nebo Bandovic
c/o St. Louis Steamers
212 North Kirkwood
St. Louis, MO 63122

Franz Beckenbauer
Feldbrunnerstrasse 16
2000 Hamburg 13
West Germany

Ricky Davis
c/o New York Express
North Village Green
School House Road
Levittown, NY 11756

Scott Manning
c/o Baltimore Blast
Civic Center
201 West Baltimore Street
Baltimore, MD 21201

Diego Maradona
Maternidad 2
Barcelona 14 Spain

Ralph Meade
c/o Federacao Portuguesa de
Futebol
Praca de Alegria N. 25
Apartado 21.000
1128 Lisboa Codex
Portugal

Pele
44 East 50th Street
New York, NY 10022

Branko Segota
c/o San Diego Sockers
3500 Sports Arena Boulevard
San Diego, CA 92110

Tatu
c/o Dallas Sidekicks
777 Sports Street
Dallas, TX 75207

Juli Veee
c/o San Diego Sockers
3500 Sports Arena Boulevard
San Diego, CA 92110

Steve Zungul
c/o Tacoma Stars
CS 2267-1121 A Street
Tacoma, WA 98401

SOFTBALL

■ ORGANIZATIONS—U.S. & CANADA

Amateur Softball Association
2801 Northeast 50th Street
Oklahoma City, OK 73111
(405) 424-5266

Canadian Amateur Softball Association
333 River Road
Ottawa, Ontario
Canada K1L 8H9
(613) 746-5735

Cinderella Softball League, Inc.
PO Box 1411
Corning, NY 14830
(607) 937-5469

National Softball Hall of Fame & Museum
2801 Northeast 50th Street
Oklahoma City, OK 73111
(405) 424-5267

National Wheelchair Softball Association
PO Box 737
Sioux Falls, SD 57101-0737
(605) 334-0000

Over the Line
Old Mission Beach Athletic Club
3990 Old Town Avenue,
Suite 2705A
San Diego, CA 92110
(619) 297-8480

Over the Line Players Association
PO Box 84964
San Diego, CA 92138

Softball Canada
333 River Road
Ottawa, Ontario, Canada
K1L 8H9
(613) 748-5668

U.S. Slo-Pitch Softball Association
3935 South Crater Road
Petersburg, VA 23805
(804) 520-3042
Mailing Address:
Box 2047
Petersburg, VA 23804

■ ORGANIZATIONS— INTERNATIONAL

British Amateur Baseball and Softball Federation
197 Newbridge Road
Hull HU9 2LR
England
(0482) 76169

International Federation of Softball
2801 Northeast 50th Street
Oklahoma City, OK 73111

International Softball Congress, Inc.
6007 East Hillcrest Circle
Anaheim Hills, CA 92807
(714) 998-5694

■ PUBLICATIONS

Balls and Strikes
2801 Northeast 50th Street
Oklahoma City, OK 73111

Sierra Softball
55 Freeport No. 17
Sparks, NV 89431

Softball News
9631 Business Center Drive, No. 5
Rancho Cucamonga, CA 91730

Softball World
PO Box 10151
Grand Lake Station
Oakland, CA 94610

CAMPS

Summer Camps
c/o Athletics Department
California Polytechnic State University
San Luis Obispo, CA 93407
(805) 546-2923
(G)

Girls' Softball Camp
University of San Diego Sports Center
Alcala Park
San Diego, CA 92110
(619) 260-4803
(G)

CSU Rams Softball Camp
Athletic Department
Colorado State University
Fort Collins, CO 80523
(303) 491-5300
(G)

Softball Camp
Office of Admissions
Culver Summer Camps
Culver, IN 46511
(219) 842-8207
(G)

Grand Slam Softball School
Mr. Bo Ruggiero
20 Main Street
Norfolk, MA 02056
(617 528-6248
(G)

Summer Sports School
Michigan State University
222 Jenison Fieldhouse
East Lansing, MI 48824-1025
(517) 355-5264
(G)

Softball Camp
Conference Services
Princeton University
Third Floor Prospect
Princeton, NJ 08544
(609) 452-3369
(609) 452-4669
(G)

Softball Camp
Brenda Marshall
Box 2268
Sam Houston University
Huntsville, TX 77341
(409) 294-1742
(G)

Summer Sports Camp
Charlie McSpiritt, Asst. Dir.
BGSU Athletic Department
Bowling Green State University
Bowling Green, OH 43404
(419) 372-2401
(G)

Teresa Wilson's Softball Camp
Athletic Department
McArthur Court
University of Oregon
Eugene, OR 97403
(503) 686-3825
(G)

Virginia Softball Camp
University of Virginia
PO Box 3785
Charlottesville, VA 22903
(804) 924-8958
(G)

TEAM HANDBALL

U.S. Team Handball Federation
1750 East Boulder Street
Colorado Springs, CO 80909
(303) 632-5551

Canadian Team Handball Federation
333 River Road
Ottawa Ontario Canada K1L 8H9
(613) 748-5676

TENNIS

- **ORGANIZATIONS— U.S. & CANADA**

American Medical Tennis Association
PO Box 841
Alton, IL 62002
(618) 462-6841

Association of Tennis Professionals
611 Ryan Plaza Drive
6th Floor, Suite 620
Arlington, TX 76011-4068
(817) 860 1166

Black Tennis Foundation
1893 Amsterdam Avenue
New York, NY 10032
(212) 926-5991

Canadian Tennis Association
3111 Steeles Avenue West
Downsview, Ontario M3J 3H2
Canada
(416) 655-9777

Intercollegiate Tennis Coaches Association
c/o Chuck Kriese
Clemson University
Athletic Department
Clemson, SC 29631
(803) 656-2101

International Tennis Hall of Fame and Museum
194 Bellevue Avenue
Newport, RI 02840
(401) 849-3990
New York Address:
100 Park Avenue
New York, NY 10017
(212) 880-4179

Men's International Professional Tennis Council
437 Madison Avenue, 4th Floor
New York, NY 10022
(212) 838-8450

National Foundation of Wheelchair Tennis
15441 Red Hill Avenue, Suite A
Tustin, CA 92680
(714) 259-1531

National Junior Tennis League
c/o USTA Education & Research
729 Alexander Road
Princeton, NJ 08540-6301
(609) 452-2580

National Senior Women's Tennis Association
1152 New York Avenue
Winter Park, FL 32789

Tennis Canada
333 River Road
Ottawa, Ontario, Canada K1L 8H9
(613) 746-5593

Tennis Foundation of North America
200 Castlewood Drive
North Palm Beach, FL 33408
(305) 848-1026

U.S. Professional Tennis Association
Saddlebrook, The Golf and Tennis Resort
PO Box 7077
Wesley Chapel, FL 34249
(813) 973-3777

U.S. Professional Tennis Registry
PO Box 5902
Hilton Head Island, SC 29938
(800) 421-6289
(813) 973-3777

U.S. Tennis Association (USTA)
1212 Avenue of the Americas
New York, NY 10036

USTA Center for Education & Recreational Tennis
729 Alexander Road
Princeton, NJ 08540
(609) 452-2580

USTA Membership and Computer Service Center
121 South Service Road
Jericho, NY 11753
(516) 333-7990

USTA REGIONAL OFFICES

NORTH ATLANTIC:

New England
PO Box 223
Needham, MA 02192
(617) 444-1332

Eastern
202 Mamaroneck Avenue
White Plains, NY 10601
(914) 946-3533

Middle States
939 Radnor Road
Wayne, PA 19087
(215) 688-4040

SOUTHERN:

Mid-Atlantic
PO Drawer F
Springfield, VA 22151-0180
(703) 321-9045

Southern
3121 Maple Drive, N.E.
Atlanta, GA 30305
(404) 237-9982

Florida
9620 Northeast Second Avenue, Suite 200
Miami Shores, FL 33138
(305) 757-8568

Caribbean
PO Box 40456 Minillas Station
Santurce, PR 00940
(809) 721-9112

CENTRAL:

Western
2242 Olympic Street
Springfield, OH 45503
(513) 390-2740

Northwestern
5525 Cedar Lake Road
St. Louis Park, MN 55416
(612) 546-0709

Missouri Valley
722 Walnut Street, Suite 1
Kansas City, MO 64106
(816) 556-0777

PACIFIC:

Texas
PO Box 192
Austin, TX 78767
(512) 443-1334

Southwestern
3228 East Indian School Road
Suite 107
Phoenix, AZ 85018
(602) 955-2546

Intermountain
1201 South Parker Road, Suite 102
Denver, CO 80231
(303) 695-4117

Pacific Northwest
10175 Southwest Barbur Boulevard
Suite 306 B
Portland, OR 97219
(503) 245-3048

Northern California
645 Fifth Street
San Francisco, CA 94107
(415) 777-5683

Southern California
PO Box 240015
Los Angeles, CA 90024-9115
(213) 208-3838

Hawaii Pacific
3538 Waialae Avenue, Room 207
Honolulu, HI 96816
(808) 735-3008

U.S. Tennis Writers' Association
c/o Steve Goldstein
Philadelphia Inquirer
400 North Broad Street
Philadelphia, PA 19130
(215) 854-2000

Volvo Tennis
369 Lexington Avenue
New York, NY 10017
(212) 370-0350

Women's International Professional Tennis Council
100 Park Avenue
New York, NY 10017
(212) 878-2250

Women's International Tennis Association
Grand Bay Plaza, Suite 1002
2665 South Bayshore Drive
Miami, FL 33133
(305) 856-4030

World Championship Tennis
2340 Thanksgiving Tower
Dallas, TX 75201
(214) 969-5554
New York Address:
150 East 58th Street
New York, NY 10022
(212) 980-0660

■ ORGANIZATIONS—
INTERNATIONAL

European Tennis Association
Dornacherstrasse 250
CH-4018 Basle, SWZ
41-61-507675

**Tennis Federation
Internationale**
Church Road
Wimbledon
London SW 19 5T1
+44+1/9479266

ARGENTINA
Asociacion Argentina de Tenis
Avda, San Juan 1317
1148 Buenos Aires, Argentina
54-1-27-0101

AUSTRALIA
**Lawn Tennis Association of
Australia**
55 Commercial Road
South Yarra 3141, Australia
61-3-267-4277

AUSTRIA
Osterreichischer Tennisverband
Hainburgstrasse 36/4
A 1030 Vienna, Austria
43-222-75-3345

BELGIUM
**Royal Belgium Tennis
Federation**
Centre Rogier
Passage International 6, BTE 522
1210 Brussels, 1 Belgium
32-2-217-2365

BRAZIL
Brazil Tennis Federation
Rua Anfilofio de Carvalho No. 29
Grupo 407/8-zC-20, 020 Centro
Rio de Janeiro, Brazil
55-21-220-5444

CHINA
**Chinese Taipei Tennis
Association**
6th Floor
120 Chun Yang Road
Nan Kang
Taipei, Taiwan

CZECHOSLAVAKIA
Na Porici 12
115 30 Prague 1
42-2-249-4514

DENMARK
Dansk Tennis Forbund
Idreattens Hus
Broendby Stadion 20
DK-2605 Broendby, Denmark
45-2-45-555

FRANCE
French Tennis Federation
Stade Roland Garros
2 Avenue Gordon Bennett
75016 Paris, France
33-14-743-9681

GERMANY
Deutscher Tennisbund e.V.
Leisewitzstrasse 266
Postfach 1403
3000 Hanover 1, West Germany
49-51-181-6065

GREECE
Hellenic Tennis Federation
89, Pattission Street
Athens, Greece
30-1-821-0478

GREAT BRITAIN
The Lawn Tennis Association
Barons Court
West Kensington
London W14 9EG, England
44-1-385-2366

ISRAEL
Israel Tennis Association
PO Box 20073
Tel Aviv, Israel 61200
972-3-61-3911

ITALY
Italian Tennis Federation
Viale Tiziano 70
00196 Rome, Italy
39-6-36858

JAPAN
Japan Tennis Association
Kishi Memorial Hall 4F
1-1-1 Jinnan
Shibuya-ku
Tokyo, Japan
81-3-481-2321

MEXICO
Mexican Tennis Federation
Durango #225 Dept. 301
Mexico 7DF
52-181-514-3759

NETHERLANDS
Koninklijke Nederlandse
Lawn Tennis Bond
PO Box 107
1200 AC Hilversum, Holland
31-35-46941

SPAIN
Real Federacion Espanola de Tenis
Avda Diagonal 618. 3D
Barcelona, Spain
34-3-250-0158

SWEDEN
Svenska Tennisforbundet
Lidingovagen 75
S-11537, Stockholm, Sweden
46-8-67-9770

SWITZERLAND
Swiss Tennis Association
Talgut-Zentrum 5
3063 Ittigen, Switzerland
41-31-58-7444

U.S.S.R.
Lawn Tennis Federation of the U.S.S.R.
Laznetskaua Naberzhnaja 8
Moscow 119270, U.S.S.R.
201-0864

YUGOSLAVIA
Tenis Savez Yugoslavike
Terazije 35
Belgrade, Yugoslavia
38-11-3336

■ PROFESSIONAL TOURNAMENTS

Argentine Open
2, Markham Square
London SW3 4UY
England
44-1-352-9135

Athens International
Greek Tennis Federation
89 Patission Street
104 34 Athens, Greece
30-1-8210-478

Australian Open
PO Box 6002
Melbourne 3004
Victoria, Australia
61-3-267-3969

Austria
c/o Hermann Fuchs
Erzbischofgasse 63A
1130 Wein, Austria
43-360-1373

Belgium Indoor Championship 1988
Belgian Olympic Committee
9 Avenue de Bouchout
1020 Bruxelles, Belgium
32-2-478-4957

Belgium Open
International Management Group
58 Queen Anne Street
London, W1M ODX, England
44-1-486-7171

Benson & Hedges New Zealand Open
PO Box 37-425
Parnell
Auckland, New Zealand
64-9-733-623

Brisbane Indoor
Sport Australia
3rd Floor
76 Berry Street
North Sydney, N.S.W. 2060
Australia
61-2-957-5668

The Bristol Trophy
The Lawn Tennis Association
Barons Court
West Kensington
London 14 9EG, England
44-1-385-2366

B.P. Nationals
New Zealand Lawn Tennis Association
Box 11541
Wellington, New Zealand
64-4-731-115

California Women's Open
Peter Herb/MCTA
645 Fifth Street
San Francisco, CA 94107
(415) 777-5683

Canadian Open
National Tennis Centre
3111 Steeles Avenue West
Downsview, Ontario M3J 3H2
Canada
(416) 665-9777

"Ebel" German Open 1988
Leisewitzstr. 26
D-3000 Hannover 1
West Germany

**Ebel Swiss Indoors Basel-
International Tennis
Championships of Switzerland**
Bettenstrasse 73
CH-4123 Allschwil
Basle, Switzerland
41-61-638-825

**Edgbaston Cup/Birmingham,
England**
Lawn Tennis Association
Barons Court, West Kensington
London W14 9EG, England
44-1-385-2366

European Open/France
15 Rue de Surene
75008 Paris, France
1-42655-292

European Open/Switzerland
Haupestrasse 23
CH-8437 Zurzach, Switzerland
56-49-3966

Federation Cup by NEC
1200 Horby Street
Vancouver, British Columbia
Canada V6Z 2E2
(604) 687-3333

French Open
French Tennis Federation
Stade Roland Garros
2 Avenue Gordon Bennett
75016 Paris, France
4-743-9681

Geneva Open
c/o Tennis Club de Geneve
Park des Eaux Vives
1207 Geneve, Switzerland
41-22-35535-1

German Open
LTCC "Rot-Wieb" e.v.
Gottfried von Cramm
Weg 47-55

**Grand Prix Passing Shot
Bordeaux**
10 Bix, place des Grands Hommes
33000 Bordeaux, France
33-56-523429

**International Championships of
Spain - Trofeo Conde de Godo**
Prvenza, 300 lo 2a
08008 Barcelona, Spain
34-3-204-5010

**International Lawn Tennis
Championships of the
Netherlands, The**
Frederik van Eedenlaan 30
1215 En Hilversum
The Netherlands
31-02158-3017

Italian Open
Federazione Italian Tennis
Viale Del Gladiatori 31
00194 Rome, Italy
6-3619041

Kim Top Line Classic
I.S.M.
Via Visconti de Modrone - 30
20121 Milan, Italy
39-2-784395

**Lipton International Players
Championships**
444 Brickel Avenue
Suite 250
Miami, FL 33131
(305) 577-3399

Masters Tournament
MIPTC
437 Madison Avenue
4th Floor
New York, NY 10022
(212) 838-8450

Monte Carlo Tournament
Monte Carlo Country Club
c/o Mr. Bernard Noat
B.P. 342
MC 98006 Monaco Cedex
33-93-782045

Newsweek Championships
World Championship Tennis
910 Allied Bank Plaza
Houston, TX 77002
(713) 739-0211

Pan Pacific Open
Group Dynamics
2601 Ocean Park Boulevard #309
Santa Monica, CA 90405
(213) 452-5056

Pilkington Glass Ladies Championships
Dale Place, Rake, Liss, Hant
GU33 7JF, England
44-073-089-3970

Rado Swiss Open Gstaad
c/o Palace Hotel
CH-3780 Gstaad, Switzerland
41-30-83131

Seiko Super Tennis Hong Kong
Hong Kong Tennis Patrons' Assn. Ltd.
Room 406, Chevalier House
45-51 Chatha Road South
Tsim Sha Tsui South
Kowloon, Hong Kong
852-3-723-8721

Seiko Tournament
Japan Professional Tennis Assoc.
Wada Bldg., 1-20-15, Jinnan
Shibuya-ku, Tokyo
Japan

Shawmut U.S. Pro Tennis Championships International Management Group
One Erieview Plaza
Suite 1300
Cleveland, OH 44114
(216) 522-1200

Shearson Lehman Brothers Tournament of Champions
World Championship Tennis
21st Floor
150 East 58th Street
New York, NY 10022
(212) 980-0660

South Australian Open
PO Box 6002
Melbourne 3004
Victoria, Australia
61-03-267-3696

Sovran Bank/DC National Bank Tennis Classic
1629 K Street, N.W.
Suite 1150
Washington, DC 20006
(202) 429-0690

Stockholm Open
c/o Messrs. Johan Flink
          Mats Laftman
Gustavlundsvagen 159
S-161 36 Bromma
Sweden
46-8-804750

Suntory Tournament
Suntory Japan Open Tennis Committee
903, Ichibancho Central Building
22-1, Ichibancho, Chiyoda-ku
Tokyo 102, Japan
81-3-262-3821

Swedish Open Bastad
The Swedish Tennis Association
Lidingovagen 75
S-115 37 Stockholm, Sweden
46-8-679770

Sydney Indoor Tournament
Sport Australia
3rd Floor
76 Berry Street
North Sydney, N.S.W. 2060
Australia
61-2-957-5668

Thriftway ATP Championship
ATP Championship
Columbia Plaza - Suite 295
250 East Fifth Street
Cincinnati, OH 45202
(513) 651-3087

Torneo Internazionale Citta' di Firenze
Via Altopiano 45/18
Sasso Marconi, Bologna
Italy
39-51-846925

United Jersey Bank Classic
c/o John Korff
505 Ramapo Valley Road
Mahwah, NJ 07430
(201) 825-9100

U.S. Hardcourt Championships
USTA
1212 Avenue of the Americas
New York, NY 10036
(212) 302-3322
OR
U.S. Hardcourt Championships
5455 West 86th Street
Suite 204
PO Box 68305
Indianapolis, IN 46268

U.S. Indoor Championships
5111 Sanderlin
Memphis, TN 38117
(901) 765-4400

U.S. Open
USTA
1212 Avenue of the Americas
New York, NY 10036
(212) 302-3322

Victoria Open
PO Box 6002
Melbourne 3004
Victoria, Australia
61-3-267-3696

Virginia Slims of Los Angeles
Tournaments Ltd.
1388 Sutter Street #710
San Francisco, CA 94109
(415) 673-2016

Virginia Slims of Newport
Tennis Hall of Fame
194 Bellevue
Newport, RI 02840
(401) 849-3990

Virginia Slims of San Diego
Promotion Sports, Inc.
Box 99937
San Diego, CA 92109
(619) 581-9166

Volvo International
PO Box 593
Stratton Mountain, VT 05155
(802) 297-2900

Volvo Ladies Event
Swedish Tennis Association
Lidingovagen 75
S-11537 Stockholm, Sweden
46-8-679770

Volvo Tennis L.A.
Southern California Tennis Association
Los Angeles Tennis Center - UCLA
PO Box 240015
Los Angeles, CA 90024-9115
(213) 208-3838

Wimbeldon/The Championships
All England Lawn Tennis &
Croquet Club
Church Road, Wimbledon
SW19 5AE, England
44-1-946-2244

WCT Finals
World Championship Tennis
2340 Thanksgiving Tower
Dallas, TX 75201
(214) 969-5554

WCT Houston Shootout
World Championship Tennis
910 Allied Bank Plaza
Houston, TX 77002
(713) 739-0211

WCT-Scottsdale Open
7000 East Camelback Road
Suite 200
Scottsdale, AZ 85251
(602) 990-9088

■ PUBLICATIONS

College and Junior Tennis
100 Harbor Road
Port Washington, NY 11050

Indiana Racquet Sports
207 South Main
PO Box 216
Frankfort, IN 46041

Inside Tennis
3561 Lakeshore Avenue
Oakland, CA 949610

International Tennis Weekly
611 Ryan Plaza Drive
Arlington, TX 76011

New Jersey Tennis
PO Box 134
West End, NJ 07740

ProTennis
2340 Thanksgiving Tower
Dallas, TX 75201

Tennis in New England
PO Box 223
Needham, MA 02192

Tennis Industry
1545 North East 123rd Street
North Miami, FL 33161

Tennis Magazine
5520 Park Avenue
Trumbull, CT 06611

Tennis Midwest
PO Box 2380
Minneapolis, MN 55402

Tennis Week
6 East 39th Street
New York, NY 10016

Tennis West
PO Box 855
Westminster, CA 92684-0855

Tournament Times
1755 Camino Corrale
PO Box 4577
Santa Fe, NM 87501

■ **CAMPS**

John Gardiner's Tennis Ranch
5700 East McDonald Drive
Scottsdale, AZ 85253
(800) 245-2051
(A)

*Adidas/Tennis Camp
U.S. Sports Development
919 Sir Francis Drake Boulevard
Kentfield, CA 94904
(800) 227-2866
(415) 459-0459 (in CA)
(J)

Lakeside Tennis Club
PO Box 5576
Incline Village, CA 89450
(800) GO-TAHOE
(702) 831-5258

Vic Braden Tennis College at Coto de Caza
22000 Plano Trabuco Canyon Road
Trabuco Canyon, CA 92678
(714) 581-2990
(800) 42-COURT
(800) CALL-VIC (in CA)

Copper Mountain Tennis Camps
Copper Mountain Racquet and
Athletic Club
PO Box 3001
Copper Mountain, CO 80443
(303) 968-2882

Australian Tennis Institute at Innisbrook
Terry Addison's ATI
Drawer 1088
Tarpon Springs, FL 33589
(813) 937-3124

*Bollettieri Tennis Camp
5500 34th Street
Bradenton, FL 33507
(813) 755-1000
(800) USA-NICK

Colony Tennis Clinics
John Knox, Director
1620 Gulf of Mexico Drive
Longboat Key, FL 33548
(800) 237-9443

Rick Macci International Tennis Academy
Rick Macci
Director of Tennis
3200 State Road 546
Grenelefe, FL 33844
(J)

Fisher Island Racquet Club
Fisher Island
Miami, FL 33109
(305) 672-4140
(A)

Gary Kesl's Inverrary Tennis Academy
3366 Spanish Moss Terrace
Fort Lauderdale, FL 33319
(305) 733-7550

Saddlebrook Golf & Tennis
Wesley Chapel, FL 34249
(813) 973-1111, ext. 4556

International Academy of Tennis, Inc.
12000 Gulf Boulevard
Treasure Island, FL 33706
(813) 367-7661
(800) 992-7797

*John Gardner Tennis Clinics
13198 Forest Hills Blvd
West Palm Beach, FL 33411
(800) 327-4204
(800) 432-4158 (in FL)
(A)

Women's International Tennis Association Tournament Camp for Girls
Grand Bay Plaza
Suite 1002
2665 South Bayshore Drive
Miami, FL 33133
(305) 856-4030
(J)

Steve Carter's/LSU Pelican Tennis Camp
1563 Audubon Avenue
Baton Rouge, LA 70806
(504) 924-0735
(J)

Irish Hills Tennis Camp
Box 36371
Grosse Pointe, MI 48236

Cornhusker Tennis Camp
Coach Kerry McDermott
University of Nebraska
Bob Devaney Sports Center
Lincoln, NE 68588
(402) 472-2271

*World Tennis Clinic on Martha's Vineyard
4821 Arlington Avenue
New York, NY 10471
(212) 549-0100

Asim's All-Star Tennis Academy Summer Camp
222 North Passaic Avenue
Chatham, NJ 07928
(201) 635-1222

Exeter Tennis School
Exeter, NJ 03833
(603) 772-4311
(J)

Adidas Tournament Training Camps
Princeton University
Box 71
Princeton, NJ 08544
(609) 452-6332
(609) 883-7442

*All American Sports Junior Tennis Academy
45 Kensico Drive
Mt. Kisco, NY 10549
(914) 666-0096 (in NY)
(800) 223-2442
(J)

*Ron Holmberg Tennis Camps
31 Roe Avenue
Suite A
Cornwall-on-Hudson, NY 12520
(914) 534-2211
(J)

The Sagamore Resort
Dack Forbush
Sagamore Resort & Conference Center
PO Box 450
Bolton Landing, NY 12814
(518) 644-9400
(A)

Total Tennis
Box 1106T
Wall Street Station
New York, NY 10268
(800) 221-6496
(718) 636-6141
(A)

Welby Van Horn Tennis at Pinehurst
Box 259
Gracie Station
New York, NY 10028
(212) 734-1037

Buckeye Tennis Camp
Dave Power Tennis School
435 Ohio Pike
Cincinnati, OH 45230
(513) 528-5700

Paul Scarpa's 18th Annual Furman Tennis Camp
Paul Scarpa
Furman University Athletic Department
Greenville, SC 29613
(803) 294-2039

Rod Laver Tennis
Box 4798
Hilton Head, SC 29938
(803) 785-1152

*Seabrook Island Tennis Camps
PO Box 32099
Charleston, SC 29407
(803) 768-2535
(800) 842-2475, ext. 535

Sea Pines Racquet Club
Hilton Head, SC 29928
(800) 845-6131
(800) 992-7042

Tournament Tough Tennis Academy
Carlos Goffi
1013 Marsh Point
Johns Island, SC 29455
(803) 768-9797
(J)

*Van Der Meer Tennis
PO Box 5902
Hilton Head, SC 29938
(800) 845-6138

John Newcombe's Tennis Ranch
Box 469
New Braunfels, TX 78130
(512) 625-9015

9th Annual International Junior Tournament Camp
Peter Burwash International
2203 Timberloch Place, Suite 126
The Woodlands, TX 77380
(713) 363-4707
(J)

4 Star Tennis Academy
Box 790, Dept TQ
McLean, VA 22101
(800) 334-STAR

Grey Rocks Tennis School
PO Box 1000
St. Jovite
Quebec, Canada J0T 2H0

Inn & Tennis Club at Manitou
821 Eglinton Avenue
West Toronto, Ontario, Canada
M5N 1E6
(416) 785-3833
(212) 772-0594
(J)

Quebec Tennis Camp
2750 Chemin Ste-Foy
Suite 251
Ste-Foy, Quebec, Canada
G1V 1V6

*Roy Emerson Tennis Clinics,
Niki Pilic Tennis Clinics
Palace Hotel
Gstaad, 3780 Switzerland

*Students Abroad Tournament Tennis Program
Edward Finn
42-E Edgewood Avenue
Mount Vernon, NY 10552
(914) 699-8335
(J)

Tennis en France
Pam Wolf
14 Gordon Street
Boston, MA 02130
(617) 524-5457

*Tennis: Europe-Juniors
Dr. Martin Vinokur
146 Cold Spring Road #13
Stamford, CT 06905
(J)

■ INDIVIDUALS

Arthur Ashe
868 17th Street N.W.
Washington, DC 20007

Tracy Austin
26406 Dunwood Road
Rolling Hills Estates, CA 90274

Boris Becker
c/o Association of Tennis Professionals
611 Ryan Plaza Drive
Arlington, TX 76011

Bjorn Borg
Liestorie Avenue
Princess Grace
Monte Carlo, Monaco

Don Budge
275 Lincoln Avenue
Brentwood, NY 11717

Jimmy Connors
8 Derold Lane
Belleville, IL 62223

Sarah Palfrey Danzig
993 Park Avenue
New York, NY 10028

Chris Evert-Lloyd
1628 Northeast 7th Place
Fort Lauderdale, FL 33304

Vitas Gerulaitis
One Erieview
Cleveland, OH 44114

Althea Gibson Darbeu
275 Prospect Street #768
East Orange, NJ 07017

Pancho Gonzales
Caesar's Palace
3570 Las Vegas Boulevard South
Las Vegas, NV 89119

Evonne Goolagong Cawley
80 Duntroon Avenue
Roseville, NSW Australia

Billie Jean King
60 West 66th Street #17A
New York, NY 10023

Ivan Lendl
800 North Street
Greenwich, CT 06830

John McEnroe
345 Park Avenue
New York, NY 10022

Martina Navratilova
643 North Buckner
Dallas, TX 75218-2708

John Newcombe
T-Bar-M Tennis Ranch
PO Box 469
New Braunfels, TX 78130

Dr. Renee Richards
1604 Union Street
San Francisco, CA 94123

Bobby Riggs
508 East Avenue
Coronado, CA 92118

Ken Rosewall
111 Pentacost Avenue
Turramurra NSW 2074
Australia

Frank Sedgeman
28 Bolton Avenue
Hampton, VIC 3188
Australia

Pancho Segura
La Costa Hotel and Spa
Carlsbad, CA 92008

Vic Seixas
716 North Beau Chere Drive
Mandeville, LA 70448

Pam Shriver
321 Hampton Drive #203
Venice, CA 90291-2653

Stan Smith
888-17th Street, N.W. #1200
Washington, D.C. 20006

Dick Stockton
Trinity College
San Antonio, TX 78284

Roscoe Tanner
1109 Gnome Trail
Lookout Mountain, TN 37350

Tony Trabert
2 Trojan Court
Rancho Mirage, CA 92270

Guillermo Vilas
Avenue Foch 86
Paris, France

Virginia Wade
Sharstead Court
Sittingbourne, Kent
England

Andrea Yeager
10695 Bardes Court
Largo, FL 33543-6429

TRACK & FIELD

■ ORGANIZATIONS—U.S. & CANADA

The Athletics Congress of the USA
200 South Capitol Avenue
Suite 140
Indianapolis, IN 46225
(317) 638-9155

Canadian Masters Track & Field Association
1220 Sheppard Avenue East
Willowdale, Ontario, Canada
M2K 2X1
(416) 495-4059

Canadian Track & Field Association
333 River Road
Vanier, Ontario, Canada
K1L 8H9
(613) 748-5678

Intercollegiate Association of Amateur Athletes of America (IC4A)
PO Box 3
Centerville, MA 02632
(617) 771-5060

Track & Field Writers of America
PO Box 5401
San Mateo, CA 94402
(415) 345-4114

U.S. Cross Country Coaches Association
c/o Bill Bergan
Iowa State University
Ames, IA 50011
(515) 294-3723

U.S. Track & Field Hall of Fame
PO Box 297
Angola, IN 46703
(219) 495-7735

■ ORGANIZATIONS—INTERNATIONAL

International Amateur Athletics Federation
3 Hans Crescent
Knightsbridge
London SW1X OLN
England

■ INVITATIONAL TRACK EVENTS

Drake Relays
Bob Ehrhart
Track Coach
Drake University
27th & Forest
Des Moines, IA 50311

Indiana National Invitational
Sam Bell, Track Coach
Indiana University
Assembly Hall
Bloomington, IN 47405

Penn Relays
James Tuppeny
University of Pennsylvania
Weightman Hall
Philadelphia, PA 19104

Prefontaine Classic
Tom Jordan
850 East 43rd Avenue
Eugene, OR 97405

Toronto Indoor Games
Paul Poce
29 Arcadian Circle
Toronto, Ontario, Canada
M8W 2Z2

USA/Mobile Outdoor Championships
Bert Bonanno
San Jose City College
2100 Moorpark Avenue
San Jose, CA 95128

Wanamaker Millrose Games
Howard Schmertz
99 Park Avenue
New York, NY 10016

■ PUBLICATIONS

Athletics Canada
333 River Road
Ottawa, Ontario, Canada
K1L 8H9

Athletics Today
U.S. Subscriptions
Clifford Frost Ltd.
Lyon Road
Windsor Avenue
Wimbledon, London SW19 25E
England

California Track and Running News
4957 East Heaton
Fresno, CA 93727

Eastern Track
141-40 84th Drive, Apartment 5L
Briarwood, NY 11435

National Masters News
PO Box 2372
Van Nuys, CA 91404

Starting Line Magazine
PO Box 878
6402 Enfield Avenue
Reseda, CA 91335

Track and Field Journal De L'Athletisme
333 River Road
Ottawa, Ontario, Canada   K1L 8H9

Track & Field News
167 South San Antonio Road
Suite 9
Los Altos, CA 94023-0296

Track Technique
167 South San Antonio Road
Suite 9
Los Altos, CA 94023

■ CAMPS

Track and Field Camp
Athletic Department
Stanford University
Stanford, CA 94305
(415) 725-0759

Track and Field Camp
Conference Services
Princeton University
Third Floor Prospect
Princeton, NJ 08544
(609) 452-3369

Penn State Track and Field/ Cross Country and Distance Running Camps
Chuck Herd
410 Keller Conference Center
University Park, PA 16802

Cougar Track and Field Camp
Athletic Department
Washington State University
Pullman, WA 99164-1610
(509) 335-0311

■ INDIVIDUALS

Sir Roger Bannister
16 Edward Square
London SW1
England

Bob Beamon
535 East 80th Street
New York, NY 10021

Joan Benoit
Freeport, ME 04302

Zola Budd
1 Church Row
Wandsworth Plain
London SW18
England

Sebastian Coe
37 Marlborough Road
Sheffield, South Yorkshire
England

Eamonn Coghlan
4 Fairway Avenue
Rye, NY 10580

Mary Decker
Athletics West
3968 West 13th Street
Eugene, OR 97402

Bob Hayes
c/o The Staubach Company
6750 LBJ Freeway
Dallas, TX 75230

Valerie Briscoe Hooks
World Class Athletes
PO Box 21053
Long Beach, CA 90801

Bruce Jenner
6342 Sycamore Canyon
Malibu, CA 90265

Rafer Johnson
4217 Woodcliff Road
Sherman Oaks, CA 91403

Carl Lewis
1801 Ocean Park Boulevard #112
Santa Monica, CA 90405

Martin Liquori
5904 NW 57th Way
Gainesville, FL 32605

Bob Mathias
3400 West 86th Street
Indianapolis, IN 46268

Billy Mills
4717 Della Robia
Fair Oaks, CT 05628

Edwin Moses
20 Kimberly Circle
Dayton, OH 45408

Willie Naulls
9753 West Pico Boulevard #307
Los Angeles, CA 90035

Bill Rogers
353-T North Market Place
Boston, MA 02109

Wilma Rudolph
3500 Centennial Boulevard
Nashville, TN 37203

Alberto Salazar
3968 West 13th Avenue
Eugene, OR 97402

Bob Seagren
120 South Thurston
Los Angeles, CA 90049

Frank Shorter
2400 Central Suite 1
Colorado Springs, CO 80302

Ria Stalman
Boylestratte 24
Den Haag, Netherlands

Dwight Stones
4790 Irvine Boulevard #105
Irvine, CA 92714

Daley Thompson
British Olympic Association
1 Church Row
Wandsworth Plain, London SW18
England

Bill Toomey
1400 Braeridge Drive
Beverly Hills, CA 90210

Greta Waits
Rovnkollbakken 79
Oslo 9 Norway

Herb Washington
642 East Austin Street
Flint, MI 48505

Dave Wottle
2273 Glenbar
Germantown, TN 38138

Emil Zatopek
112 93 Prague 1
Czechoslovakia

TRIATHLON

■ ORGANIZATIONS—U.S. & CANADA

Association of Professional Triathletes
666 Baker Street, Suite 367
Costa Mesa, CA 92626
(714) 432-8226

Triathlon Federation/USA
915 Third Street
Davis, CA 95616
(916) 757-2831
Mailing Address:
PO Box 1963
Davis, CA 95617-1963

■ PUBLICATIONS

Great Lakes Triathlete
7990 West Grand River, Suite C
Brighton, MI 48116
(313) 227-4200

Running & Triathlon News
5111 Santa Fe Street
Suite 206
San Diego, CA 92109
(619) 270-4974

The Beast
Box 789
Wainscott, NY 11975
(516) 324-2027

Triathlete Magazine
8461 Warner Drive
Culver City, CA 90230
(213) 558-3321

Tri-Fed/USA
PO Box 1963
Davis, CA 95617-1963
(916) 757-2831

Tri-Fit
575 Burns Street
Penticton, BC, Canada V2A 4W9
(604) 493-5181

■ EVENTS

Bud-Light Chicago Triathlon
I.A.A.
PO Box 805
Barrington, IL 60010

Ironman Triathlon World Championship
1100 Ward Avenue #815
Honolulu, HI 96814

■ CAMPS

National Triathlon Training Camp
1015 Gayley Avenue
Suite 217
Los Angeles, CA 90024

TUG-OF-WAR

■ ORGANIZATIONS— INTERNATIONAL

Tug-of-War International Federation
Hon. Secretary General:
P. F. J. Edlin
'Spire Gate', Steep Hollow
Dinton, Salisbury,
Wilts, England

VOLLEYBALL

■ ORGANIZATIONS—U.S. & CANADA

Association of Volleyball Professionals
1021 Sepulveda Boulevard, Suite I
Manhattan Beach, CA 90266
(213) 545-3836

Canadian Volleyball Association
333 River Road
Vanier, Ontario, Canada
K1L 8H9
(613) 748-5681

Major League Volleyball
2 Harbor Drive
Sausalito, CA 94965
(415) 332-6922

National Outdoor Volleyball Association
936 Hermosa Avenue
Hermosa Beach, CA 90254
(213) 379-3636

U.S. Volleyball Association
1750 East Boulder Street
Colorado Springs, CO 80909
(303) 632- 5551, Ext. 3312.

■ ORGANIZATIONS— INTERNATIONAL

Federation Internationale De Volleyball
Correspondence:
Headquarters
Place Chauderson No. 7 (Annexe)
1003 Lausanne
Switzerland

■ PUBLICATIONS

Volleyball Monthly
2308 Broad Street
San Luis Obispo, CA 93401
(805) 541-2294
Mailing Address:
PO Box 3137
San Luis Obispo, CA 93403

■ CAMPS

*Al Scates Instructional Volleyball Camp
UCLA Athletic Department
405 Hilgard Avenue
Los Angeles, CA 90024
(818) 981-3939

*Al Scates Instructional Volleyball Camp
15236 Burbank Boulevard
Suite 216
Van Nuys, CA 91411
(818) 981-3939

Volleyball Camp
Clarie Duffey
Extension Coordinator
Office of Continuing Education
Humboldt State University
Arcata, CA 95521
(707) 826-3731

CSU Lady Rams Volleyball Camp
Athletic Department
Colorado State University
Fort Collins, CO 80523
(303) 491-5300
(G)

Volleyball Office
University of Northern Colorado
Greeley, CO 80639
(303) 351-1719
(G)

Summer Camps Program
Yates Field House
Georgetown University
Washington, DC
(202) 625-3504
(G)

Volleyball Camp
Cecile Reynaud
Florida State University
PO Box 2195
Tallahassee, FL 32316-2915
(904) 644-1091
(G)

Lady Jayhawk Volleyball Camp
221 Allen Field House
University of Kansas
Lawrence, KS 66045
(913) 864-3417
(G)

Summer Camps Program
Room 41 Boyden Building
University of Massachusetts
Amherst, MA 01003
(413) 545-3522
(G)

*Sports Camps International
4489 East Paris, S.E.
Grand Rapids, MI 49509
1-800-253-6074 (outside MI)
1-800-632-8653 (in MI)
(616) 698-2008

Volleyball Camp
Geri Knortz
Hamilton College
Clinton, NY 13323
(G)

Gerry Gregory's Oregon Volleyball Camp
Athletic Department
University of Oregon
Eugene, OR 97403
(503) 686-4459
(G)

Penn State Volleyball Camp
Chuck Herd
The Pennsylvania State University
410 Keller Conference Center
University Park, PA 16802

***Al Scates International
Volleyball Camp**
Southwest Texas State University
Attn: Karen Chisum
Strahan Coliseum
San Marcos, TX 78666

■ INDIVIDUALS

Karch Kiraly
3991 Sequoia Street
San Diego, CA 92109

Andrew Smith
Smithers
2523 Wilshire Boulevard
Santa Monica, CA 90403

Sinjin Smith
Smithers
2523 Wilshire Boulevard
Santa Monica, CA 90403

WALKING ━━━━━━

**■ ORGANIZATIONS—U.S. &
CANADA**

Walker's Club of America
445 East 86th Street
New York, NY 10128
(212) 722-9255

■ PUBLICATIONS

The Walking Magazine
711 Boylston Street
Boston, MA 02116

WATER SPORTS ━━━━━━

SWIMMING AND DIVING

**■ ORGANIZATIONS—U.S. &
CANADA**

**American Swimming Coaches
Association**
One Hall of Fame Drive
Fort Lauderdxale, FL 33316
(305) 462-6267

**Aquatic Hall of Fame and
Museum of Canada, Inc.**
436 Main Street
Winnipeg,Manitoba, Canada
R3B 1B2
(204) 947-0131

Canadian Amateur Diving Association
333 River Road
Ottawa,Ontario,Canada
K1L 8H9
(613) 748-5631

Canadian Amateur Swimming Association
333 River Road
Ottawa, Ontario, Canada
K1L 8H9
(613) 748-5673

Canadian Amateur Synchronized Swimming Association
333 River Road
Ottawa, Ontario, Canada
K1L 8H9
(613) 748-5674

Iceberg Athletic Club
3046 West 22nd Street
Brooklyn, NY 11224
(718) 372-8457

International Swimming Hall of Fame
1 Hall of Fame Drive
Ft. Lauderdale, FL 33316
(305) 462-6536

National Association of Diving Schools
641 West Willow Street
Long Beach, CA 90806
(213) 595-5361

National Association of Underwater Instructors
4650 Arrow Highway
Suite F-1
Montclair, CA 91763
(714) 621-5801
Mailing Address:
PO Box 14650
Montclair, CA 91763-1150

Polar Bear Club-Winter Swimmers
Chamber of Commerce Building
Coney Island, NY 11224
(718) 492-9075

Professional Association of Diving Instructors (PADI)
1243 East Warner Avenue
Santa Ana, CA 92705
(714) 540-7234

Underwater Society of America
PO Box 628
Daly City, CA 94017
(415) 583-8942

U.S. Diving, Inc.
901 West New York Street
Indianapolis, IN 46202
(317) 634-3040

U.S. Swimming, Inc.
1750 East Boulder Street
Colorado Springs, CO 80909
(303) 578-4578

■ ORGANIZATIONS— INTERNATIONAL

Confederation Mondiale Des Activities Subaquatic
34, rue du Colisee
75008 Paris
France

Federation Internationale De Amateur Swimming
3540 West 41st Avenue
Vancouver, B.C., Canada
V6N 3E6

Federation Internationale De Life Saving/Utilitarian Sports
DLRG Bundesgeschaftsstelle
Alfredstrasse 73
43000 Essen 1
R.F.A.
West Germany

WATER POLO

■ ORGANIZATIONS—U.S. & CANADA

Canadian Water Polo Association
333 River Road
Ottawa, Ontario, Canada
K1L 8H9
(613) 748-5682

U.S. Water Polo, Inc.
1750 East Boulder Street
Colorado Springs, CO 80909
(303) 578-4549

WATER SKIING

■ ORGANIZATIONS—U.S. & CANADA

American Water Ski Association
PO Box 191
Winter Haven, FL 33880
(813) 324-4341

Canadian Water Ski Association
333 River Road
Ottawa, Ontario, Canada
K1L 8H9
(613) 748-5683

■ ORGANIZATIONS— INTERNATIONAL

Union Mondiale Water Ski
Via Verza 4
22035 Canzo (Como)
Italy

Water Ski Industry Association
200 Castlewood Drive
North Palm Beach, FL 33408
(305) 842-3600

■ SKI SCHOOLS

Academy of Professional Show Skiing
PO Box 21809
Fort Lauderdale, FL 33335
(615) 453-9473

Bill Peterson Ski School
PO Box 835
Windermere, FL 32786
(305) 876-5966

McCormick's Ski School
Seffner, FL 33584
(800) 237-5599

Linda Giddens Ski School
Route 5
Eastman, GA 31023
(912) 374-2517

SURFING AND WIND SURFING

■ ORGANIZATIONS—U.S. & CANADA

Association of Surfing Professionals
PO Box 309
Huntington Beach, CA 92648
(714) 842-8826

National Scholastic Surfing Association
5209 Surfrider Way
Oxnard, CA 93030
(805) 985-6214

U.S. Board Sailing Association
PO Box 206
Oyster Bay, NY 11771
(516) 922-1047

U.S. Surfing Federation
11 Adams Point Road
Barrington, RI 02806
(401) 245-5067

■ ORGANIZATIONS— INTERNATIONAL

International Council of Associations of Surfing (ICAS)
Surf House
Box 2174
Palm Beach, FL 33480
(305) 832-4420

International Women's Boardsailing Association
PO Box 44549
Washington, DC 20026
(703) 920-9583

Surfing Association International
"Sunridge" 109,
Winston Ave.
Branksome
Poole, Dorset
England

■ PUBLICATIONS

Diver Magazine
PO Box 1312
Delta, B.C., Canada V4M 3Y8

The Diver
PO Box 249
Cobalt, CT 06414

Scuba Times
147 Drew Circle
Pensacola, FL 32503
(904) 478-5288

Skin Diver Magazine
8490 Sunset Boulevard
Los Angeles, CA 90069

Surfer Magazine
33046 Calle Aviador
San Juan Capistrano, CA 92675

Surfing
2720 Camino Capistrano
PO Box 3010
San Clemente, CA 92672

Swim Magazine
PO Box 2168
Simi Valley, CA 93062

Swimming Technique
116 West Hazel
Inglewood, CA 90302

Swimming World
116 West Hazel Street
Inglewood, CA 90302

Undercurrent
2315 Broadway
New York, NY 10024

The Water Skier
799 Overlook Drive
Winter Haven, FL 33882

Wind Surf Magazine
Box 561
Dana Point, CA 92629

World Water Skiing
809 S. Orlando Avenue, Suite H
Winter Park, FL 32789

■ CAMPS

Don Gambril Swim Camps, Inc.
2 Old Northriver Point
Tuscaloosa, AL 35406
(205) 752-7027

Swimming Camp
Matt Coffey
Assistant Director-SAR
California State University-
Long Beach
1250 Bellflower Boulevard
Long Beach, CA 90840
(213) 498-4650

Yale Sports Camps
402A Yale Station
New Haven, CT 06520
(203) 436-4158

St. Pete Diving
c/o Breck, Amick
1200 Fourth Street North
St. Petersburg, FL 33701
(813) 822-3340

*The Sports Group, Inc.
PO Box 7009
Evanston, IL 60204
(312) 869-6860
(G)

Swimming Camp
Counsilman Co., Inc.
3806 Cameron Avenue
Bloomington, IN 47401
(812) 332-5247

Summer Camps Program
Room 41 Boyden Building
University of Massachusetts
Amherst, MA 01003
(413) 545-3522

Summer Swimming School
St. Lawrence University
Augsbury Physical Education Center
St. Lawrence University
Canton, NY 13617
(315) 379-5421

**Tennessee Swimming and
Diving Camps**
2106 Andy Holt Avenue
Knoxville, TN 37996-2905

Virginia Cavalier Swim Camp
University Hall
PO Box 3785
University of Virginia
Charlottesville, VA 22903
(804) 924-3676
(804) 977-8445
(804) 971-5994

EWU Swim Camp
University Conference Center
Eastern Washington University
Cheney, WA 99004
(509) 359-2406

■ **INDIVIDUALS**

Tracy Caulkins
213 Ocella Street
Nashville, TN 37209

Rowdy Gaines
3822 Gaines Cove
Winter Haven, FL 33880

Michael Gross
Paul Erlich Strasse 6
D-6000 Frankfurt 70
West Germany

Micki King
PO Box 155
Air Force Academy, CO 80840

Greg Louganis
PO Box 4068
Malibu, CA 90265

Patricia McCormick
PO Box 250
Seal Beach, CA 90740

John Nabor
PO Box 50107
Pasadena, CA 91105

Diana Nyad
c/o Uptown Racquet Club
151 East 86th Street
New York, NY 10028

Mark Spitz
383 Dalehurst
Los Angeles, CA 90024

Esther Williams
9377 Readcrest Drive
Beverly Hills, CA 90210

WINTER SPORTS ━━━━━━

SKIING

■ **ORGANIZATIONS—U.S. & CANADA**

Alpine Ski Team (Canada)
333 River Road
Ottawa, Ontario, Canada K1L 8H9
(613) 748-5661

American Ski Federation
207 Constitution Avenue N.E.
Washington, DC 20002
(202) 543-1595

American Ski Teachers Association
PO Box 34
Marshalls Creek, PA 18335
(717) 223-0730

Association of Ski Racing Professionals
G-5 Stonehedge Drive
South Burlington, VT 05401

Canadian Ski Association
333 River Road
Ottawa, Ontario, Canada K1L 8H9
(613) 748-5660

Cross Country Canada
333 River Road
Vanier, Ontario, Canada K11 8H9
(613) 748-5662

Cross Country Ski Areas of America
RD No. 2
Bolton Road
Manchester, NH 03451
(603) 239-6387

Eastern Ski Representatives Association
4154 West Lake Road
Canandaigua, NY 14424
(716) 394-3070

Midwest Ski Areas Association
PO Box 20287
Bloomington, MN 55420
(612) 884-9687

National Ski Credit Association, Inc.
150 Causeway Street, Room 908
Boston, MA 02114
(617) 742-4380

National Ski Hall of Fame
PO Box 1981
Ishpeming, MI 49849
(906) 486-9281

New England Ski Representatives Association
RD 2
Stowe, VT 05672
(802) 253-8335

North American Pro Ski, Inc.
PO Box 680
Bath, ME 04530
(207) 443-4461/2743

Pacific Northwest Ski Association
PO Box 3448
Kirkland, WA 98083
(206) 822-1770

Professional Ski Instructors of America
5541 Central Avenue
Boulder, CO 80301
(303) 447-0842

Ski Council of America Inc.
600 Madison Avenue
New York, NY 10022
(212) 874-3030

Ski For Light, Inc.
1455 West Lake Street
Minneapolis, MN 55408
(612) 827-3232

National Ski Industries Association
1822A Sherbrooke Street West
Montreal, Quebec, Canada H3H 1E4
(514) 937-6356

National Ski Patrol System, Inc.
133 South Van Gordon Street
Lakewood, CO 80228
(303) 237-2737

Ski Industries America
8377-B Greensboro Drive
McLean, VA 22102
(703) 556-9020

**Southeastern Ski
Representatives Association**
PO Box 183
Rocky Ridge, MD 21778
(301) 631-6474

U.S. Deaf Skiers Association
159 Davis Avenue
Hackensack, NJ 07601
(201) 489-3777

U.S. Ski Association
1750 East Boulder Street
Colorado Springs, CO 80909
(303) 578-4572

U.S. Ski Coaches Association
PO Box 1747
Park City, UT 84060
(801) 649-9090

**U.S. Ski Team/U.S. Ski
Education Foundation**
PO Box 100
Park City, UT 84060
(801) 649-9090

U.S. Ski Writers Association
7 Kinsington Road
Glen Falls, NY 12801
(518) 793-1201

Women in Skiing, Inc.
90 Farm Chase
Farmington, CT 06032
(203) 677-7121

**Women's Professional
Ski Racing, Inc.**
42 East 23rd Street
New York, NY 10010
(212) 673-4500

World Wide Ski Corporation
PO Box 4580
Aspen, CO 81612
(303) 925-7864

■ **ORGANIZATIONS—
INTERNATIONAL**

**Ski Federation Internationale
De Worbstrasse 210**
CH-3073 Gumligen b. Bern
Switzerland
+41+31/525815

AUSTRALIA
Australian Ski Federation
PO Box 210
South Melbourne, VIC 3189
Australia
(03) 553-1447

FRANCE
Federation Francaise de Ski
34 rue Flachat
75017 - Paris
France
(1) 742.82.27

GERMANY, FEDERAL REPUBLIC OF
Deutscher Skiverband
Hubertstrasse 1
8033 Planegg
Germany
089/85790-0

SKATING

■ ORGANIZATIONS—U.S. & CANADA

Amateur Skating Union of the United States
1033 Shady Lane
Glen Ellen, IL 60137
(312) 469-2107

Biathlon Ski (Canada)
333 River Road
Ottawa, Ontario, Can K1L 8H9
(613) 748-5608

Canadian Amateur Speed Skating Association
333 River Road
Ottawa, Ontario, Canada K1L 8H9
(613) 748-5669

Canadian Figure Skating Association
333 River Road
Vanier, Ontario, Canada K1L 8H9
(613) 748-5635

Ice Skating Institute of America
1000 Skokie Boulevard
Wilmette, IL 60091
(312) 256-5060

Professional Skaters Guild of America
PO Box 5904
Rochester, MN 45903
(507) 281-5122

U.S. Figure Skating Association
20 First Street
Colorado Springs, CO 80906
(303) 635-5200

U.S. Figure Skating Association Hall of Fame and Museum
20 First Street
Colorado Springs, CO 80906-3697
(303) 635-5200

■ ORGANIZATIONS— INTERNATIONAL

International Skating Union
Promenade 73
Postfach
CH-7270 Davos-Platz, Switzerland
+41+83/3 75 77
or
Marmorveien 1
Oslo, Norway

International Speed Skating
One East Liberty Street, Suite 412
Reno, NV 89501

U.S. International Speedskating Association
17060 Patricia Lane
Brookfield, WI 53005
(414) 782-3533

World Figure Skating
Championships (Canada)
333 River Road
Ottawa, Ontario, Canada K1L 8H9
(613) 746-2868

OTHER WINTER SPORTS

■ ORGANIZATIONS—U.S. & CANADA

Curl Canada
River Road
Ottawa, Ontario, Canada K1L 8H9
(613) 741-7126

Curling Hall of Fame and Museum of Canada
15 May Street
Winnipeg,Manitoba,Canada R3B 0G8
(204) 837-3621

Pro Bobsledding, Inc.
340 Cornelia Street
Plattsburgh, NY 12901
(518) 563-5237

U.S. Biathlon Association
PO Box 5515
Essex Junction, VT 05453
(802) 655-4592/4524

U.S. Curling Association
PO Box 971
Stevens Point, WI 54481
(715) 344-1199

U.S. Luge Association
PO Box 651
Lake Placid, NY 12946
(518) 523-2071

U.S. Women's Curling Association
Route No. 1
Box 100
Drayton, ND 58255
(218) 455-3863

USA National Bobsled Federation, Inc.
PO Box 828
Lake Placid, NY 12946
(518) 523-1842

Western Winter Sports Representatives Association
2621 Thorndyke Avenue West
Seattle, WA 98199
(206) 284-0751

■ INTERNATIONAL ORGANIZATIONS

Federation Internationale De Bobsleigh Et De Tobogganing
Via Piranesi 44/b
20137   Milan, Italy
+39+2/719751

Federation Internationale De Luge De Course
A-8786 Rottenmann 168 a
Autriche

Union Internationale De Biathlon Pentathlon Moderne Et De Briger
Jarlsgatan 113:C, 3 tr.
S11356 Stockholm
Sweden

■ PUBLICATIONS

Canadian Skater
333 River Road
Ottawa,Ontario,Canada K1L 8H9

Cross Country Skier
33 East Minor Street
Emmaus, PA 18049

Great Lakes Skier
7990 W. Grand River, Suite C
Brighton, MI 48116

Nordic West
PO Box 7077
Bend, OR 97708-7077

North American Curling News
214 Summit Street
Portage, WI 53901

Northwest Skier
903 Northeast 45th
Seattle, WA 98105

Skating
20 First Street
Colorado Springs, CO 80906

Ski America
737 Riverview Road
Lenox, MA 01240

Ski Magazine
380 Madison Avenue
New York, NY 10017

Ski New England
537 Post Road
Darien, CT 06820

Snow Week
11812 Wayzata Blvd, Suite 100
Minnetonka, MN 55343

Winter Sports News Magazine
117 Marlboro Road
Delmar, NY 12054

■ **EVENTS**

American Birkebeiner
Cable, WI 54821
(715) 798-3811

Aspen Winternational
Aspen Skiing Company
PO Box 1248
Aspen, CO 81612
(303) 925-1220

U.S. Ski Team/Celebrity Classic
PO Box 100
Park City, UT 84060
(801) 649-9090

■ **CAMPS**

FIGURE SKATING
Town of Vail
Dobson Ice Arena
Attn: Summer Skating School
321 East Lionshead Circle
Vail, CO 81657
(303) 476-1560

Sport-O-Rama
18 College Road
Monsey, NY 10952

Skating School
Mrs. Judy Mattke
2051 Pinewood Drive
Eagle River, WI 54521
(715) 479-4502

Skating School
JoAnn Maizitis
Huronia School of Skating
PO Box 110
Wasaga Beach
Ontario L0L SP0
Canada
(705) 429-3321
(705) 429-3327

SNOW SKIING
Lathrop Ski and Race Camps
1430 Massachusetts Avenue
Suite 310
Cambridge, MA 02138
(617) 497-7744
1-800-222-LATH

Ski School
Andy Stern
357 East 57th Street
New York, NY 10022
(212) 355-1385

Ski School
Edward Finn, Director
42-N Edgewood Avenue
Mount Vernon, NY 10522
(914) 699-8335

Timberline Ski School
Timberland Lodge, OR 97028
(503) 231-5402

Craftsbury Nordic Ski Center
Box 31-M
Craftsbury Common, VT 05827
(802) 586-2514

■ **INDIVIDUALS**

Dr. Tenley Albright
110 Francis Street
Boston, MA 02108

Tai Babilonia
13889 Valley Vista Blvd.
Sherman Oaks, CA 91423

Dick Button
888 7th Avenue #650
New York, NY 10106

Suzie Chaffee
5106 Woodwind Lane
Anaheim, CA 92807

John Curry
John Curry Skating Company
155 E. 55th Street
New York, NY 10022

Peggy Fleming
Box 173
Los Gatos, CA 95031

Linda Fratianne
18214 Septo Street
Northridge, CA 91324

Dorothy Hamill
2569 Benedict Canyon Drive
Beverly Hills, CA 90210

Beth Heiden
3505 Blackhawk Drive
Madison, WI 53705

Eric Heiden
3505 Blackhawk Drive
Madison, WI 53705

Jean-Claude Killy
73 Val d'Isere
France

Janet Lynn
4215 Marsh Avenue
Rockford, IL 61111

Phil Mahre
White Pass Drive
Naches, WA 98937

Steve Mahre
2408 North 52nd Avenue
Yakima, WA 98908

Toni Sailer
A-6370 Kitzbuhel
Tirol, Austria

Ingemar Stenmark
Tarnaby, Sweden

WRESTLING ━━━━━━━

■ ORGANIZATIONS— U.S., CANADA & INTERNATIONAL

Canadian Amateur Wrestling Association
333 River Road
Vanier, Ontario, Canada K1L 8H9
(613) 748-5686

Federation Internationale De Amateur Wrestling
Avenue Ruchonnet 3
CH-1 3 Lausanne
SuisseMountain Intercollegiate

National Wrestling Coaches Association
Foothill Station
Salt Lake City, UT 84108

National Wrestling Hall of Fame
405 West Hall of Fame Avenue
Stillwater, OK 74075
(405) 377-5339

New England University Wrestling Association
c/o Garry N. Barton
University of Rhode Island
Kingston, RI 02881
(401) 792-2029

USA Wrestling
405 West Hall of Fame Avenue
Stillwater, OK 74075
(405) 377-5242

World Wrestling Federation
Sub of: Titan Sports
1055 Summer Street
Stamford, CT 06905
(203) 352-8600

Wrestling Association
3702 Forsythia Drive
Boise, ID 83703
(208) 342-5084

■ PUBLICATIONS

Amateur Wrestling News
PO Box 60397
Oklahoma City, OK 73146

Championship Wrestling
1115 Broadway
New York, NY 10010

Pro Wrestling Illustrated
PO Box 48
Rockville Centre, NY 11571

Ring Wrestling
PO Box 304
Pleasantville, NY 10570

USA Wrestler
405 West Hall of Fame Drive
Stillwater, OK 74075

Wrestling Magazine
Route 1, Box 103
Vernon Center, MN 56090

Wrestling Revue
PO Box 304
Pleasantville, NY 10570

Wrestling U.S.A.
PO Box 128
M.S.U.
Bozeman, MT 59717

■ CAMPS

Wrestling Camp
Jim Humphrey
Indiana University
Assembly Hall
Bloomington, IN 47405
(812) 335-6941
(B)

Wrestling Camp
Continuing Education and
Community Services
Rowe Hall No. 126
Central Michigan University
Mount Pleasant, MI 48859
(517) 774-3718
(B)

J. Robinson Iowa Intensive Camps
1313 Fifth Street S.E., Suite 303
PO Box 13040
Dinkytown Station
Minneapolis, MN 55414
(612) 379-3919
(B)

UNO Maverick Wrestling Clinic
University of Nebraska at Omaha
Omaha, NE 68182
(402) 554-2300
(B)

Bronco Wrestling Camp
Gary Taylor
Rider College
2083 Lawrenceville Road
Lawrenceville, NJ 08648
(609) 896-5201
(215) 860-2205
(B)

Summer Sports Camps
West Gymnasium, SUNY/
Binghamton
Vestal Parkway East
Binghamton, NY 13901
(B)

Wrestling Camp
Bob Guzzo
Weisiger-Brown Athletic Facility
North Carolina State University
Raleigh, NC 27695-8501
(919) 737-3548
(B)

Wrestling Camp
Jerry Stanley
180 West Brooks
Room 201
University of Oklahoma
Norman, OK 73069
(405) 325-8273
(B)

Ron Finley's Wrestling Camp
c/o Athletic Department
University of Oregon
Eugene, OR 97403
(503) 686-3825
(B)

Penn State Wrestling Camp
Chuck Herd
The Pennsylvania State University
410 Keller Conference Center
University Park, PA 16802

*BYU Sports Camps, Conferences and Workshops
154 Harman Building
Provo, UT 84602
(801) 378-4903
(B)

■ INDIVIDUALS

AMATEUR

Stan Abel
University of Oklahoma
Athletic Department
Norman, OK 73069

Dan Gable
RR 2 Box 55
Iowa City, IA 52240

Jim Gibbons
206 State Gymnasium
Iowa State University
Ames, IA 50011

Bob Guzzo
Box 8501
North Carolina State
Raleigh, NC 27695

Joe Seay
Oklahoma State University
Stillwater, OK 74074

Thad Turner
Taylor Gymnasium
Lehigh University
Bethlehem, PA 18015

PROFESSIONAL

Captain Lou Albano
c/o Wrestling Revue
PO Box 304
Pleasantville, NY 10570

Rick Flair
c/o Jim Crockett Promotions Inc.
421 Briar Bend Drive
Charlotte, NC 28209

Gorgeous Ladies of Wrestling
G.L.O.W.
6121 Santa Monica Boulevard
Hollywood, CA 90038

Hulk Hogan
c/o Gerald Singleton (F.G.K.& S.)
485 Madison Avenue
New York, NY 10022

Dusty Rhodes
c/o Jim Crockett Promotions Inc.
421 Briar Bend Drive
Charlotte, NC 28209

The Road Warriors (Animal & Hawk)
c/o Jim Crockett Promotions Inc.
421 Briar Bend Drive
Charlotte, NC 28209

Sargeant Slaughter
c/o Richard MacLean
191 Post Road West
Westport, CT 06880

GENERAL DIRECTORY

COLLEGE SPORTS ORGANIZATIONS AND CONFERENCES

■ U.S. AND CANADA

Arkansas Intercollegiate Conference
4801 North Hills Boulevard
North Little Rock, AR 72116
(501) 758-6688

Atlantic Coast Conference
PO Box 29169
Greensboro, NC 27408
(919) 282-1108

Atlantic 10 Conference
201 Route 17 North
Rutherford, NJ 07070
(201) 933-5450

Bay Area Intercollegiate Athletic Conference
c/o Brett Smith
College of Notre Dame
1500 Ralston Avenue
Belmont, CA 94002
(415) 593-1601

Big East Conference
321 South Main Street
Heritage Building
Penthouse
Providence, RI 02903
(401) 272-9108,9109

Big Eight Conference
600 East Eighth Street
Kansas City, MO 64106
(816) 471-5088

Big Sky Athletic Conference
PO Box 1736
409 West Jefferson
Boise, ID 83701
(208) 345-5393

Big State Intercollegiate Conference
c/o Dr. Tex Kassen
809 Country Club Road
Georgetown, TX 78626
(512) 863-5276

Big Ten Athletic Conference
1111 Plaza Drive
Suite 600
Schaumburg, IL 60173-4900
(312) 885-3933

California Collegiate Athletic Association
40 Via di Roma Walk
Long Beach, CA 90803
(213) 433-2672

Canadian Colleges Athletic Association
333 River Road
Tower A, 11th Floor
Vanier, Ontario, Canada
K1L 8H9
(613) 748-5626

Canadian Interuniversity Athletic Union
333 River Road
Ottawa, Ontario, Canada K1L 8H9
(613) 748-5619

Carolina's Intercollegiate Athletic Conference
Catawba College
Salisbury, NC 28144
(704) 637-4474

Cascade Collegiate Conference
c/o Sally Jones, Pres.
Southern Oregon State College
Ashland, OR 97520

Central Collegiate Conference
Western Michigan University
1705 Evanston
Kalamazoo, MI 49008
(616) 383-1338

Central Intercollegiate Athletic Association
2013 Cunningham Drive
Suite 241
Hampton, VA 23666
(804) 838-8801

Chicagoland Intercollegiate Athletic Conference
c/o Bill Brucks
Rosary College
7900 West Division
River Forest, IL 60305
(312) 366-2490

College Athletic Business Managers Association
c/o Bernard R. Meese, Jr.
Athletic Business Manager
University of Cincinnati
Cincinnati, OH 45221
(513) 475-5601

College Athletic Conference
c/o Walter Bryant
2327 Bonnieview Drive
Ormond Beach, FL 32074
(904) 441-7343

College Conference of Illinois and Wisconsin
c/o Dennis Prikkel
North Park College
Chicago, IL 60625
(312) 579-6300

College Sports Information Directors of America
Campus Box 114
Kingsville, TX 78363
(512) 595-3908

Collegiate Commissioner's Association
c/o Ken Germann
Southern Conference
Suite 220
5 Woodlawn Green
Charlotte, NC 28210
(704) 527-0314

CUNY Athletic Conference
c/o Wallace Pina
John Jay College
444 West 56th Street
New York, NY 10019
(212) 489-3351

Dixie Intercollegiate Athletic Conference
c/o Nelson Bobb
University of North Carolina/
Greensboro
Greensboro, NC 27412
(804) 379-3000

East Coast Conference
Athletic Department, Building 14
Drexel University
Philadelphia, PA 19104
(215) 222-2700

Eastern College Athletic Conference
PO Box 3
Centerville, MA 02632
(617) 771-5060

Frontier Conference
c/o Sonny Holland
Montana State University
Huffman Building
Bozeman, MT 59717
(406) 994-2401

Gateway Collegiate Athletic Conference
7700 Clayton Road, Suite 107
St. Louis, MO 63117
(314) 645-8760

Georgia Intercollegiate Athletic Conference
c/o James Landrum
Kennesaw College
PO Box 444
Marietta, GA 30061
(404) 429-2984

Golden State Conference
321 Golf Club Road
Pleasant Hill, CA 94523
(415) 685-1230, Ext 258

Great Lakes Intercollegiate Athletic Conference
1141 Three Mile Road N.E.
Grand Rapids, MI 49505
(616) 363-2981

Great Lakes Valley Conference
PO Box 1012, College Station
Rensselaer, IN 47978
(219) 866-5217

Greater Boston League
Athletic Department
Brandeis College
South Street
Waltham, MA 02254
(617) 647-2000

Greater Ohio Athletic Conference
c/o Diane Plas
Box 46457
Peck-Wadsworth Road
Weelington, OH 44090

Gulf Coast Athletic Conference
c/o Thomas Howell
216 Myrtle Street
Pineville, LA 71360
(318) 487-7102

Gulf South Conference
4 Office Park Circle, Suite 218
Birmingham, AL 35223
(205) 870-9750

Heart of America Athletic Conference
c/o William R. George
307 Rothrock
Richmond, MO 64085
(816) 776-5041

Heartland Collegiate Conference
2905 West Torquay Road
Muncie, IN 47304
(317) 285-6574

Independent College Athletic Conference
c/o Robert F. Ducatte
RPI
Troy, NY 12181
(518) 266-6685

International Collegiate Sports Foundation, Inc.
PO Box 866
Plano, TX 75074
(214) 424-8227

Iowa Intercollegiate Athletic Conference
1615 West Schrock Road
Waterloo, IA 50701
(319) 296-2227

Ivy League
70 Washington Road
Princeton, NJ 08540
(609) 452-6426

Keystone Athletic Conference
c/o Reuben M. Smitley
Penn State Capitol Campus
Middletown, PA 17057
(717) 948-6267

Lone Star Conference
c/o Garvin Beauchamp
ACU Station Box 7868
Abilene, TX 79699
(915) 674-2000

Massachusetts State College Athletic Conference
c/o F. Paul Bogan
Westfield State College
Westfield, MA 01085
(413) 568-3311, Ext 405

Mayflower Conference
c/o Darrel Pound
Lyndon State College
Lyndonville, VT 05851
(802) 626-9371

Metro-Atlantic Athletic Conference
1 Lafayette Circle
Bridgeport, CT 06604
(203) 368-6969

Metropolitan Collegiate Athletic Conference
One Ravinia Drive, Suite 1120
Atlanta, GA 30346
(404) 577-3700

Michigan Intercollegiate Athletic Conference
PO Box 63
Spring Lake, MI 49456
(616) 842-7865

Mid-American Athletic Conference
Four SeaGate, Suite 501
Toledo, OH 43604
(419) 249-7177

Mid-Central College Conference
c/o Harold Yoder, Pres.
Goshen College
Goshen, IN 46526
(219) 533-3161

Middle Atlantic States Collegiate Athletic Conference
26 Parker Street
Carlisle, PA 17013
(717) 243-3018

Mid-Eastern Athletic Conference
1304 East Wendover Avenue
Greensboro, NC 27405
(919) 275-9961
Mailing Address:
PO Box 21205
Greensboro, NC 27420-1205

Mid-Ohio Conference
c/o Carol Cosby
558 Magie Avenue
Fairfield, OH 45014
(513) 895-7289

Midwest Athletic Conference For Women
47 Cherry Hill Road N.W.
Cedar Rapids, IA 52405
(319) 396-4004

Midwest Collegiate Athletic Conference
c/o Ralph L. Shively
Lake Forest College
Lake Forest, IL 60045
(312) 234-3100

Midwestern Collegiate Conference
Landmark Center, Suite 642
1099 North Meridian Street
Indianapolis, IN 46204
(317) 630-3690

Minnesota Intercollegiate Athletic Conference
405 Laurie Lane
Stillwater, MN 55082
(612) 439-7768

Missouri Intercollegiate Athletic Association
430 West Lincoln
PO Box 508
Maryville, MO 64468
(816) 582-5655

Missouri Valley Conference
200 North Broadway
Suite 1905
St. Louis, MO 63102
(314) 421-0339

National Association of Academic Advisors for Athletics (NAAAA)
c/o Brian Mand, Pres
Florida State University
Moore Athletics
Tallahassee, FL 32303
(904) 644-1060

National Association of College Directors of Athletics (NACDA)
1229 Smith Court
PO Box 16428
Cleveland, OH 44116
(216) 892-4000

National Association of Intercollegiate Athletics (NAIA)
1221 Baltimore Avenue
Kansas City, MO 64105
(816) 842-5050

National Association of Intercollegiate Commissioners
1221 Baltimore Avenue
Kansas City, MO 64105
(816) 842-5050

National Christian College Athletic Association
1815 Union Avenue
Chattanooga, TN 37404
(615) 699-7980
Mailing Address:
PO Box 80454
Chattanooga, TN 37411

National College Athletic Association (NCAA)
Nall Avenue at 63rd Street
PO Box 1906
Mission, KS 66201
(913) 384-3220

National Junior College Athletic Association (NJCAA)
1831 Austin Bluff Parkway
Suite 200
Colorado Springs, CO 80907
(303) 590-9788
Mailing Address:
PO Box 7305
Colorado Springs, CO 80933-7305

National Little College Athletic Association
c/o Charles Trafton
5510 Winston Road
Evansville, IN 47110
(812) 422-0066

Nebraska Athletic Conference
c/o John Gibbs
Peru State College
Peru, NE 68421
(402) 872-3815

New England College Athletic Conference
c/o Athletic Department
Attn: Dick Lipe
Bentley College
Waltham, MA 02254
(617) 891-2256

New England Collegiate Conference
c/o Geoff Wheeler
Washington Bible College
6511 Princess Garden Parkway
Lanham, MD 20706
(301) 552-1400

North Central Intercollegiate Athletic Conference
Ramkota Inn
2400 North Louise
Sioux Falls, SD 57107
(605) 338-0907

Northeast-8 Conference
c/o Bentley College
Waltham, MA 02254
(617) 891-2256

Northeastern Athletic Conference
c/o Berkshire Community College
West Street
Pittsfield, MA 01201
(413) 499-4660, Ext 367

Northern California Athletic Conference
3415 Nathan Court
Rocklin, CA 95677
(916) 624-1181

Northern California Christian College Athletic Conference
800 Bethany Drive
Scotts Valley, CA 95066
(408) 438-3800

Northern Illinois Intercollegiate Conference
c/o William Langston
Aurora College
Aurora, IL
(815) 226-4085

Northern Intercollegiate Conference
Dr. David J. Rislove, Exec. Secy.
Winona State University
Winona, MN 55987
(507) 457-5295

Ohio Athletic Conference
Four SeaGate, Suite 501
Toledo, OH 43604
(419) 249-7179

Ohio Valley Conference
50 Music Square West, Suite 307
Nashville, TN 37203
(615) 327-2557

Old Dominion Athletic Conference
PO Box 971
Salem, VA 24153
(703) 389-7373

Pacific Coast Athletic Association
1700 East Dyer Road
Suite 140
Santa Ana, CA 92705
(714) 261-2525

Pacific-10 Conference
800 South Broadway
Suite 400
Walnut Creek, CA 94596
(415) 932-4411

Pennsylvania State Athletic Conference
c/o Rod C. Kelchner, Chmn.
Alumni Hall, Room 118
Mansfield University
Mansfield, PA 16933
(717) 662-4046

President's Athletic Conference
Men's Division:
c/o Jerry Schweickert
John Carroll University
University Heights, OH 44118
(216) 397-4662
Women's Division:
c/o Kathleen Manning
John Carroll University
University Heights, OH 44118
(216) 397-4662

Rocky Mountain Athletic Conference
2940 East Bates Avenue
Denver, CO 80210
(303) 753-0600

Sooner Athletic Conference
c/o John Hudson
120 North Fourth Street
Chickasaw, OK 73018
(405) 224-7575

South Atlantic Conference
c/o Dr. Alan White, Pres.
Elon College
Elon, NC 27244
(919) 584-2316

South Dakota Intercollegiate Conference
c/o Jack Schuver
719 West 9th
Sioux Falls, SD 57104
(605) 332-8683

Southeastern Conference
900 Central Bank Building
Birmingham, AL 35233
(205) 252-7415

Southern Conference, The
Ten Woodfin Street, Suite 206
Asheville, NC 28801
(704) 255-7872

Southern Intercollegiate Athletic Conference
c/o Howard Davis
Tuskegee University, Logan Hall
Tuskegee Institute, AL 36088
(205) 727-8848

Southern States Conference

c/o Neal Posey
Huntingdon College
Box 141
Montgomery, AL 36106
(205) 262-3017

Southland Conference

5195 Oriole Drive
Beaumont, TX 77707
(409) 892-0070

Southwest Athletic Conference

1300 West Mockingbird, Suite 444
PO Box 47420
Dallas, TX 75247
(214) 991-1016

Southwestern Athletic Conference

c/o James Frank
6400 Press Drive
New Orleans, LA 70126
(504) 283-0791

State University of New York Athletic Conference

c/o Dr. Patrick R. Damore
Fredonia State
Fredonia, NY 14063
(716) 673-3105

Sun Belt Conference

1408 North Westshore Boulevard
Suite 1010
Tampa, FL 33607
(813) 872-1511

Sunshine State Conference

2453 Kingfisher Lane, G-202
Clearwater, FL 33520
(813) 577-9166

Tennessee Collegiate Athletic Conference

c/o E.L. Hutton
5050 Popular Avenue, Suite 1722
Memphis, TN 38157
(901) 756-4030

Tennessee Valley Athletic Conference

c/o Dr. Earl Brooks, Pres.
LMU
Harrogate, TN 37752

Texas Intercollegiate Athletic Association

Reed Richmond
Tarleton State University
Stephenville, TX 76401
(817) 968-9077

Trans America Athletic Conference

337 South Milledge
Suite 215
Athens, GA 30605
(404) 548-3369

U.S. Collegiate Sports Council

Blatt PE Center
University of South Carolina
Columbia, SC 29208

West Coast Athletic Conference

5421 Geary Boulevard
San Francisco, CA 94121
(415) 751-9190

West Virginia Intercollegiate Athletic Conference

2 Smiley Drive
St. Albans, WV 25177
(304) 755-8201

Western Athletic Conference
14 West Dry Creek Circle
Littleton, CO 80120
(303) 795-1962

Wisconsin State University Conference
PO Box 8010
Madison, WI 53708
(608) 263-4402

Wisconsin Women's Intercollegiate Athletic Conference
PO Box 8010
Madison, WI 53708
(608) 263-4407

Women's Athletic Conference of North Dakota
c/o Linda J. Roberts, Pres.
Valley City State College
Valley City, ND 58072

■ **INTERNATIONAL**

British Universities Sports Federation
28 Woburn Square
London WC1H 0AD
England
01-580 3618

Universities Athletic Union
28 Woburn Square
London WC1H 0AA
England
01-637 4828

Australian Universities Sports Association
173 Epping Road
N. Ryde, NSW 2113
Australia
(02) 88 2196

Deutscher Sportlehrerverband
Am Rasselberg 16
6330 Wetzlar
Germany
06441/28444

University Sport, Federation Internationale du
Correspondence:
Secretariat F.I.S.U.
Rue General Thys 12
1050 Bruxelles
Belgium

FANTASY GIFTS ━━━━━━━

■ CAMPS AND TOURS

Baltimore Orioles Dream Week
c/o Orioles
Memorial Stadium
Baltimore, MD 21218

Baseball Fantasies Fulfilled
Sportsworld
5764 Paradise Drive, Suite 7
Corte Madera, CA 94925

Boston Red Sox Cruise
Boston Red Sox Marketing
Department
4 Yawkee Way
Boston, MA 02215
(617) 262-1915

Boston Red Sox Fantasy Camp
The Sox Exchange
PO Box 145
Montpelier, VT 05602
(802) 223-6666

Chicago Cubs Fantasy Camp
Randy Hundley Baseball
Camps, Inc.
605 North Court, Suite 200
Palatine, IL 60067
(312) 991-9595

Chicago White Sox Fantasy Camp
324 West 35th Street
Chicago, IL 60616

Cincinnati Reds Dream Week
100 Riverfront Stadium
Cincinnati, OH 45202

Detroit Tigers Fantasy Camp
Sports Fantasies Inc.
19111 West Ten Mile Road
Suite A21
Southfield, MI 48075

Los Angeles Dodgers Adult Baseball Camp
PO Box 2887
Vero Beach, FL 32961-2887

Mickey Mantle/Whitey Ford Fantasy Baseball Camp
PO Box 2500
Ashland, KY 41105-2500
(212) 382-1660

New York Mets Dream Week
Shea Stadium
Flushing, NY 11368
(718) 507-METS

Philadelphia Phillies Caribbean Cruise
Whiteland West Travel, Inc.
300 C North Pottstown Pike
(215) 363-5830

Philadelphia Phillies Dream Week
PO Box 115
Huntingdon Valley, PA 19006
(215) 938-0517

San Francisco Giants Fantasy Camp
Sportsworld
5764 Paradise Drive, Suite 7
Corte Madera, CA 94925

St. Louis Cardinals Baseball Camp
Randy Hundley's Baseball
Camps, Inc.
605 North Court, Suite 200
Palatine, IL 60067
(314) 621-8989 or (312) 991-9595

■ TAPES AND VIDEOS

DJ Fantasy
PO Box 28606
San Diego, CA 92128

Fantasy Tapes
2124 North Military Road
Arlington, VA 22207

Los Angeles Lakers Fantasy Video
PO Box 10
Inglewood, CA 90306

GENERAL SPORTS ORGANIZATIONS ▬▬▬▬▬

Academy for Psychology of Sports
4222 Airport Highway, Suite 11
Toledo, OH 43615
(419) 381-0044

Afro-American Hall of Fame
149 California
Highland Park, MI 48203
(313) 345-5621

Amateur Athletic Foundation of Los Angeles
2141 West Adams Boulevard
Los Angeles, CA 90402
(213) 730-9600

Amateur Athletic Union of the U.S. (AAU)
AAU House
3400 West 86th Street
PO Box 68207
Indianapolis, IN 46268
(317) 872-2900

American Association For Leisure and Recreation
1900 Association Drive
Reston, VA 22091
(703) 476-3400

American Council on International Sports
817 23rd Street Northwest
Washington, DC 20052
(202) 676-7246
(703) 476-3462

American Recreation Coalition
1915 Eye Street NW, Suite 700
Washington, DC 20006
(202) 466-6870

American Sports Education Institute/Booster Clubs of America
200 Castlewood Road
North Palm Beach, FL 33408
(305) 842-3600

American Sportscasters Association, Inc.
150 Nassau Street
New York, NY 10038
(212) 227-8080

Associated Exhibitors of AAHPERD (American Alliance for Health, Physical Education, Recreation, and Dance)
30 Mystic Isle Way
Becket, MA 01223
(413) 623-6696

Association of Representatives of Professional Athletes
9111 South La Cienega Boulevard
Suite 205
Los Angeles, CA 90301
(213) 670-8448
Mailing Address:
PO Box 90053
World Way Postal Center
Los Angeles, CA 90009

Association of Sports Museums and Halls of Fame
c/o Al Cartwright, Exec. Dir.
4 West Dale Road
Wilmington, DE 19810
(302) 475-7068

Athletes in Action
Mailing Address:
4749 Irvine Boulevard, 105-325
Irvine, CA 92714
Street Location:
4840 Irvine Boulevard, 206
Irvine, CA 92714
(714) 669-1720

Athletic Equipment Managers Association
723 Keil Court
Bowling Green, OH 43402

Athletic Goods Team Distributors
1699 Wall Street
Mount Prospect, IL 60056
(312) 439-4000

Athletic Institute
200 Castlewood Drive
North Palm Beach, FL 33408
(305) 842-3600

British Columbia Sports Hall of Fame and Museum
PO Box 69020, Station K
Vancouver, BC , Canada V5K 4W3
(604) 253-2311

Canada's Sports Hall of Fame
Exhibition Place
Toronto, Ontario, Canada M6K 3C3
(416) 595-1046

Canadian Amateur Sports Hall of Fame
c/o Canadian Olympic Assn
2380 Ave Pierre Dupuy
Cite du Havre
Montreal, Quebec, Canada
H3C 3R4
(514) 861-3371

Canadian Association For Sport Heritage
B.C. Sports Hall of Fame &
Museum
PO Box 69020, Station K
Vancouver, B.C., Canada V5K 4W3
(604) 253-2311

Canadian Intramural Recreation Association
333 River Road
Ottawa, Ontario, Canada K1L 8H9
(613) 748-5639

Canadian Olympic Association
Olympic House
Cite du Havre
Montreal, Quebec, Canada H3C 3R4
(514) 861-3371

Canadian Parks/Recreation Association
333 River Road
Ottawa, Ontario, Canada K11 8H9
(613) 748-5651

Canadian Society for Psychomotor Learning and Sport Psychology
c/o Alan Salmoni
Division of Psysical Education
Laurentian University
Sudbury, Ontario, Canada P3E 2C6
(705) 675-1151 Ext. 509

Canadian Sporting Goods Association
1315 de Maisonneuve Blvd West
Suite 702
Montreal, Quebec, Canada H3G 1M4
(514) 845-6113

Club Managers Association of America
7615 Winterberry Place
Bethesda, MD 20817
(301) 229-3600

Coaching Association of Canada
333 River Road
Ottawa, Ontario, Canada
K1L 8H9
(613) 748-5624

Comite International des Sports des Sourds (CISS)
800 Florida Avenue N.E.
Washington, DC 20002
(202) 651-5393

Comite Internationale Labour Sport
Correspondence:
11, Bd de l'Empereur
1000—Bruxelles
Belgium

Commonwealth Games Association of Canada, Inc.
c/o Neil J. Farrell, Hon. Secy.
PO Box 3763
Postal Station "C"
Hamilton, Ontario, Canada L8H 7N1

Consolidated Athletic Commission
851 North Leavitt Street
Chicago, IL 60622
(312) 276-3762

Delaware Sports Hall of Fame
402 Lee Trail
Wilmington, DE 19803
(302) 478-2863

Fellowship of Christian Athletes
8701 Leeds Road
Kansas City, MO 64129
(816) 921-0909

The General Association of International Sports Federations
Villa Henri
7 Boulevard de Suisse
Monte Carlo, Monaco
(93) 50-74-13

Georgia Sports Hall of Fame
1455 Tullie Circle, Suite 117
Atlanta, GA 30329
(404) 634-9138

Grover Cleveland Sports Hall of Fame Foundation, Inc.
1209 Cleveland Heights Boulevard
Cleveland Heights, OH 44121
(216) 781-0678

Indiana Sports Corporation
251 North Illinois Street, Suite 910
Indianapolis, IN 46204
(317) 237-2200

International Athletic Footwear and Apparel Manufacturer's Association
c/o SGMA
200 Castlewood Drive
North Palm Beach, FL 33408
(305) 842-4100

International Jewish Sports Hall of Fame
9200 Sunset Boulevard, Suite 1101
Los Angeles, CA 90069
(213) 276-1014

International School Sport Federation
Correspondence:
c/o Bundeminister fur Unterricht und Kunst
Abt 15 c, Postfach 65
A-1014 Vienna, Austria

International Senior Athletics
200 Castlewood Drive
North Palm Beach, FL 33408
(305) 842-4100

International Society For Sports Information
L. v. Meerdervoort la
The Hague, Holland
632964

Internationale Sport Facilities
Arbeitskreis
Neusser Strasse 26
D-5000 Koln 1
RFA
West Germany

International Sports Exchange
5982 Mia Court
Plainfield, IN 46168
(317) 839-9257

Irish American Sports Foundation
740 North Main Street, Suite M
West Hartford, CT 06117
(203) 233-3692

Maccabi World Union
Correspondence:
Kfar Hamaccabiah
52 105 Ramat Gan
Israel

Maine Sports Hall of Fame
3 Delano Park
Cape Elizabeth, ME 04107

Manitoba Sports Hall of Fame
1700 Ellice Avenue
Winnipeg, Manitoba, Can. R3H 0B1
(204) 786-5641

Michigan Jewish Sports Hall of Fame
6600 West Maple Road
West Bloomfield, MI 48033
(313) 661-1000

Muskegon Area Sports Hall of Fame Inc.

The Muskegon Chronicle
981 Third Street, PO Box 59
Muskegon, MI 49443
(616) 722-3161

National Academy of Sports

220 East 63rd Street
New York, NY 10021
(212) 838-5860

National Association for Girls and Women in Sport

1900 Association Drive
Reston, VA 22091
(703) 476-3450

National Association of Police Athletic Leagues

200 Castlewood Drive
North Palm Beach, FL 33408
(305) 842-4100

National Association of Sports Officials

2017 Lathrop Avenue
Racine, WI 53405
(414) 632-8855

National Club Association

1625 I Street N.W., Suite 609
Washington, DC 20006
(202) 466-8424

National Employee Services and Recreation Association

2400 South Downing Avenue
Westchester, IL 60153
(312) 562-8130

National Federation of Interscholastic Coaches Association

11724 Plaza Circle
PO Box 20626
Kansas City, MO 64195
(816) 464-5400

National Federation of Interscholastic Officials Association

11724 Plaza Circle
PO Box 20626
Kansas City, MO 64195
(816) 464-5400

National Federation of State High School Associations

PO Box 20626
11724 Plaza Circle
Kansas City, MO 64195
(816) 464-5400

National High School Athletic Coaches Association

1515 East Silver Springs Blvd
PO Box 1808
Ocala, FL 32678-1808
(904) 622-3660

National High School Sports Hall of Fame

11724 Plaza Circle, Box 20626
Kansas City, MO 64195
(816) 464-5400

National Interscholastic Athletic Administrations Association (NIAAA)

PO Box 20626
11724 Plaza Circle
Kansas City, MO 64195
(816) 464-5400

National Intramural Recreational Sports Association (NIRSA)
c/o Will Holsberry, Exec. Secy.
Gill Coliseum, Room 221
Oregon State University
Corvallis, OR 97331
(503) 754-2088

National Italian American Sports Hall of Fame
7906 West Grand Ave
Elmwood Park, IL 60635
(312) 452-4812

National Operating Committee on Standards for Athletic Equipment (NOCSAE)
11724 Plaza Circle
PO Box 20626
Kansas City, MO 64195
(816) 464-5400

National Polish-American Sports Hall of Fame & Museum
13450 Keystone
Detroit, MI 48212
(313) 552-9001

National Recreation & Parks Association
3101 Park Center Drive
Alexandria, VA 22302
(703) 820-4940

National Senior Sports Association
317 Cameron Street
Alexandria, VA 22314
(703) 549-6711

National Sport and Recreation Centre
333 River Road
Ottawa, Ontario, Canada
K1L 8H9
(613) 746-0060

National Sporting Goods Association
1699 Wall Street
Mt. Prospect, IL 60056
(312) 439-4000

National Youth Sports Coaches Association
2611 Old Okeechobee Rd
West Palm Beach, FL 33409
(305) 684-1141

New Brunswick Sports Hall of Fame
PO Box 6000, Queen Street
Fredericton, N.B., Canada E3B 5H1
(506) 453-3747

New England Museum of Sport
1175 Soldiers Field Road
Boston, MA 02134
(617) 782-2692

New England Sports Agents Association
PO Box 196
Needham, MA 02192
(617) 444-3373

North American Society for the Psychology of Sport and Physical Activity
c/o Dr. Maureen Weiss
University of Oregon
Department of Physical Education
Eugene, OR 97403
(503) 686-4108

North American Society for the Sociology of Sport

c/o Susan Greendorfer
University of Illinois
Department of Physical Education
Urbana, IL 61801

North American Youth Sport Institute

4985 Oak Garden Drive
Kernersville, NC 27284-9520
(919) 784-4926

North Carolina Sports Hall of Fame

3316 Julian Drive
Raleigh, NC 27604
(919) 872-9289

North Country Trail Association

c/o Virginia Wunsch
PO Box 311
White Cloud, MI 49349
(616) 689-6876

Oregon Sports Hall of Fame

PO Box 4381
Portland, OR 97208-4381
(503) 227-7466

Participation

Suite 805
80 Richmond Street West
Toronto, Ontario, Canada M5H 2A4
(416) 361-0514

Pennsylvania Sports Hall of Fame

PO Box 2034
Cleona, PA 17042-1322
(717) 272-3644

People-to-People Sports Committee, Inc.

40 Cutter Mill Road
Great Neck, NY 11021
(516) 482-5158

Philosophic Society for the Study of Sport

c/o Prof. Joy DiSensi, Secy/Treas
The University of Tennessee
School of HPER
Knoxville, TN 37996-2700

Prince Edward Island Sports Hall of Fame

19 Edinburgh Drive
Charlottetown, P.E.I , Canada
C1A 3E9
(902) 894-6300

Pro Athletes Outreach

PO Box 1044
Issaquah, WA 98027
(206) 392-6300

Recreation Safety Institute

100 Arrival Avenue
Ronkonkoma, NY 11779
(516) 588-2626

Recreational Industries Council on Exporting

200 Castlewood Drive
North Palm Beach, FL 33408
(305) 842-4100

Rome Sports Museum and Hall of Fame

City Hall Building
Rome, NY 13440
(315) 336-6000

St. Louis Sports Hall of Fame, Inc.
100 Stadium Plaza
St. Louis, MO 63102
(314) 421-6790

San Diego Hall of Champions, Inc.
1649 El Prado—Balboa Park
San Diego, CA 92101-1689
(619) 234-2544

Saskatchewan Sports Hall of Fame
2205 Victoria Avenue
Regina, Saskatchewan, Canada
S4P 0S4
(306) 522-3651

Shamrock Games
740 North Main Street, Suite M
West Hartford, CT 06117
(203) 233-3692

Sporting Goods Agents Association
PO Box 998
Morton Grove, IL 60053
(312) 296-3670

Sporting Goods Manufacturers Association
200 Castlewood Drive
North Palm Beach, FL 33408
(305) 842-4100
Washington Office:
1625 K Street Northwest
Suite 900
Washington, DC 20006
(202) 775-1762

Sports Ambassadors
25 Corning Avenue
Milpitas, CA 95053
(408) 263-1101

Sports America
Prog. of: USIA
301 4th Street S.W., Room 566
Washington, DC 20547
(202) 485-6671

Sports Business Press International
Katzheimerstrasse 1A
Bamberg, Federal Republic of
Germany
D-8600
(0951) 14881

Sports Federation of Canada
333 River Road
Ottawa, Ontario, Canada
K1L 8H9
(613) 748-5670

Sports Foundation, Inc.
1699 Wall Street
Mount Prospect, IL 60056
(312) 439-4000

Sports Lawyers Association
5300 South Florida Avenue
PO Box 5684
Lakeland, FL 33807
(813) 646-5091

Sports Summit
372 Fifth Avenue
New York, NY 10018
(212) 502-5306

State of Michigan Sports Hall of Fame
1010 Joanne Court
Bloomfield Hills, MI 48013
(313) 646-2216

Texas Sports Hall of Champions & Tennis Museum
PO Box 3475
Waco, TX 76707
(818) 756-2307

Timekeepers, Federation International des
Correspondence:
Secretariat General
Viale Tiziano, 70
00100 Rome
Italy

Trophy Dealers & Manufacturers Association, Inc.
4644 West Jennifer
Fresno, CA 93711
(209) 275-5100

U.S. Amputee Athletic Association
Route 2, County Line Road
Fairview, TN 37062
(615) 5 670-5453

U.S. Athletes Association
555 Simpson Street
St. Paul, MN 55104
(612) 642-9363

U.S. Cultural Exchange and Sports Society
PO Box 3602
Thousand Oaks, CA 91360
(805) 497-9628

U.S. Committee Sports For Israel
275 South 19th Street, Suite 1203
Philadelphia, PA 19103
(215) 546-4700

Veterans Park District Sports Museum
1203 North 24th Avenue
Melrose Park, IL 60160
(312) 343-5151

Virginia Sports Hall of Fame, Inc.
420 High Street
Portsmouth, VA 23704
(804) 397-5273
Mailing Address:
PO Box 370
Portsmouth, VA 23705

Women's Equity Action League
1250 Eye Street N.W., Suite 305
Washington, DC 20005
(202) 898-1588

Women's Sports Foundation
342 Madison Avenue
New York, NY 10017
(212) 972-9170

World Federation of the Sporting Goods Industry
USA Office
200 Castlewood Drive
North Palm Beach, FL 33408
(305) 842-4100

World Leisure and Recreation Association
559 King Edward Avenue,
Room 108
University of Ottawa Campus
Ottawa, Ontario, Canada
K1N 7N6
(613) 564-6812

Youth-to-Youth Committee International, Inc.
1649 Bay Drive
Miami Beach, FL 33141
(305) 866-6120

GENERAL SPORTS PUBLICATIONS

Academic-Athletic Journal
c/o Jerry Gruney
Southern Methodist University
Ownby Stadium
Dallas, TX 75275

Action Now Magazine
33046 Calle Aviador
San Juan Capistrano, CA 92675

Adirondack Life Magazine
PO Box 97
Jay, NY 12941

American Sports
8926 Valley Boulevard
PO Box 6100
Rosemead, CA 91770

Athletic Advisor Newsletter
8090 Engineer Road
San Diego, CA 92111

Athletic Business Magazine
1842 Hoffman Suite 201
Madison, WI 53704

Black College Sports Review
617 North Liberty Street
PO Box 3154
Winston-Salem, NC 27102

The Blue Chips
PO Box 20688
Oklahoma City, OK 73120

Cass Sports Program Network
1633 Central Street
Evanston, IL 60201

City Sports Monthly
Box 3693
San Francisco, CA 94119

The Coaching Clinic
117 Cuttermill Road
Great Neck, NY 11021

Field & Stream
1515 Broadway
New York, NY 10036

High School Sports
1230 Avenue of the Americas
Suite 5450
New York, NY 10020

Host Communications, Inc.
546 East Main Street
Lexington, KY 40502

Info AAU
3400 West 86th Street
Indianapolis, IN 46268

Journal of Sport Behavior
University of South Alabama
Department of HPERS
Mobile, AL 36688

Journal of Sport History
101 White Building
Penn State University
University Park, PA 16802

Journal of Sport Psychology
1607 North Market
Champaign, IL 61920

MacGregor Sports News
5326 Bluemound Road
Waukesha, WI 53186

Metro Sports, Dallas/Ft. Worth
3105 East Carpenter Freeway
Irving, TX 75062

Nationwide Sports Publications, Inc.
9255 Sunset Boulevard
Suite 200
Los Angeles, CA 90069

New England Sports Magazine
332 Congress Street
Boston, MA 02210

Northwest Sports
PO Box 51190
Seattle, WA 98115

The Olympian
c/o U.S. Olympic Committee
1750 East Boulder Street
Colorado Springs, CO 80909

Outdoor America Magazine
1701 North Fort Myer Drive
Suite 1100
Arlington, VA 22209

Outdoor Life
380 Madison Avenue
New York, NY 10017

The Racer
2-1263 Nicola Street
Vancouver, B.C., Canada
V6G 2E8

Red, White & Green Sports
7906 West Grand Avenue
Elmwood Park, IL 60635

Referee Magazine
PO Box 161
Franksville, WI 53126

Scholastic Coach
730 Broadway
New York, NY 10003

Shepherd's Pro Sports
3979 Medina Road
Akron, OH 44313

Sierra Magazine
730 Polk Street
San Francisco, CA 94109

Sociology of Sport Journal
PO Box 5076
Champaign, IL 61820

Special Events Report
213 West Institution Place
Suite 303
Chicago, IL 60610

Sport & Recreation Index
333 River Road
Ottawa, Ontario, Canada
K1L 8H9

The Sport Psychologist
PO Box 5076
Champaign, IL 61820

Sport Scene
4985 Oak Garden Drive
Kernersville, NC 27284

The Sporting News
1212 North Lindbergh
PO Box 56
St. Louis, MO 63132

Sports Afield
250 West 55th Street
New York, NY 10019

Sports Collectors Digest
Krause Publications
700 East State Street
Iola, WI 54990

Sports Heritage
PO Box 1831
Harrisburg, PA 17105

Sports History
PO Box 183
Leesberg, VA 22075

Sports Illustrated
Time-Life Bldg.
1271 Sixth Avenue
New York, NY 10020

Sports Inc.
3 Park Avenue
New York, NY 10017

The Sports Journal
3505 14th Street S.W.
Calgary Alberta Canada
T2T 3W3

The Sports Journal
105 Berkley Place
Glen Rock, NJ 07452

Sports Marketing News
1460 Post Road East
Westport, CT 06880

Sports Parade
1720 Washington Boulevard
Ogden, UT 84401

Sports Weekly Newsletter
1206 Redeemer Drive
Hawahan, SC 29406

Sportscan
141 Fifth Avenue
New York, NY 10010

Sportscape
1415 Beacon Street
Boston, MA 02146

Ultrasport Magazine
711 Boylston Street
Boston, MA 02116

Western Outdoor News
PO Box 2027
Newport Beach, CA 92663

Western Outdoors
PO Box 2027
Newport Beach, CA 92663

Winner Magazine
4 East 8th Street, Suite 2F
New York, NY 10003

The Wolfpacker
PO Box 50357
Raleigh, NC 27650

Women's Coaching Clinic
117 Cuttermill Road
Great Neck, NY 11021

Women's Sports & Fitness
310 Town & Country Village
Palo Alto, CA 94301

HALLS OF FAME ━━━━━

Afro-American Hall of Fame
149 California
Highland Park, MI 48203
(313) 345-56221

**American Museum of
Fly Fishing**
PO Box 42
Manchester, VT 05254
(802) 362-3300

**Aquatic Hall of Fame and
Museum of Canada, Inc.**
436 Main Street
Winnipeg, Manitoba R3B 1B2
Canada
(204) 947-0131

**Association of Sports Museums
and Halls of Fame**
c/o Al Cartwright
4 West Dale Road
Wilmington, DE 19810
(302) 475-7068

Canada's Sports Hall of Fame
Exhibition Palace
Toronto, Ontario M6K 3C3
Canada
(416) 595-1046

**Canadian Amateur Sports Hall
of Fame**
c/o Canadian Olympic Association
2380 Avenue Pierre Dupuy
Cite Du Havre
Montreal, Quebec H3C 3R4
Canada
(514) 861-3371

**Canadian Lacrosse Hall of
Fame**
333 River Road
Vanier, Ontario K1L 8H9
Canada

**Curling Hall of Fame and
Museum of Canada**
15 May Street
Winnipeg, Manitoba R3B 0G8
Canada
(204) 837-3621

Delaware Sports Hall of Fame
402 Lee Trail
Wilmington, DE 19803
(302) 478-2863

Georgia Sports Hall of Fame
1455 Tullie Circle, Suite 117
Atlanta, GA 30329
(404) 634-9138

Green Bay Packer Hall of Fame
1901 South Oneida
PO Box 10567
Green Bay, WI 54307-0567
(414) 499-4281

Hall of Fame of the Trotter
240 Main Street
Goshen, NY 10924
(914) 294-6330

**Hockey Hall of Fame and
Museum**
Exhibition Palace
Toronto, Ontario
Canada M6K 3C3
(416) 595-1345

Indiana Football Hall of Fame
PO Box 1035
Richmond, IN 47374
(317) 966-2235

**International Boxing Hall of
Fame**
PO Box 425
Canastota, NY 13032
(315) 697-7095

International Hockey Hall of Fame and Museum
York and Alfred Streets, PO Box 92
Kingston, Ontario K7L 4V6
Canada

International Jewish Sports Hall of Fame
9200 Sunset Boulevard, Suite 1101
Los Angeles, CA 90069
(213) 276-1014

International Swimming Hall of Fame
1 Hall of Fame Drive
Fort Lauderdale, FL 33316
(305) 462-6536

International Tennis Hall of Fame and Museum
194 Bellevue Avenue
Newport, RI 02840
(401) 849-3990

Kentucky Derby Museum
704 Central Avenue
PO Box 3513
Louisville, KY 40201
(502) 637-1111

Lacrosse Hall of Fame and Museum
Newton H. White Athletic Center
Baltimore, MD 21218
(301) 235-6882

Maine Sports Hall of Fame
3 Delano Park
Cape Elizabeth, ME 04107

Manitoba Sports Hall of Fame
1700 Ellice Avenue
Winnipeg, Manitoba R3H 0B1
Canada

Michigan Jewish Sports Hall of Fame
6600 West Maple Road
West Bloomfield, MI 48033
(313) 661-1000

Muskegon Area Sports Hall of Fame
The Muskegon Chronicle
Muskegon, MI 49443
(616) 722-3161

Naismith Memorial Basketball Hall of Fame
PO Box 179, Highland Station
1150 West Columbus Avenue
Springfield, MA 01101-0179
(413) 781-6500

National Baseball Hall of Fame & Museum
Box 590
Cooperstown, NY 13326
(607) 547-9988

National Bowling Hall of Fame and Museum
111 Stadium Plaza
St. Louis, MO 63102
(314) 231-6340

National Football Foundation Hall of Fame
Kings Island, OH 45034
(513) 241-5600

National Freshwater Fishing Hall of Fame
PO Box 33
One Hall of Fame Drive
Hayward, WI 54843
(715) 634-4440

National High School Sports Hall of Fame
11724 Plaza Circle
PO Box 20626
Kansas City, MO 64195
(816) 464-5400

National Italian American Sports Hall of Fame
7906 West Grand Avenue
Elmwood Park, IL 60635
(312) 452-4812

National Motor Sports Hall of Fame
20 Division Street
Coldwater, MI 49036
(517) 278-7223

National Polish American Sports Hall of Fame & Museum
13450 Keystone
Detroit, MI 48212
(313) 552-9001

National Ski Hall of Fame
PO Box 191
Ishpeming, MI 49849
(906) 486-9281

National Soccer Hall of Fame
58 Market Street
Oneonta, NY 13820
(607) 432-3351

National Softball Hall of Fame & Museum
2801 Northeast 50th Street
Oklahoma City, OK 7311
(405) 424-5267

National Wrestling Hall of Fame
405 West Hall of Fame Avenue
Stillwater, OK 74075
(405) 377-5339

New Brunswick Sports Hall of Fame
PO Box 6000, Queen Street
Fredericton, New Brunswick E3B 5H1
Canada
(506) 453-3747

New England Museum of Sport
1175 Soldiers Field Road
Boston, MA 02134
(617) 782-2692

North Carolina Sports Hall of Fame
3316 Julian Drive
Raleigh, NC 27604
(919) 872-9289

Oregon Sports Hall of Fame
PO Box 4381
Portland, OR 97208-4381
(503) 227-7466

Pennsylvania Sports Hall of Fame
PO Box 2034
Cleona, PA 17042-1322
(717) 272-3644

Prince Edward Island Sports Hall of Fame
19 Edinburgh Drive
Charlottetown, P.E.I. C1A 3E9
Canada
(902) 894-6300

Pro Football Hall of Fame
2121 George Hallas Drive, N.W.
Canton, OH 44708
(216) 456-8207

Pro Golfers' Association Hall of Fame
PO Box 12458
100 Avenue of the Champions
Palm Beach Gardens, FL 33410
(305) 626-3600

Rome Sports Museum and Hall of Fame
City Hall Building
Rome, NY 13440
(315) 336-6000

St. Louis Sports Hall of Fame, Inc.
100 Stadium Plaza
St. Louis, MO 63102
(314) 421-6790

San Diego Hall of Champions, Inc.
1649 El Prad-Balboa Park
San Diego, CA 92101-1689
(619) 234-2544

Saskatchewan Sports Hall of Fame
2205 Victoria Avenue
Regina, Saskatchewan S4P 0S4
Canada
(306) 522-3651

State of Michigan Sports Hall of Fame
1010 Joanne Court
Bloomfield Hills, MI 48013
(313) 646-2216

Texas Sports Hall of Champions and Tennis Museum
PO Box 3475
Waco, TX 76707
(818) 756-2307

U.S. Figure Skating Association Hall of Fame and Museum
20 First Street
Colorado Springs, CO 80906-3697
(303) 635-5200

U.S. Golf Association Hall of Fame
Golf House
Far Hills, NJ 07931
(201) 234-2300

U.S. Hockey Hall of Fame
Hat Trick Avenue
PO Box 657
Eveleth, MN 55734
(218) 744-5167

U.S. Track & Field Hall of Fame
PO Box 297
Angola, IN 46703
(219) 495-7735

Virginia Sports Hall of Fame, Inc.
420 Highland Street
Portsmouth, VA 23704
(804) 397-5273

World Golf Hall of Fame
PO Box 1908
Gerald Ford Boulevard
Pinehurst, NC 28364
(919) 295-6651

HANDICAPPED SPORTS ORGANIZATIONS

National Handicapped Sports & Recreation Association
4405 East-West Highway
Suite 603
Bethesda, MD 20814
(301) 652-7505
Mailing Address:
1145 19th Street N.W.
Suite 717
Washington, DC 20036

United States Cerebral Palsy Athletic Association
34518 Warren Road, Suite 264
Westland, MI 48185
(313) 425-8961

National Wheelchair Athletic Association
3617 Betty Drive
Suite S
Colorado Springs, CO 80907
(303) 597-8330

National Handicapped Sports & Recreation Association
1145 19th Street N.W.
Suite 717
Washington, DC 20036
(301) 652-7507
Mailing Address:
Capitol Hill Station
PO Box 18664
Denver, CO 80218
(303) 232-4575

U.S. Association for Blind Athletes
4708 46th Street N.W.
Washington, DC 22016
(202) 393-3666

Special Olympics
1350 New York Avenue N.W.
Suite 500
Washington, DC 20005
(202) 628-3630

United States Amputee Athletic Association
Suite 149-A Bell Forest Circle
Nashville, TN 37221
(615) 356-0144

American Athletic Association of the Deaf
President:
Lyle Mortensen
10604 E. 95th Street Terrace
Kansas City, MO 64134
(816) 274-1725 (B)
(816) 765-5520 (H)

Adaptive Sports Program
Kinesiotherapy Clinic
c/o Dr. Leonard Greninger
University of Toledo
2801 West Bancroft Street
Toledo, OH 43606
(419) 537-2755

Adolescent and Young Adult Amputee Programs
c/o Dr. Leonard Greninger
PO Box 99776
Pittsburgh, PA 15233
(419) 537-2755

American Therapeutic Recreation Association, Inc.
c/o Peg Conley
3417A Sapula Road, Box 377
Sand Springs, OK 74063
(904) 644-6014

Blind Outdoor Leisure Development (BOLD)
c/o Peter Maines
533 East Main Street
Aspen, CO 81611
(303) 985-2086

Boy Scouts of America
Scouting for the Handicapped
c/o John E. Hunt
PO Box 16030
Dallas-Fort Worth Airport
Dallas, TX 75261
(214) 659-2000

Canadian Special Olympics, Inc.
40 St. Claire Avenue West
Suite 209
Toronto, Ontario, Canada
M4V 1M6
(416) 928-8100

Canadian Wheelchair Sports Association
333 River Road
Ottawa, Ontario, Canada
K1L 8H9
(613) 748-5685

Courage Center
c/o Jim Beaton, Dir.
3915 Golden Valley Road
Golden Valley, MN 55422
(612) 588-0811

Disabled Sportsmen of America, Inc.
PO Box 5496
Roanoke, VA 24012

Eastern Amputee Athletic Association
2080 Ennabrock Road
North Bellmore, NY 11710
(516) 221-0610

Far West Wheelchair Athletic Association
c/o Bruce Schreber
PO Box 26483
San Jose, CA 95159
(408) 987-2828

Girl Scouts, U.S.A.
Scouting for the Handicapped
Services
c/o Cindy Ford
830 Third Avenue
New York, NY 10022
(212) 940-7500

International Committee of Silent Sports
Record Management Office
c/o Gerald M. Jordan, Pres.
Gallaudet College
800 Florida Avenue, N.E.
Washington, DC 20002
(202) 851-5114

International Games for the Disabled
Eisenhower Park
c/o Tony Giustino
East Meadow, NY 11554
(516) 542-4420

International Sports Organization for the Disabled
International Stoke Mandeville
Games Federation
Stoke-Mandeville Spinal Injury
Center
Aylesbury, England

International Sports Organization for the Disabled
S-12387 RARSTA
Sweden

Joseph P. Kennedy, Jr. Special Olympics Foundation
c/o Robert Montague
1350 New York Avenue N.W.
Washington, DC 20006
(202) 393-1250

National Association of Handicapped Outdoor Sportsmen, Inc.
PO Box 25
Carterville, IL 62918
(618) 985-3579

National Association of Sports for Cerebral Palsy
c/o Cynthia Good, Dir.
66 East 34th Street
New York, NY 10016
(212) 481-6345

National Organization on Disability
2100 Pennsylvania Avenue N.W.
Suite 232
Washington, DC 20037
(202) 343-3674

National Rehabilitation Information Center
c/o Ed Rorie, Information Specialist
Catholic University of America
4407 8th Street N.E.
Washington, DC 20422
(202) 635-5826

Paralyzed Veterans of America
c/o Jack Powell, Exec. Dir.
801 18th Street N.W.
Washington, DC 20006
(202) 872-1300

ARCHERY, CROSSBOW AND DARTCHERY
National Archery Association
c/o Christine McKarthy
1750 East Boulder Street
Colorado Springs, CO 80909
(303) 578-4576

BASEBALL/SOFTBALL
American Special Recreation Association
c/o John Nesbitt, Ed.D.
Recreation Education Program
University of Iowa
Iowa City, IA 52240
(319) 353-2121

National Wheelchair Softball Association
PO Box 737
Sioux Falls, SD 57101

National Wheelchair Softball Association
John Speake
PO Box 22478
Minneapolis, MN 55422
(612) 437-1792

BASKETBALL
Mike Glenn Basketball Camp for the Hearing Impaired
3166 Big Spring Court
Decatur, GA 30034

National Wheelchair Basketball Association
c/o Stan Labanowich
110 Seaton Building
University of Kentucky
Lexington, KY 40506
(606) 257-1623

Rolling Warhawk Wheelchair Basketball Camp and Coaching Clinic
c/o Lou Zahn, Summer Camp Office
Roseman Building 1004
University of Wisconsin
Whitewater, WI 53190
(414) 472-1508

BICYCLING

Adaptive Sports Program
Kinesiotherapy Clinic
c/o Dr. Leonard Groninger
University of Toledo
2801 West Bancroft Street
Toledo, OH 43606
(419) 537-2755

BOATING

Canadian Recreational Canoeing Association
c/o Steve Secco, Project Dir.
PO Box 500
Hyde Park
Ontario N0M 1Z0 Canada
(519) 473-2109

Water Safety and Boating Program for the Disabled Office of Parks and Recreation
c/o Glo Webel
Sailboat House
1520 Lakeside Drive
Oakland, CA 94612
(415) 444-3807

BOWLING

American Blind Bowling Association
150 North Bellaire Avenue
Louisville, KY 40206
(502) 896-8039

American Wheelchair Bowling Association
Daryl Pfister
N54 W15858 Larkspur Lane
Menomonie Falls, WI 53501

FLYING

American Wheelchair Pilots Association
c/o Dave Graham
1621 East 2nd Avenue
Mesa, AZ 85204
(602) 831-4262

FOOTBALL

Recreation and Athletic Rehabilitation-Education Center
c/o Brad Hedrick
University of Illiniois
1207 South Oak Street
Champaign, IL 61820
(217) 333-4606

GOLF

International Senior Amputee Golf Society, Inc.
c/o Dale Bourisseau
14039 Ellesmere Drive
Tampa, FL 33624
(813) 961-3275

National Amputee Golf Association
c/o Bob Wilson
5711 Yearling Court
Bonita, CA 92002
(619) 479-4578

Project Fore, Golf for the Physically Disabled
c/o John Klein
Singing Hills Country Club
3007 Dehesa Road
El Cajon, CA 92021
(619) 442-3425

U.S. Blind Golfers Association
c/o Patrick Browne, Jr.
225 Baronne Street, 28th Floor
New Orleans, LA 70112

HIKING

National Easter Seal Society
2023 West Ogden Avenue
Chicago, IL 60612

HORSEBACK RIDING

National Foundation for Horsemanship for the Handicapped
c/o Maudie Hunter-Warfel
Box 462
Malvern, PA 19355
(215) 644-7414

North American Riding for the Handicapped Association
Leonard Warner, Exec. Dir.
Box 100
Ashburn, VA 22011
(703) 471-1621
(703) 777-3540

ICE SKATING

Skating Association for the Blind and Handicapped
c/o Elizabeth O'Donnell, Pres.
3236 Main Street
Buffalo, NY 14214
(716) 833-2994

MARATHON RACING

International Wheelchair Road Racers Club, Inc.
Joseph M. Dowling, Pres.
30 Myano Lane
Stamford, CT 06902
(203) 967-2231

National Wheelchair Marathon
c/o Bob Hall
15 Marlborough Street
Belmont, MA 02178
(617) 489-3246

MARTIAL ARTS

American Alliance for Health, Physical Education, Recreation and Dance Programs for the Handicapped
c/o Dr. Razor, Exec. VP
1900 Association Drive
Reston, VA 22091
(703) 476-3461

MOTORCYCLING

Wheelchair Motorcycle Association, Inc.
c/o Dr. Eli Factor
101 Torrey Street
Brockston, MA 02401

MOUNTAIN CLIMBING

S.O.A.R. (Shared Outdoor Adventure Recreation)
c/o Linda Besant
PO Box 14583
Portland, OR 97214
(503) 238-1613

RACQUETBALL

National Wheelchair Racquetball Association
Jim Leatherman
c/o AARA
815 North Weber, Suite 203
Colorado Springs, CO 80903
(301) 732-1881

United States Wheelchair Racquetball Association
Chip Parmelly
1941 Viento Verano Drive
Diamond Bar, CA 91765
(714) 861-7312

ROLLER SKATING

U.S. Amateur Confederation Roller Skating Association
Special Olympics
c/o Nancy Kirk
PO Box 81846
Lincoln, NE 68501
(402) 483-7551

RUNNING

Recreation and Athletic Rehabilitation-Education Center
University of Illinois
c/o Brad Hedrick
1207 South Oak Street
Champaign, IL 61820
(217) 333-4606

SCUBA DIVING

Handicapped Scuba Association
c/o Jim Gatacre
1104 El Prado
San Clemente, CA 92672

SKYDIVING

United States Parachute Association
c/o Mike Johnston
1440 Duke Street
Alexandria, VA 22314
(703) 836-3495

SNOWMOBILING

Winter Park Sports and Learning Center
c/o Hal O'Leary
PO Box 36
Winter Park, CO 80482

SNOW SKIING

Alberta Association for Disabled Skiers
Box 875, Station M
Calgary, Alberta T2P 2J6
Canada

Alpine Alternatives
c/o Mary Decker
1634 West 13th Street
Anchorage, AK 99501

British Amputee Ski Association
Box 1373
Banff, Alberta T0L 0C0
Canada

Canadian Association for Disabled Skiing
Box 307
Kimberley, B.C. VIA 249
Canada

Chicagoland Handicapped Skiers
c/o Josie Krass
PO Box 115B
R.R. 1
Sandwich, IL 60548
(815) 786-8059

United States Deaf Skiers Association
Two Sunset Hill Road
Simsbury, CT 06070
(203) 244-3341

SOCCER

International Games for the Disabled
c/o Michael Mushett (Wheelchair Soccer)
Eisenhower Park
East Meadow, NY 11554

United Cerebral Palsy of Detroit
c/o Jeffrey Jones (Ambulant Soccer)
7700 Second Avenue
Detroit, MI 48202
(313) 871-0177

United States Quad Rugby Association
811 Northwestern Drive
Grand Forks, ND 58201
(701) 775-0790

SWIMMING

National Association of Swimming Clubs for the Handicapped
63 Dunnegan Road
Eltham, London SE9
England

TENNIS

International Foundation of Wheelchair Tennis
c/o Peter Burwash International, Ltd.
2203 Timberloch Place, Suite 126
The Woodlands, TX ;77380
(713) 363-4707

National Foundation of Wheelchair Tennis
c/o Brad Park
3857 Birch Street, Suite 411
Newport Beach, CA 92660
(714) 851-1707

U.S. Tennis Association, Inc.
Education and Research Center
c/o Eve Kraft, Director
729 Alexander Road
Princeton, NJ 37062
(615) 670-5453

UNICURL

Ahlqvist Agentur Ab
Argongatan 8
431 33 Molndal
Sweden

WATER SKIING

Advisory Panel on Water Sports for the Disabled
The Sports Council
70 Brompton Road
London SW3 IEX
England

American Water Ski Association
c/o Bruce Kistler
State Road 550 and Carl Floyd
Road
PO Box 191
Winter Haven, FL 33880
(813) 324-4341

British Disabled Water Ski Association
Warren Wood, The Warren
Ashtead, Surry KT212 SN
England

WEIGHTLIFTING

Iron Athlete Training Center
c/o Mark Lescoe
1940 East University Avenue
Tempe, AZ 85281
(602) 839-7872

■ **SPORT WHEELCHAIR MANUFACTURERS**

American Rollers
c/o Loretta Butler
PO Box 987
Paramount, CA 90723
(213) 634-4083

Bair Enterprises
c/o Lewis Bair
Route 1, Box 682
Esparto, CA 95627
(916) 787-3902

Everest and Jennings, Inc.
3233 East Mission Oaks Boulevard
Camarillo, CA 93010
(805) 987-6911

Invacare Corporation
c/o Jerry Smith
4457 63rd Circle North
Pinellas Park, FL 33565
(813) 526-9419

Ortop Meditech, Inc.
Ortop Limited
c/o Matin Silver
544 10th Street
Palisades Park, NJ 07650
(201) 947-0500

INTERNATIONAL OLYMPIC COMMITTEES

National Olympic Committee of Afghanistan
Kabul, Afghanistan

Comite Olympique de la Republique Populaire Socialiste d'Albanie
Rruga Kongresii Permetit Nr. 41
Tirana, Albania

ALGERIA
Comite National Olympique Algerien
Cite Olympique
B.P. 64, El Biar
Algeria

ANDORRA
Comite Olympique Andorran
c/o Babot Camp No. 2-3-2
Andorre-la-Vieille, Andorra

ANGOLA
Comite Olimpico Angolano
B.P 5466
Luanda, Angola

ANTIGUA
Antigua Olympic and Commonwealth Games Association
PO Box 747
St. John's, Antigua W.I.

ANTILLES, NETHERLAND
Nederlands Antilliaans Olympisch Comite
PO Box 3495
Willemstad, Curacao

ARGENTINA
Comite Olimpico Argentino
Codigo Postal 1062
Juncal No. 1662
Buenos Aires
Argentina

ARUBA
Aruba Olympic Committee
PO Box 253
San Nicolaas, Aruba

AUSTRALIA
Australian Olympic Federation
PO Box 284
South Melbourne, Victoria 3205
Australia

AUSTRIA
Osterreichisches Olympishes Komitee
Prinz-Eugen-Strasse 12
1040 Vienna
Austria

BAHAMAS
Bahamas Olympic Association
PO Box 6250 (SS)
Nassau
Bahamas

BAHRAIN
Bahrain Olympic Committee
PO Box 26406
Bahrain

BANGLADESH
Bangladesh Olympic Association
Tennis Complex
Ramna Green
Dacca 2
Bangladesh

BARBADOS
Barbados Olympic Association
PO Box 659
Bridgeton
Barbados

BELGIUM
Comite Olympique et Interfederal Belge
Avenue de Bouchout 9
1020 Bruxelles
Belgium

BELIZE
Belize Olympic and Commonwealth Games Association
P.O. Box 103
Belize City
Belize

BENIN
Comite Olympique Beninois
B.P. No. 032767
Contonou
Benin

BERMUDA
Bermuda Olympic Association
PO Box 1665
Hamilton 5, Bermuda

BHUTAN
Bhutan Olympic Committee
PO Box No. 103
Thimphu, Bhutan

BOLIVIA
Comite Olimpico Boliviano
Casilla 448L
La Paz
Bolivia

BOTSWANA
Botswana National Olympic Committee
PO Box 1404 Gaborone
Botswana

BRAZIL
Comite Olimpico Brasileiro
Rua da Assembleia 10-32 Andar
Salas 3209/11
20011 Rio de Janeiro
Brazil

BRITISH VIRGIN ISLANDS
British Virgin Islands Olympic Committee
PO Box 35
Road Town
Tortola, British Virgin Islands

BRUNEI
Brunei National Olympic Council
PO Box 2008
Bandar Seri Begawan
Negara Brunei Darussalam

BULGARIA
Comite Olympique Bulgare
rue Anghel Kantchev 4
100 Sofia
Bulgaria

BURKINA FASO
Counseil National Olympique et des Sports Burkinabe
B.P 3925
Ouagadougou
Burkina Faso

BURMA
Burma Olympic Committee
Aungsan Stadium
Mingala Taungnyunt Township
Rangoon Division 11221
Burma

CAMEROON
Comite National Olympique du Cameroun
B.P. 528
Yaounde
Cameroon

CANADA

Canadian Olympic Association

Olympic House, Cite du Havre
Montreal, Quebec H3C 3R4
Canada

CAYMAN ISLANDS

Cayman Islands Olympic Committee

PO Box 309
Grand Cayman/British West Indies

CENTRAL AFRICAN REPUBLIC

Comite Olympique Centrafricain

B.P. 1541
Banqui, Central African Republic

CHAD

Comite Olympique Tchadien

B.P. 519
N'Djamena, Chad

CHILE

Comite Olimpico de Chile

Casilla 2239
Vicuna Mackenna 44
Santiago
Chile

CHINA, PEOPLE'S REPUBLIC OF

Chinese Olympic Committee

9 Tiyuguan Road
Beijing
China

COLOMBIA

Comite Olimpico Colombiano

Carrera 16 No. 37-20
Apartado Aereo (Postal) 5093
20 Bogota, Colombia

CONGO, PEOPLE'S REPUBLIC OF THE

Comite Olympique Congolais

B.P. 1007, Brazzaville
The Congo

COOK ISLANDS

Cook Islands Sports and Olympic Association

PO Box 569
Rarotonga

COSTA RICA

Comite Olimpico de Costa Rica

Apartado 5388
1000 San Jose
Costa Rica

CUBA

Comite Olimpico Cubano

Zona Postal 4
Calle 13, No. 601
La Habana
Cuba

CYPRUS

Cyprus National Olympic Committee

19 Nikitara Street
Nicosia
Cyprus

CZECHOSLOVAKIA

Comite Olympique Tchecoslovaque

Narodni Trida 33
11293 Prague, Czechoslovakia

DENMARK

Danmarks Olympiske Komite

Idraettens Hus
Brondby Stadion 20
2605 Brondby
Denmark

DJIBOUTI, REPUBLIC OF
Comite National Olympique Djiboutien
Cite Miniserielle
B.P. 16
Djibouti

DOMINICAN REPUBLIC
Comite Olimpio Dominicano
Estadio Olimpico 3 Piso
Centro Olimpico Juan Pablo Duarte
Apartado Postal 406
Santo Domingo
Dominican Republic

EAST GERMANY
Nationales Olympisches Komitee der Deutschen Demokratischen Republic
Behrenstrasse 40/41
1080 Berlin, East Germany

ECUADOR
Comite Olimpico Ecuatoriano
PO Box 4567
Ecuador

EGYPT
Comite Olympique Egyptien
PO Box 2055
Rue Kasr-el-Nil 13
Le Caire
Egypt

EL SALVADOR
Comite Nacional Olimpico de El Salvador
Apartado Postal 759
Gimnasio Nacional Jose Adlolfo Pineda
San Salvador, El Salvador

ETHIOPIA
Comite Olympique Ethiopien
B.P. 3241
Addis-Ababa
Ethiopa

FIJI
Fiji Amateur Sports Association & National Olympic Committee
PO Box 127
Suva
Fiji

FINLAND
Finnish Olympic Committee
Radiokatu 12
SF-00240 Helsinki
Finland

FRANCE
Comite National Olympique et Sportif Francais
23 rue d'Anjou
75008 Paris
France

GABONESE REPUBLIC
Comite Olympigue Gabonais
B.P. 2266 Libreville
Gabonese Republic

GAMBIA
Gambia National Olympic Committee
Commonwealth Games Association
Independence Stadium
PO Box 666, Bakau
Kombo St. Mary Division
Gambia

GHANA
Ghana Olympic Committee
PO Box M 439
Ministries Branch
Accra
Ghana

GREAT BRITAIN
The British Olympic Assocation
1 Wandsworth Palin
London SW 18 1 EH
England

GREECE
Comite Olympique Hellenique
4 rue Kapsali
Athenes 138
Greece

GRENADA
Grenada Olympic Association
c/o Ministry of Sports
Carenage
St. George's
Grenada

GUAM
Guam Amateur Sports Federation
PO Box 21815
GMF Guam /MI 96921

GUATEMALA
Comite Olimpico Guatemalteco
Palacio de Ceportes, Zona 5
Guatemala C.A.
Guatemala

GUINEA
Comite Olympique Guineen
Ministere de la Jeunesse du Sport et
des Arts Populaires
B.P. 262
Conakry, Guinea

GUINEA, REPUBLIC OF EQUATORIAL
Comite National Olympique Equato-Guineen
c/o Ministerio de Educacion y
Deportes
Malabo, Equatorial Guinea

GUYANA
Guyana Olympic Association
PO Box 10133
Georgetown, Guyana

HAITI
Comite Olympique Hatien
PO Box 1796
Av. marie-Jeanne No. 21,
Cite de l'Exposition
Port-au-Prince, Haiti

HONDURAS
Comite Olimpico Hondureno
C.A. Apartado Postal 36 C
Tegucigalpa
Honduras

HONG KONG
Amateur Sports Federation and Olympic Committee of Hong Kong
Prince's Building 908
Hong Kong

HUNGARY
Comite Olympique Hongrois
Rosenberg Hazspar U.I
1054 Budapest

ICELAND
Olympiunefnd Islands
Lthrottamidstodin
Laugardal
105 Reykjavik, Iceland

INDIA
Indian Olympic Assocation
Room No. 1104– Block No. "F"
Jawaharlal Nerhu Stadium
110003 New Delhi
India

INDONESIA
Komite Olympiade Indonesia
c/o Koni Pusat Pintu 1 Senayan
Djakarta, Indonesia

IRAN
**National Olympic Committee
of the Islamic Republic of Iran**
Enghelab venue Forsat Street
Araste Alley 9
PO Box 15815/1589
Teheran, Iran

IRAQ
**Iraqi National Olympic
Committee**
PO Box 441
Kherbandha
Baghdad, Iraq

IRELAND
Olympic Council of Ireland
14 Herbert Street
Dublin 2, Ireland

ISRAEL
Olympic Committee of Israel
6 Ha-arbaa Street
Tel-Aviv 64739
Israel

ITALY
**Comitato Olimpico Nazionale
Italiano**
Foro Italico
Rome, Italy

IVORY COAST
Comite Olympique Ivoirien
B.P. 979
Abidjan 08
Ivory Coast

JAMAICA
Jamaica Olympic Association
PO Box 544
Kingston 10, Jamaica

JAPAN
**The Japanese Olympic
Committee**
1-1-1, Kinnan, Shibuya-ku
Tokyo 150
Japan

JORDAN
Jordan Olympic Committee
PO Box 5348
Amman, Jordan

KENYA
Kenya Olympic Association
PO Box 46888
Nairobi, Kenya

KOREA
Korean Olympic Committee
C.P.O. Box 1106
Seoul
Korea

KOREA, PEOPLE'S REPUBLIC OF
**Olympic Committee of the
Democratic People's Republic
of Korea**
PO Box 56
Pyong Yang, Korea

KUWAIT
Kuwait Olympic Committee
PO Box No. 795
Safat Postal Code 32042
Kuwait

LAOS
Comite Olympique Lao
B.P. 819
Vientiane, Laos

LEBANON
Comite Olympique Libanais
PO Box 4300
Hazmieh-Beyrouth, Liban

LESOTHO
Lesotho Olympic Committee
PO Box 138, Maseru
Lesotho

LIBERIA
Liberian National Olympic Committee
PO Box 481, Monrovia
Liberia

LIBYA
National Olympic Committee Socialist People's Libyan rab Jamahiriya
PO Box 879
Jamahiriya St., Tripoli
Libya

LIECHTENSTEIN
Comite Olympique du Liechtenstein
Essanestr, 423 Haus Mano
FL-9492 Eschen, Liechtenstein

LUXEMBOURG
Comite Olympique et Sportif Luxembourgeois
7 avenue Victor-Hugo
1750 Luxembourg

MADAGASCAR
Comite Olypique Malgache
B.P. 4188 Tananarive
Madagascar

MALAWI
Olympic and Commonwealth Games Association of Malawi
PO Box 867 Blantyre
Malawi

MALAYSIA
Olympic Council of Malaysia
Stadium Negara
Hang jebat Road, Kuala Lumpur
05-05
Malaysia

MALDIVES
Maldives Olympic Committee
Male, Republic of Maldives

MALI
Comite Olympique Malien
B.P. 88, Bamako
Mali

MALTA
Malta Olympic Committee
PO Box 39, Valletta
Malta

MAURITANIA
Comite Olympique Mauritanien
B.P. 1360
Nouakchott, Mauritania

MAURITIUS

Mauritius Olympic Committee
8 Felicien Mallefille Street
Port-Louis, Mauritius

MEXICO

Comite Olimpico Mexicano
Apartado postal 36-24
Ae. del conscripto y Anillo
Periferico
Mexico 10 DF

MONACO

Comite Olympiqe Monegasque
Nouveau Stade Louis 11
Av. Prince Hereditaire Albert
98000 Monaco

MONGOLIA

Comite National Olympique de la Republique Populaire de Mongolie
Baga Toirog 55, Oulan Bator
Mongolia

MOROCCO

Comite Olympique Morocain
Immeuble des Federations Royales
Sportives Marocaines
Centre de Belle-vue
Rabat–Aguedal
Morocco

MOZAMBIQUE

Comite Olimpico Nacional de Mocambique
Caixa postal 1404
19 r/c avenida Mao Tse Tung
Maputo, Mozambique

NEPAL

Nepal Olympic Committee
Dashrath Rangashala
Tripureswore, P.B. 2090
Katmandou, Nepal

NETHERLANDS, THE

Netherland Olympic Committee
Surinamestraat 33
2585 La Haye
The Netherlands

NEW GUINEA, PAPUA

Papua New Guinea Olympic Committee and Commonwealth Games Association
PO Box 467
Papua, New Guinea

NEW ZEALAND

New Zealand Olympic and Commonwealth Games Association
PO Box 643
Wellington, New Zealand

NICARAGUA

Comite Olimpico Nicaraguense
PO Box 4981
Civico Camilo Ortega Saavedra
modulo R
Managua, Nicaragua

NIGERIA

Comite Olypique Nigeria
B.P. 11975
Maimey, Nigeria

NORWAY

Norwegian Olympic Committee
Hauger Skolevei 1
1351 Rud
Norway

OMAN
National Olympic Committee of Oman
PO Box 5842 Ruwi
Muscat, Oman

PAKISTAN
Pakistan Olympic Association
Olympic House
Temple Road 2
Lahore, Pakistan

PANAMA
Comite Olimpico de Panama
apartado 2927
Panama 3

PARAGUAY
Comite Olimpico Paraguayo
Edificio Ministerio de Salud Publica
y Bienstar Social—Oficina 151
Avda. pettirossi y Brasl
Casilla postal 1420
Asuncion, Paraguay

PERU
Comite Olimpico Peruano
Estadio Nacional
Puerta 4
Lima, Peru

PHILIPPINES
Philippine Olympic Committee
Rizal Memorial Sports Complex
PO Box 2272
Adminstration Building
2800 Manila
Philippines

POLAND
Comite Olympique Polonais
rue Frascati, 4
00483 Varsovie
Poland

PORTUGAL
Comite Olimpico Portugues
Rue Braamcamp 12, R.C. esq.
1200 Lisbonne, Portugal

PUERTO RICO
Comite Olimpico de Puerto Rico
Apartado 8
San Juan, Puerto Rico 00902

QATAR
Qatar National Olympic Committee
PO Box 7494
Doha, Qatar

ROMANIA
Comite Olympique Roumain
Str. Vasile Conta nr. 16
Bucarest
section 1
Romania

RWANDA
Comite National Olympique du Rwand
B.P. 1044
Kigali, Rwanda

SAINT-MARTIN
Comitato Olimpico Nazionale Sammarinese
Via Del Bando
Borgo Maggiore
47031 Saint-Martin

SAMOA
Western Samoa Amateur Sports Federation
c/o Ministry of Youth, Sports and
Cultural Affairs
Private Bag, Apia
Samoa

SAUDIA ARABIA

Saudi Arabia Olympic Committee
PO Box 6040
Riyadh 11442
Saudi Arabia

SENEGAL

Comite National Olympique et Sportif Senegalais
B.P. 356
72 Boulevard de la Republique
Dakar, Sengal

SEYCHELLES

Seychelles Olympic Committee
PO Box 580
Victoria–Mahe
Seychelles

SIERRA LEONE

Sierra Leone Olympic and Overseas Games Committee
c/o National Sports Council
PO Box 1181
Siaka Stevens Stadium
Freetown, Sierra Leone

SINGAPORE

Singapore National Olympic Council
National Stadium
Singapore 1439

SOLOMON ISLANDS

Solomon Islands National Olympic Committee
c/o National Sports Council
PO Box 532
Honiara, Solomon Islands

SOMALI

Somali National Olympic Committee
PO Box 523
Mogadiscio, Somali

SPAIN

Comite Olimpico Espanol
Nunez de Balboa 120
28006 Madrid
Spain

SRI LANKA

National Olympic Committee of Sri Lanka
Rakshana Mandiraya
21, Vauxhall Street
Colombo 2, Sri Lanka

SUDAN

Sudanese Olympic Committee
PO Box 1938
Baladia Street
Khartoum, Sudan

SURINAME, REPUBLIC OF

Surinaams Olympisch Comite
PO Box 1171
Van Roosmalenstraat 30 - Sunecon
Paramaribo, Suriname

SWAZILAND

Swaziland Olympic and Commonwealth Games Association
3rd Floor
Mbabane House
Mbabane, Swaziland

SWEDEN
The Swedish Olympic Committee
Idrottens Hus
12387 Farsta
Sweden

SWITZERLAND
Comite Olympique Suisse
Case Postale
8907 Wettswill
Switzerland

SYRIA
Comite Olympique Syrien
PO Box 3375
Damas, Syria

TAIPEI
Chinese Taipei Olympic Committee
PO Box 34-20
Nr. 3, Lane 153
Chang An East Road
Section 2
Taipei

TANZANIA
Tanzanie Olympic Committee
PO Box 2182
Dar-es-Salaam, Tanzania

THAILAND
Olympic Committee of Thailand
226 Ban Ampawan
Sri Ayudhya Road
Bangkok 3, Thailand

TOGO
Comite National Olympique Togalais
B.P. 1320
Lome, Togo

TRINIDAD & TOBAGO
Trinidad and Tobago Olympic Association
PO Box 529
Port-of-Spain

TUNISIA
Comite Olympique Tunisien
2bis, rue Pierre-de-Coubertin
Tunis

TURKEY
Turkish Olympic Committee
Sisli, Buyukdee Cad No. 18
Tankaya
Apt. Daire 10
Istanbul, Turkey

UGANDA
Uganda Olympic Committee
PO Box 2610
Kampala, Uganda

UNITED ARAB EMIRATES
United Arab Emirates Olympic Committee
PO Box 4350
Dubai
United Arab Emirates

UNITED STATES
United States Olympic Committee
1750 East Boulder Street
Colorado Springs
Colorado 80909

URUGUAY
Comite Olimpico Uruguayo
PO Box 161
Canelones 1044
Montevideo, Uruguay

USSR
Comite Olympique d'U.R.S.S.
Luzhnetskaya Nab. 8
Moscow, U.S.S.R.

VENEZUELA
Comite Olimpico Vanezolano
Apartado postal 6370
Caracas 101, Venezuela

VIETNAM
Comite Olympique du Vietnam
36 Boulevard Tran Phu
Hanoi, Vietnam

VIRGIN ISLANDS
Virgin Islands Olympic Committee
PO Box 1576
Frederiksted, Sainte Croix
Virgin Islands 00840

WEST GERMANY
Nationales Olympisches Komitee fur Deutschland
Postfach 710130
Otto-Fleck-Schneise 12
600 Francfort-sur-le-Main 71
West Germany

YEMEN ARAB REPUBLIC
The Yemen Arab Republic Committee
PO Box 2701
Sanaa, Yemen

YEMEN, DEMOCRATIC REPUBLIC
Yemen Olympic Committee
PO Box 933
Crater - Aden

YUGOSLAVIA
Comite Olympique Yougoslave
Ada Ciganlija 10
11030 Belgrade
Yugoslavia

ZAIRE
Comite National Olympique et Sportif Zairois
B.P. 3626
Gombe
Kinshasa, Zaire

ZAMBIA
National Olympic Committee of Zambia
PO Box 20728
Kitwe, Zambia

ZIMBABWE
National Olympic Committee of Zimbabwe
PO Box 4718
Harare, Zimbabwe

MILITARY SPORTS

■ ORGANIZATIONS—U.S. & CANADA

Air Force Sports
AFMPC/MPCSOS
Randolph AFB, TX 78150
(512) 652-3471

Army Sports
HQDA, DAAG-MSP
2461 Eisenhower Avenue
Alexandria, VA 22331
(202) 325-9715

Marine Corps Sports Unite
Headquarters Marine Corps
(Code MSR)
Washington, DC 20380
(202) 694-2655/2450

Naval Military Personnel Command N111
Commonwealth Building
Room 932
1300 Wilson Boulevard
Arlington, VA 22209
(202) 694-0596/7

U.S. Armed Forces Sports Committee
HQDA (DACF-AFS) Alexandria, VA 22331-0522
(703) 325-8871

■ ORGANIZATIONS— INTERNATIONAL

International Du Conseil Military Sport
2 av. des Abeilles
B-1050 Bruxelles
Belgique

SPORTING GOODS MANUFACTURERS

Adidas U.S.A., Inc.
Sub. of: Adidas
200 Sheffield Street
Suite 300
Mountainside, NJ 07092
General equipment

Alamo Athletics, Inc.
Sub. of: Rust Enterprises
6846 Alamo Downs Parkway
San Antonio, TX 78238
Football equipment

All American Scoreboard Div.
Sub. of: General Indicator Corp.
2701 International Lane
Suite 200
Madison, WI 53704
Timing devices

All Lacrosse, Inc.
68 Forest Street
Montclair, NJ 07042
Lacrosse equipment

All Star Sporting Goods
Sub. of: George Frost Co.
Leominster Road
PO Box 428
Shirley, MA 01464
General equipment

American Fencers Supply
1180 Folsom Street
San Francisco, CA 94103
Fencing equipment

AMF American Athletic Equipment
Div. of: AMF, Inc.
200 American Avenue
Jefferson, IA 50129
General equipment

AMF Ben Hogan Company
Div. of Minstar, Inc.
2912 West Pafford Street
Fort Worth, TX 76110
Golf equipment

AMF Bowling Products Group
Sub. of: Minstar, Inc.
Jericho Turnpike
Westbury, NY 11590
Bowling equipment

AMF Head Racquet Sports Div.
Div. of: Minstar, Inc.
4801 North 63rd Street
Boulder, CO 80301
Racquet equipment

Bjorn Bengston
PO Box 71
S-124 21 Bandhagen
Stockholm, Sweden
Archery equipment

Bear Archery
4600 Southwest 41st Boulevard
Gainesville, FL 32601
Archery equipment

Canadian Hockey Industries (1975), Inc.
Sub. of: Amer Sport Int'l
2155 Canadian
Drummondville, Quebec
Canada S2B 6V2
Ice hockey equipment

Canterbury of New Zealand
Sub. of: Lane Walker Rudkin, Ltd.
600 Lincoln Centre Drive
Foster City, CA 94404
General sports equipment

Capital Industries, Inc.
PO Box 689
De Soto, TX 755115
Uniforms

Carron Net Co., Inc.
PO Box 177
Two Rivers, WI 54241
General equipment

Champion Products, Inc.
PO Box 850
3141 Monroe Avenue
Rochester, NY 14603
General apparel

Coat Marketing Group/SBC Sports
Sub. of: CMG Holding Corp.
2294 Quimby
PO Box 61022
San Jose, CA 95122
General equipment

Concept II, Inc.
RR No. 1, Box 1100
Morrisville, VT 05661
Rowing/crew equipment

Converse, Inc.
1 Fordham Road
North Reading, MA 01864
General apparel, shoes

Cosby, Gerry Co., Inc.
3 Pennsylvania Plaza
New York, NY 10001
General equipment

Court 1 Sports Products
Sub. of: Int'l Cordage Systems, Ltd.
6750 Cote De Liesse
St. Laurent, Quebec, Canada
General equipment

Croquet International Ltd.
100 Devonshire Way
Palm Beach Gardens, FL 33418
Accessories, sets

Cycles Peugeot, USA, Inc.
Sub. of: Cycles Peugeot
555 Gotham Parkway
Carlstadt, NJ 07072
General equipment

Danskin, Inc.
Sub. of: Playtex International
350 Fifth Avenue
Suite 5400
New York, NY 10118
General equipment, apparel

Debeer, J. & Son, Inc.
PO Box 11-570
Albany, NY 12211
Baseball, softball equipment

Dunlop Sports Corp.
Sub. of: Dunlop Slazenger Int'l, Ltd.
PO Box 3070
Greenville, SC 29602
Golf, racquet sports equipment

Durham Boat Company
RFD No. 2
Newmarket Road
Durham, NJ 03824
Rowing/crew equipment

Easton Aluminum
7800 Haskell Avenue
Van Nuys, CA 91406
Baseball/softball bats, field/ice hockey sticks, ski poles, archery equipment

Ebonite International, Inc.
PO Box 746
Highway 68 West
Hopkinsville, KY 42240
Bowling equipment

Elmer's Weights, Inc.
Sub. of: Bollinger Ind., Inc.
PO Box 16326
Lubbock, TX 79490
Training/conditioning weights

Etonic, Inc.
Sub. of: The Aritmos Group
147 Centre Street
Brockton, MA 02403
General equipment

Everlast Sporting Goods Manufacturing Company
750 East 132nd Street
Bronx, NY 10454
General equipment

Excel, The Exercise Co.
Sub. of: Rocket Ind., Inc.
9935 Beverly Boulevard
Pico Rivera, CA 90660
Training/conditioning weights

Exel, Inc.
Sub. of: Exel Oy-Finland
10-D Roessler Road
Woburn, MA 01801
Skiing-Nordic accessories, sailboard masts

Felco Athletic Wear Co., Inc.
Sub. of: Felco Sports Products, Inc.
900 Passaic Avenue
Harrison, NJ 07029
General uniforms

Fibersport, Inc.
6308 East 102 Terrace
Kansas City, MO 64134
Track & field/running equipment

Fila Sports, Inc.
Sub. of: Fila Sport SPA
821 Industrial Road
San Carlos, CA 94070
General apparel

Flags International
10845 U.S. Highway 20-SG
Osceola, IN 46561
General equipment

Fleming Gray Limited
690 Bishop Street
Cambridge, Ontario
Canada H3H 4S6
Ice hockey/ice skating equipment

Franklin Sports Industries, Inc.
PO Box 508
17 Campanelli Parkway
Stoughton, MA 02072
General equipment

Gold Medal Recreational Products
Sub. of: Hanson Trust
Blue Mountain Industries
Blue Mountain, AL 36201
General equipment

Granada Pitching Machines
PO Box
5055 Dobrot Way
Central Point, OR 97502
Baseball/softball pitching machines

Gravity Guidance, Inc.
1540 Flower Avenue
Duarte, CA 91010
Training/conditioning - ankle holders, doorway support rods, exercisers, etc.

GSC Athletic Equipment, Inc.
PO Box 1710
600 North Pacific Avenue
San Pedro, CA 90733
General equipment

Haden Industries, Inc.
2707 Satsuma
Dallas, TX 75229
Training/conditioning equipment

Haggar Co.
6113 Lemmon Avenue
Dallas, TX 75209
Golf apparel

Hang Ten Int'l
Sub. of: Ratner Clothes
705 12th Avenue
San Diego, CA 92101
General apparel

Harley-Davidson Golf Car Division
PO Box 653
3700 West Juneau Avenue
Milwaukee, WI 53201
Golf cars-electric cars-gasoline

Har-Tru Corp.
PO Box 569
Hagerstown, MD 21741
Racquet/tennis equipment

Harv-Al Athletic Mft., Inc.
PO Box 91
409 West Main Street
Ranger, TX 76470
General apparel

Heierling of Switzerland, Ltd.
59 Maple Street
Warwick, RI 02888
Skiing-Alpine boots-after ski; skiing-Nordic boots

Hillerich & Bradsby Co., Inc.
PO Box 35700
Louisville, KY 40232
General equipment

Hudson Racing Shells Ltd.
R.R. 3
Komaka, Ontario
Canada N0L 1R0
Rowing/crew racing shells

Hyde Athletic Ind., Inc.
Centennial Drive
Peabody, MA 01960
Shoes, apparel

Ibsen Water Ski Company
3224 78th Place Northeast
Bellevue, WA 98004
Water ski plags, water ski fins

Izod/Lacoste Golf & Tennis
Airport Industrial Park West
Route 183
Reading, PA 19605
Golf, racquet sports, track/field apparel

Jantzen, Inc.
Sub. of: Bluebell, Inc.
PO Box 3001
Portland, OR 97208
General apparel

Jayfro Corporation
Sub. of: Unified Sports
976 Hartford Turnpike
PO Box 400
Waterford, CT 06385
General equipment

Jesco Athletic Co.
Sub. of: James E. Short Co.
PO Box 1716
316 Rose Street
Williamsport, PA 17701
General apparel

Johar of California
15934 South Figueroa
Gardena, CA 90248
Baseball/racquet grips, tapes, bicycle saddles/seats, etc.

John Jaques and Sons Ltd.
361 White Horse Road
Thornton Heath, Surrey
England
Cricket/croquet equipment

Jugs Pitching Machines
PO Drawer 365
Tualatin, OR 97062
Baseball/softball nets, pitching
machines

Kangaroo Products Co.
Highway 108
Columbus, NC 28722
Golf carts-electric, motorized golf
bag carriers

Karhu-Titan USA
55 Green Mountain Drive
South Burlington, VT 05401
Ice hockey sticks, skiing-Nordic
accessories, bindings, boots, etc.

Kayak Specialties, Inc.
PO Box 152
Buchanon, MI 49107
Rowing/crew cartop shell carriers,
elec. speedometers

Keds Corp. (Pro-Keds)
Sub. of: Stride Rite, Inc.
5 Cambridge Center
Cambridge, MA 02142
General shoes

Kenneth Smith Golf Club
Company
PO Box 41
Kansas City, MO 64141
Golf clubs

Kitchener Hockey Sticks Ltd.
176 Forfar Avenue
Kitchener, Ontario
Canada N2B 3A1
Ice hockey sticks

Life Sports, Ltd.
3829 Plyers Mill Road
Kensington, MD 20895
Rugby/soccer balls, shoes, goal-
posts, etc.

Little River Marine Co.
PO Box 12722
Gainesville, FL 32604
Rowing/crew cartop shell carriers,
oarlocks, oar carriers, oars, etc.

MacGregor Sporting Goods
25 East Union Avenue
East Rutherford, NJ 07073
General equipment

Master Industries, Inc.
17222 VonKarman Avenue
Irvine, CA 92713
Bowling accessories

Master Pitching Machine, Inc.
4200 Birmingham Road
Kansas City, MO 64117
Baseball/softball pitching machines,
balls, etc.

Match Mate
Sub. of: Crown Manufacturing
8600 Darby Avenue
Northridge, CA 91325
Racquet sports equipment

Matman Wrestling Company
12724 Pacific Highway S.W.
Tacoma, WA 98499
Wrestling head guards, knee/elbow
pads, shoes, trunks, warm-up suits

Muehleisen Mfg. Co.
Sub. of: Baldwin/Green, Inc.
PO Box 1326
1100 North Johnson Avenue
El Cajon, CA 92022
General equipment

National Fabricators
937 Saw Mill River Road
Yonkers, NY 10710
Exercise bikes, machines, etc.

Nautilus Sports/Medical Ind.
Sub. of: Ward Int'l Corp.
PO Box 1783
Deland, FL 32720
Exercisers/exercise machines

Nielsen-Kellerman Co.
201 East Tenth Street
Marcus Hook, PA 19061
Rowing/crew digital strokewatch 8-lap/place timer, etc.

Nike
3900 Southwest Murray Boulevard
Beaverton, OR 97005
General equipment

Nissen Corporation
Sub. of: Kidde, Inc.
930 27th Avenue South West
Cedar Rapids, IA 52406
Gymnastics/volleyball/wrestling equipment

North American Recreation
Sub. of: BSN Corporation
PO Box 430
FH Station
New Haven, CT 06513
General equipment

Northland Products, Inc.
117 Troy Street
Richford, VT 05476
General equipment

Olympia Sports
745 State Circle
PO Box 1941
Ann Arbor, MI 48106
General equipment

Orbit Skates of Canada
Div. of: Sport Maska, Inc.
6500 Trans-Canada Highway
Suite 208
St. Laurent, Quebec
Canada H4T 1X4
Ice hockey/ice skating skates

Owens, R.S. Trophy Co., Inc.
5535 North Lynch Avenue
Chicago, IL 60630
Trophies/awards components, medals, plaques, ribbons, trophies

Pacer Track & Field
Sub. of: Harry Gill Co.
715 Industrial Parkway Drive
Carson City, NV 89701-5499
Track & field/running equipment

Paramount Fitness Equipment Corp.
6450 East Bandini Boulevard
City of Commerce, CA 90040
Training/conditioning equipment

Parker Sweeper Company
PO Box 1728
Springfield, OH 45501
Tennis court equipment

Pins & Patches, Ltd.
PO Box 897
Dillon, CO 80435
Golf/skiing-Nordic/Alpine accessories

Plough, Inc.
Sub. of: Schering/Plough Corp.
3030 Jackson Avenue
Memphis, TN 38151
Skiing-Nordic/Alpine accessories

Polaris by Iron Company
PO Box 1458
Spring Valley, CA 92077
Training/conditioning equipment

Pony Sports & Leisure, Inc.
201 Route 17 North
Rutherford, NJ 07070
General equipment

Powderhorn Mountainering, Inc.
Sub. of: B.W. Harris Co.
1777 Oakdale Avenue
PO Box 64946
West St. Paul, MN 55164
Skiing-Alpine/Nordic accessories

Precise International
3 Chestnut Street
Suffern, NY 10901
Timing devices

Prince Manufacturing, Inc.
Sub. of: Chesebrough-Pond's Inc.
PO Box 2031
Princeton, NJ 08540
Racquet sports - apparel, bags, etc.

Puma USA, Inc.
Sub. of: Puma Sportschuhfabriken KG
429 Old Connecticut Path
PO Box 1369
Framingham, MA 01701
General sports shoes

Rawlings Sporting Goods Co.
Div. of: Figgie International
1859 Intertech
Fenton, MO 63026
Mailing Address:
PO Box 22000
St. Louis, MO 63126
General equipment

Recreation Equipment Corp.
PO Box 2188
Anderson, IN 46018
Baseball-cages/backstops; basketball-backstops; football-goalposts

Reebok International Ltd.
150 Royall Street
Canton, MA 02021
General shoes, apparel

Regent Sports Corp.
45 Ranick Road
Hauppauge, NY 11787
General equipment

Rol-Sweep
33 Greenwood Avenue
Midland Park, NJ 07432
Racquet sports - sponge water removers, tennis court equipment

Rossignol Ski Company
Sub. of: Skis Rossignol S.A.
Industrial Avenue
PO Box 298
Williston, VT 05495
Skiing/Alpine-Nordic - gloves, poles, apparel

Round Trampoline USA
Highway 90E
PO Drawer 505
Quincy, FL 32351
Gymnastics - trampolines

Rugby Imports, Ltd.
885 Warren Avenue
East Providence, RI 02914
Rugby - balls, jerseys, shoes/boots, shorts, socks, uniforms

Russell Athletic
Div. of: Russell Corp.
Alexander City, AL 35010
General uniforms

Salomon/North America, Inc.
Sub. of: Salomon S.A. (France)
444 Salomon Circle
Sarks, NV 89431
Skiing accessories

Schwinn Bicycle Company
217 North Jefferson Street
Chicago, IL 60601
*Bicycling equipment, training/
conditioning equipment*

Seaway Mats, Inc.
Sub. of: Seaway Plastic-Quebec
PO Box 407
Lower Park Street
Malone, NY 12953
Mats

Shorter, Frank Sports Wear
Sub. of: Levi Strauss & Co.
2400 Central Avenue
Suite L
Boulder, CO 80301
General equipment

Skis Dynastar
PO Box 25
Hercules Drive
Colchester, VT 05446
Skis & accessories

Soccer Sport Supply Co., Inc.
1745 First Avenue
New York, NY 10028
General equipment

Spalding Sports Worldwide
Sub. of: Questor Corp.
425 Meadow Street
Chicopee, MA 01013
General equipment

St. Lawrence Manufacturing Co., Inc.
3030 Boulevard St. Anne
Beauort, Quebec
Canada G1E 6N1
Ice hockey/skating - blades

Stadiums Unlimited, Inc.
PO Box 627
Grinnell, IA 50112
*Benches, bleachers, seating-
permanent/portable*

Stebco Industries, Inc.
Sub. of: Stebco Products Corp.
1020 West 40th Street
Chicago, IL 60609
Bowling/ice hockey/skating bags

Table Tennis America
PO Box 32111
Oklahoma City, OK 73123
Table tennis equipment

Titan Bodybuilding, Inc.
6254 Powers Avenue
Suite 39
Jacksonville, FL 32217
*Exercisers/exercise machines,
weights, weight stacking machines*

Titleist Golf
Div. Acushnet
Sub. of: American Brands, Inc.
PO Box B965
New Bedford, MA 02741
Golf equipment

Trampolking Trampolines
Sub. of: Rich Enterprises
PO Box 3828
Albany, GA 31706
*Rebounders, wall mats, spring-
boards, trampolines, benches, etc.*

True Temper Sports, Inc.
Div. of: Emhart Corp.
871 Ridgeway Loop Road
Suite 201
Memphis, TN 38119
Bicycling - components, golf - components

U.S. Net Batting Cage Co.
819 Miraflores Avenue
San Pedro, CA 90731
Batting cages/backstops, nets

Victoriaville Hockey Sticks
35 Campagna
Victoriaville,Quebec
Canada G6P 5H9
Hockey sticks

Victory Sports Nets
Sub. of: FNT Industries
927 First Street
Menominee, MI 49858
Nets, badminton equipment

Voit Sports, Inc.
45 Gould Street
Rochester, NY 14610
General equipment

Wilson Sporting Goods Co.
Sub. of: Wesray Capital Corp.
2233 West Street
River Grove, IL 60171
General equipment

Windsurfing International
2006 Gladwick Street
Compton, CA 90220
Sailboards

Wolverine World Wide
9341 Coutland Drive
Rockford, MI 49351
Bowling, golf, track & field running shoes

Worcester Oar 7 Paddle Co.
660 Franklin Street
Worcester, MA 01604
Oarlocks, oars, outriggers, shells/ sculls

Yamaha International Corp.
Sporting Goods Division
Sub. of: Yamaha Int'l Corp.
6600 Orangethorpe Avenue
PO Box 6600
Buena Park, CA 90622
General equipment

York Barbell Co.
Box 1707
York, PA 17405
General equipment

Zamboni, Frank J. & Co., Inc.
15714 Colorado Avenue
Paramount, CA 90723
Ice rinks, resurfacing

SPORTS AGENTS AND ATTORNEYS

■ ASSOCIATIONS

Associations of Representatives of Professional Athletes
9111 South LaCienega Boulevard
Suite 205
Los Angeles, CA 90301
(213) 670-8448

New England Sports Agents Association
PO Box 196
Needham, MA 02192
(617) 444-3373

Sports Lawyers Association
5300 South Florida Avenue
PO Box 5684
Lakeland, FL 33807
(813) 646-5091

■ SPORTS AGENTS & ATTORNEYS

ALABAMA

Kickliter, George D. P.A.
166 North Gay Street
Auburn, AL 36830
(205) 821-4250

M.V.P. Management Services, Inc.
PO Box 5753
Tuscaloosa, AL 35405
(205) 556-1204

*PASS
203 East Side Square #23
Huntsville, AL 35801
(205) 556-1204

CALIFORNIA

A I M S
PO Box 422
Montrose, CA 91020

American Sports Network, Inc.
8926 Valley Boulevard
PO Box 6100
Rosemead, CA 91770
(818) 572-4727

Auchincloss & Turner, Inc.
195 Moulton Street
San Francisco, CA 94123
(415) 563-7549

DK Sports
284 Greenwood Place
Bonita, CA 92002
(619) 470-3269

First Team Marketing
2049 Century Park East, Suite 3050
Los Angeles, CA 90067

Landaal & Baer
Attorneys at Law
2029 Century Park East
Suite 3250
Los Angeles, CA 90067
(213) 553-6900

Moriarty Pro Management
5796 Encina Road, #6
Goleta, CA 93117
(805) 683-1815

Muller Enterprises
10504 Fuerte Drive
La Mesa, CA 92041
(619) 440-3000

Nationwide Professional Football Search
24252 Bellerine Circle
Laguna Niguel, CA 92677
(714) 495-4336

Phillips Organization, The, Ltd.
5030 Camino De La Siesta
San Diego, CA 92108
(619) 692-9900

Pro Sports, Inc.
4386 Paradise Drive
Tiburon, CA 94920
(415) 435-1211

Professional Sports Planner
1101 Quail Street, Suite C-2
Newport Beach, CA 92660
(714) 752-1035

Professional Stars, Inc.
9807 Haas Avenue
Los Angeles, CA 90047
(213) 777-5046

Schot, Tom, Sports
PO Box 73
Capitola, CA 95010
(408) 462-5293

Shapiro Management
2147 North Beachwood Drive
Los Angeles, CA 90068
(213) 469-9452
Mailing Address:
PO Box 69813
Los Angeles, CA 90069

Siegal, Joel H., Attorney
1285 8th Avenue, No. 2
San Francisco, CA 94122
(415) 986-6489; 661-4626

Simpson Management Co.
1519 Valleda Lane
Encinitas, CA 92024
(619) 436-3914

Sports & Media Services
PO Box 495
Huntington Beach, CA 92648
(714) 841-3253

Sports Communications, Inc.
8610 Sunset Boulevard
Hollywood, CA 90069
(213) 544-1988

Sports Depot
2950 Airway Avenue, Unit D3
Costa Mesa, CA 92626
(714) 641-0610

Sports Plus, Inc.
1330 Broadway, Suite 1428
Oakland, CA 94612
(415) 839-2793

Stanley, James K., Attorney
1516 West Redwood Street,
Suite 110
San Diego, CA 92101
(619) 295-2135

Sunwest Sports & Associates
7883 North Pershing Avenue
Stockton, CA 95207
(209) 952-9922

Technical Athletic Programs
1922 The Alameda
San Jose, CA 95126
(408) 246-7502

Technical Equities Corp.
1922 The Alameda #400
San Jose, CA 95126
(408) 246-7502

Wallach Enterprises, Inc.
8821 Beverly Boulevard
Los Angeles, CA 90048
(213) 278-4574

World Class Sports
9171 Wilshire Boulevard
Suite 404
Beverly Hills, CA 90212
(213) 278-2010
New York Address:
110 East 59th Street, 11th Floor
New York, NY 10022
(212) 593-6340

Zlaket Sports Enterprises, Inc.
2518 North Santiago Boulevard
Orange, CA 92667
(714) 921-0370

CANADA
J. W. & Associates
1400 Ghent Avenue
Burlington, Ontario, Canada
(416) 637-5198

Rae-Con
65 Queen Street West, Suite 1000
Toronto, Ontario, Canada
M5H 2M5
(416) 863-6000

Sierra Sports Group
288 Lawrence Avenue West
Toronto, Ontario, Canada
M5M 1B3
(416) 789-7624

Sports Management Ltd.
65 Queen Street West
Suite 1000
Toronto, Ontario, Canada
M5H 2M5

DISTRICT OF COLUMBIA
Advantage International
1025 Thomas Jefferson Street N.W.
Washington, DC 20007
(202) 333-3838
Los Angeles:
Marvin Demoff (Mng. Dir.)
11377 West Olympic Boulevard
Los Angeles, CA 90064
(213) 312-3290

ProServ. Inc.
888 Seventeenth Street NW
Suite 1200
Washington, DC 20006
(202) 457-8800
New York Office:
369 Lexington Avenue
New York, NY 10017
(212) 370-0350

COLORADO
Michaels, Bill, and Company, Inc.
1666 Race Street
Denver, CO 80206
(303) 399-9005

Western Pro Sports, Inc.
PO Box 12354
Aspen, CO 81612-9237
(303) 292-0153

CONNECTICUT
International Sports & Entertainment, Inc.
One State Street, Suite 2310
Hartford, CT 06103
(203) 548-2666

Sports Marketing
Sub of: Robustelli Corporate Services Ltd.
30 Spring Street
Stamford, CT 06901
(203) 965-0275
(212) 792-9252

Sports Support Services
201 Hazel Street
New Haven, CT 06511
(203) 624-0179

FLORIDA
Career Sports Management, Inc.
6601 Southwest 116th Court
No. 401
Miami, FL 33173
(305) 279-5502

Hafner, Doug, Asssociates, Inc.
1421 Sopera Avenue
Coral Gables, FL 33134
(305) 667-2692

Holthus Sports Management
8701 Southwest 137th Avenue
One Tower Suite
Miami, FL 33183
(305) 387-1937

Neader Sports Management, Inc.
1200 Eden Isle Drive NE
St. Petersburg, FL 33704
(813) 823-4412

Pro Athletes Management
357 South Atlantic Avenue
Daytona Beach, FL 32018
(904) 252-1177

Sports Management Associates, Inc.
Sub of: Zimbler & Cutler
300 Sevilla Avenue, Suite 313
Coral Gables, FL 33134
(305) 446-0100

Stauder, Michael H. Attorney
1201 U.S. Highway 1, Suite 310
North Palm Beach, FL 33408
(305) 627-8899

Witlin Professional Management
1100 Northeast 125th Street, Suite 109
North Miami, FL 33161
(305) 891-0941

ILLINOIS
Flair Communications Agency
214 West Erie Street
Chicago, IL 60610
(312) 943-5959

Pro Football Associates
5041 West 95th Street
Oak Lawn, IL 60453
(312) 636-9700

Sports Group, The, Inc.
PO Box 7009
Evanston, IL 60204
(312) 869-6860

Talent Network, Inc.
5200 Main Street
Suite 210
Skokie, IL 60077
(312) 679-2700

Talent Services, Inc.
5200 West Main Street
Skokie, IL 60077
(312) 679-2700

Universal Sports Associates, Inc.
12 South First Avenue
St. Charles, IL 60174
(312) 377-7430

LOUISIANA
Action Ink, Inc.
c/o Michael L. Eckstein
430 Notre Dame Street
New Orleans, LA 70130
(504) 524-9714

Tanana, Kenneth W.
Attorney at Law
1214 Saint Mary Street
New Orleans, LA 70130
(504) 523-2584

MARYLAND
Athletes Management Co-operative
2202 Chantilla Road
Baltimore, MD **21228**
(301) 747-1239

PM Associates
711 West 40th Street #450
Baltimore, MD 21211
(301) 467-6300

Sportsworld Consultants
14 Supreme Court
Gaithersburg, MD 20878
(301) 258-9689

MASSACHUSETTS
First Council of Boston, The, Inc.
120 Tremont Street, 5th Floor
Boston, MA 02108
(617) 542-4141

Grabill & Ley, P.C.
155 Federal Street
Boston, MA 02110
(617) 292-9500

Mula, Jack & Associates
6 New England Executive Park, Suite 400
Burlington, MA 01803
(617) 273-1605

Pender Sports Corporation
560 Turnpike Street
PO Box 527
Canton, MA 02021
(617) 821-1310

Sports Advisors Group
One Union Street
Boston, MA 02108
(617) 227-5535

Woolf, Bob Associates, Inc.
4575 Prudential Tower
Boston, MA 02199
(617) 437-1212

MICHIGAN
Contract Management Group
19640 Harper
Grosse Point, MI 48236
(313) 883-6260

Ping's Professional Sports Agency
PO Box 343
Saline, MI 48176
(213) 429-1266

Sports Stars International Inc.
18485 Mack Avenue
Detroit, MI 48236
(313) 886-9140

Universal Management Co.
1000 West University Drive #105
Rochester, MI 48063
(313) 656-1006

MINNESOTA
Henline, Roy B.
3434 Lexington Avenue North
Shoreview, MN 55126
(612) 482-7900

Northstar Consultants, Inc.
2222 Park Avenue
Minneapolis, MN 55404
(612) 872-1300

Sports Films and Talents, Inc.
Div of: Carlson Co. Marketing
Group
12755 Highway 55
Minneapolis, MN 55441
(612) 540-5972

MISSOURI
Photo Promotion Associates
229 Route 59
St. Louis, MO 63146
(800) 325-4876

Proworld Sports Management, Inc.
393 North Euclid, No. 301
St. Louis, MO 63108
(314) 361-2986

Vision Consultants, Inc.
8631 Delmar Boulevard
St. Louis, MO 63124
(314) 993-1400

MONTANA
Staninger Sports Agency
PO Box 4865
Missoula, MT 59806
(406) 728-8850

NEBRASKA
New Dawn Marketing and Financial Services
3522 Allendale Drive
Lincoln, NE 68516-9801
(402) 643-4690

Rembolt, Ludtke, Parker, Milligan & Berger
1201 Lincoln Mall, Suite 102
Lincoln, NE 68508
(402) 475-5100

Vacanti, Alfred C.
11414 West Center Road
Omaha, NE 68144
(402) 333-4774

Watson, Tom, Enterprises
1313 Commerce Tower
Kansas City, MO 64105
(816) 421-4770

NEVADA
Professional Kicking Services, Inc.
PO Box 2747
Sparks, NV 89431
(702) 359-5973

NEW JERSEY
Ard & Schumacher Associates
90 Hughes Lane
Watchung, NJ 07060
(201) 756-6172
Mailing Address:
PO Box 7064
Watchung, NJ 07060

Athletic Enterprises, Inc.
15 Wendover Drive
Mt. Laurel, NJ 08050
(201) 874-8497

Madigan, Richard E. and Associates, Inc.
311 Claremont Avenue
Montclair, NJ 07042
(201) 746-8381

Select Sports Inc.
17 Ridge Road
Hawthorne, NJ 07506
(201) 423-2468

Spotlight on Sports
PO Box 1851
Guarantee Trust Building
Atlantic City, NJ 08404
(609) 347-1128

NEW YORK
Ack Sports, Inc.
521 Madison Avenue
New York, NY 10022
(212) 688-2130

Action Sports Marketing
100 North Village Avenue
Rockville Centre, NY 11570
(516) 536-2130

Arnold, Steve, Enterprises
300 East 40th Street, Suite 9-S
New York, NY 10016
(212) 986-3188

BBDO Promotion-Sports Marketing
Sub of: BBDO Inc.
383 Madison Avenue
New York, NY 10017
(212) 415-5000

Blackman & Raber
545 Fifth Avenue
New York, NY 10017
(212) 986-1420

Capital Sports, Inc.
805 Third Avenue, 8th Floor
New York, NY 10022
(212) 319-7770

Davis, Steve Public Relations
380 Lexington Avenue
New York, NY 10017
(212) 697-3521

Equisport Marketing, Inc.
174 Hegemans Lane
PO Box 231
Old Brookville, NY 11545
(516) 626-9249/626-1539

First Investor Corporation
Two Penn Plaza, Suite 1050
New York, NY 10121
(212) 563-2600

Fishof, David Productions, Inc.
1775 Broadway, 7th Floor
New York, NY 10019
(212) 757-1605

GVD Professional Management, Inc.
1 Pennsylvania Plaza, Suite 100
New York, NY 10199
(212) 621-9786

Henry, Rene A., Jr.
220 East 6th Street No. 3-G
New York, NY 10021
(212) 832-1597

International Management Group
22 East 71st Street
New York, NY 10021
(212) 772-8900

International Talent Services, Ltd.
15 Columbus Circle, 6th Floor
New York, NY 10023
(212) 586-1117

Island Professional Sports Services
133 Main Street
Port Washington, NY 11050
(516) 944-9281

JB Sports Enterprises, Ltd.
185 Kneeland Avenue
Yonkers, NY 10705
(914) 476-2692

King, Don Productions, Inc.
32 East 69th Street
New York, NY 10021
(212) 794-2900

Machol Media Services
21 West Main Street, Suite 300
Oyster Bay, NY 11771
(516) 922-2100

Mattgo Enterprises, Inc.
185 East 85th Street
New York, NY 10028
(212) 427-4444

Mega Sports, Inc.
287 Northern Boulevard
Great Neck, NY 11021
(516) 466-5400

Momentum Enterprises, Inc.
250 West 57th Street, No. 603
New York, NY 10019
(212) 265-4621

Morris, William, Agency
1350 Avenue of the Americas
New York, NY 10019
(212) 586-5100

Pro-Mark Services, Inc.
2464 Elmwood Avenue
Kenmore, NY 14217
(716) 873-6765

Pro Players Enterprises, Inc.
575 Madison Avenue
New York, NY 10022
(212) 751-4300

Pro Tect Management Corp.
80 Wall Street
New York, NY 10005
(212) 809-3232

Rome, Thomas & Company
574 Fifth Avenue
New York, NY 10036

Roundball Enterprise
336 West End Avenue #15- A
New York, NY 10023
(212) 362-3322

Ruder Finn & Rotman Sports Marketing
Sub of: Ruder Finn & Rotman, Inc.
110 East 59th Street
New York, NY 10022
(212) 593-6352

Silverman, Warren/Kremer Inc.
2 Park Avenue
New York, NY 10016
(212) 686-5983

Target Market Sports

Affil. of: Ann Wright Representatives, Inc.
136 East 57th Street, Penthouse
New York, NY 10022
(212) 832-0157

Taylor, John A. Associates

2600 Netherland Avenue,
Suite 30001
Riverdale, NY 10463
(212) 704-3434

Tri-Star Enterprises

2 Penn Plaza, Suite 100
New York, NY 10121
(212) 244-3100

Walsh, James C.

300 East 51st Street
New York, NY 10022
(212) 688-6310

W.F. Sports Enterprises, Inc.

9 South 1st Avenue
Mount Vernon, NY 10550-3409

World Sports & Entertainment

Sub of: Norby Walters Associates
200 West 51st Street
New York, NY 10019
(212) 245-3939

World Sports Group

133 East 58th Street, Suite 100
New York, NY 10022
(212) 308-5001
Office in Holland:
Hofstede Oud Bussem
Flevolaan 41
1411 KC Naarden
Holland

NORTH CAROLINA

Carolina Sports Consultants

2427 Rosewood Court
Chapel Hill, NC 27514
(919) 942-0895

OHIO

Brooks, Jeffrey M. & Co., Inc.

21625 Chagrin Boulevard, No. 120
Beachwood, OH 44122
(216) 752-4600

Elias, Eddie Enterprises

1720 Merriman Road
Akron, OH 44313
(216) 867-4388

International Management Group

One Erieview Plaza
Cleveland, OH

International Sports Group

Sub of: ISG Inc.
78 East Chestnut Street, Suite 303
Columbus, OH 43215
(614) 228-0777
(800) 527-6446 (OH only)

Keating, Edward J. Management Agency

747 Statler Office Tower
Cleveland, OH 44114
(216) 621-2021

Lustig Pro Sports Enterprises, Inc.

2620 Ridgewood, Suite 300
Akron, OH 44313
(216) 867-0231

McDonald ProSports, Inc.

2100 Society Building
Cleveland, OH 44114
(216) 443-2300

Pro Sports Management, Inc.
11260 Chester Road, Suite 650
Cincinnati, OH 45246
(513) 771-4499

**Worldwide Management
Group, Inc.**
23200 Chagrin Boulevard,
Suite 600
Cleveland, OH 44122
(216) 292-8282

OKLAHOMA

AllPro Enterprises, Ltd.
4201 North Classen Blvd.
Oklahoma City, OK 73118
(405) 524-3215

**Intersouth Sports Management
Corp.**
6124 South Memorial
Tulsa, OK 74133
(918) 250-2681

OREGON

**International Basketball
Services**
2905 Broadway
Portland, OR 97232
(503) 281-0375

PENNSYLVANIA

PDS, Inc.
430 Hochberg Road
Monroeville, PA 15146
(412) 325-1642

SOUTH CAROLINA

SE Sports Consultants, Inc.
Box 21232
Columbia, SC 29221
(803) 772-8100

**Smelkinson, Cerrati &
Company, Inc.**
PO Box 6069
Hilton Head Island, SC 29938
(803) 785-5038

TENNESSEE

**Mid-America Professional
Sports Company**
100 North Main Building,
Suite 3204
Memphis, TN 38103
(901) 523-7788

Sports Management Group
303 Church Street, Suite 201
Nashville, TN 37201
(615) 255-5374

TEXAS

**All Pro Sports Management,
Inc.**
13355 Noel Road, Suite 1710
Dallas, TX 75240
(214) 738-6464

American Sports
1600 East Lamar Boulevard
Arlington, TX 76011
(817) 461-3355

Athletic Associates, Inc.
Sub of: Sherwood Blount
Companies
15303 Dallas Parkway
Suite 800, LB 18
Dallas, TX 75248
(214) 960-1616

Boyd, Veigel & Hance P.C.
218 East Louisiana
McKinney, TX 75069
(214) 542-0191
Mailing Address:
PO Drawer B
McKinney, TX 75069

Burwash, Peter International
2203 Timberloch Place
Suite 126
The Woodland, TX 77380
(713) 363-4707

Champion Players, Inc.
PO Box 3375
Fort Worth, TX 76113
(817) 246-0511

Coaches Sports Techniplex, Inc.
9931 Harwin Drive
Houston, TX 77036
(713) 772-9314

Cornerstone Sports
Glen Lakes Tower, Suite 510
Lock Box 154
9400 North Central Expressway
Dallas, TX 75231
(214) 369-3876

Hendricks Sports Management
Div of: Hendricks Management
Company, Inc.
400 Randal Way, Suite 106
Spring, TX 77388
(713) 440-3000

PRO
PO Box 470031
Fort Worth, TX 76147
(817) 334-0184

ProFile, Inc.
Sub of: True Distance
5818 Beverly Hill Lane
Houston, TX 77057
(713) 784-1280

Star's Choice, Inc.
516 South Post Oak Lane, Suite 17
Houston, TX 77056
(713) 266-6986

Witt Stewart Sports
815 Brazos Suite 703
Austin, TX 78701-2514
(512) 474-5136

UTAH

Pro Search
311 South State Street #280
Salt Lake City, UT 84111
(801) 531-1300

VIRGINIA

The Austin Group, Inc.
105 North Washington Street
Suite 300
Alexandria, VA 22314
(703) 684-1380

**Professional Management
Group, Ltd.**
PO Box 2549
Fairfax, VA 22031
(703) 278-9174

Pros, Incorporated
100 Shockoe Slip
PO Box 673
Richmond, VA 23206
(804) 643-7600

Sports Development Ltd.
2000 West Club Lane, Suite C
Richmond, VA 23226
(804) 288-2258

Trigon Sports International, Inc.
3819 Plaza Drive
Fairfax, VA 22030
(703) 273-9332

WASHINGTON
Bonneville, Viert, Morton & McGoldrick
820 "A" Street, Suite 600
Tacoma, WA 98402
(206) 627-8131
Mailing Address:
PO Box 1533
Tacoma WA 98401

Rozzini & Associates
PO Box 6998
Bellevue, WA 98008
(206) 641-5202

SPORTS MEDIA ━━━━━━━━

■ ORGANIZATIONS

ABC Radio Network Sports
Sub of: Capital Cities/ABC, Inc.
125 West End Avenue, 6th Floor
New York, NY 10023
(212) 887-4333

ABC Sport, Inc.
Sub of: Capital Cities/ABC Inc.
1330 Avenue of the Americas
New York, NY 10019
(212) 887-7777

Black Entertainment Television
1232 31st Street N.W.
Washington, DC 20007
(202) 337-5260
Production Address:
4217 Wheeler Avenue
Alexandria, VA 22304
(703) 461-0344

Cable News Network
Div of: Turner Broadcasting
Systems, Inc.
1050 Techwood Drive N.W.
PO Box 105264
Atlanta, GA 30348-5264
(404) 827-1500

Cablevision Sports
One Media Crossways
Woodbury, NY 11797
(516) 496-1376

Canadian Broadcasting Company
Box 500
Station A
Toronto, Ontario
Canada M5W 1E6
(416) 975-3311

CBS Radio Network
51 West 52nd Street
New York, NY 10019
(212) 975-4321

CBS Sports
Sub of: CBS, Inc.
51 West 52nd Street, 30th Floor
New York, NY 10019
(212) 975-5230

Cox Cable
1400 Lake Hehran Drive
Atlanta, GA 30319

Dodgervision/Angelvision
5746 Sunset Boulevard
Los Angeles, CA 90028
(213) 856-1305

Dynocomm Sports
Sub of: Dynocomm Productions
27285 Las Ramblas, No. 130
Mission Viejo, CA 92691
(714) 582-1834
Mailing Address:
PO Box 6331
Laguna Niguel, CA 92677

Eastman Radio, Inc.
One Rockefeller Plaza
New York, NY 10020
(212) 581-0800, Ext. 208

ESPN-Entertainment & Sports Programming Network
Sub of: ABC Inc.
ESPN Plaza
Bristol, CT 06010
(203) 584-8477
New York Office:
355 Lexington Ave.
New York, NY 10017
(212) 661-6040

Gould Entertainment Corporation
101 West 57th Street
New York, NY 10019
(212) 586-5760

Group W Satellite Communications
Sub of: Westinghouse Broadcasting
and Cable, Inc.
41 Harbor Plaza Drive
Stamford, CT 06904
(203) 965-6000
New York Address:
90 Park Avenue
New York: NY 10016
(212) 557-6550

Home Box Office
Sub of: Time Inc.
1271 Avenue of the Americas
New York, NY 10020
(212) 484-1500

Home Sports Entertainment
5251 Gulfton Street
Houston, TX 77081
(713) 661-0078

Home Team Sports
111 18th Street N.W.
Suite 200
Washington, D.C. 20036
(202) 728-5300

Hughes Television Network
Sub of: Madison Square Garden
Network
Four Penn Plaza
New York, NY 10001
(212) 563-8903

International Sport Summit
372 Fifth Avenue
New York, NY 10018
(212) 502-5306

King, Don Sports & Entertainment Network
32 East 69th Street
New York, NY 10021
(212) 794-2900

Lorimar Sports Network
7475 Skillman, Suite 101B
Dallas, TX 75231
(214) 340-1404

Lorimar-Telepictures Corp.
1 Dag Hammarskjold Plaza
New York, NY 10017
(212) 735-1500

Madison Square Garden Network
Two Pennsylvania Plaza
New York, NY 10121
(212) 563-8000

Main Event Productions, Inc.
214 Lackawanna Avenue
West Paterson, NJ 07424
(201) 785-4477

Manhattan Cable TV
120 East 23rd Street
New York, NY 10010
(212) 598-7200

Mizlou Television Network, Inc.
350 Fifth Avenue, Suite 6400
New York, NY 10118
(212) 244-3750

NBA Entertainment, Inc.
Sub of: National Basketball
Association
1650 Broadway, Suite 402
New York, NY 10019
(212) 541-9339

NBC Radio Network
Sub of: RCA Corp.
30 Rockefeller Plaza
New York, NY 10112
(212) 664-4444

NBC Sports Division
Sub of: RCA Corp.
30 Rockefeller Plaza
New York, NY 10112
(212) 664-4444

New England Sports Network
70 Brookline Avenue
Fenway Park
Boston, MA 02215
(617) 536-9233

New York Times Syndication Sales Corp.
130 Fifth Avenue, 9th Floor
New York, NY 10011
(212) 645-3000

NFL Films
Sub of: National Football League
330 Fellowship Road
Mt. Laurel, NJ 08054
(609) 778-1600

Pennzoil Products Company
Div of: Pennzoil Company
Pennzoil Place
PO Box 2967
23rd Floor
Houston, TX 77252-2967
(713) 546-6699

Proserv Television
1540 Eastgate Drive, Suite 200
Garland, TX 75041
(214) 270-7601

Raycom, Inc.
801 East Trade Street
Charlotte, NC 28233-3367
(704) 331-9494
Mailing Address:
PO Box 33367
Charlotte, NC 28233-3367

SIN Television Network
460 West 42nd Street
New York, NY 10036
(212) 502-1300

Sports Legends, Inc.
27 City Line Avenue
Bala Cynwyd, PA 19004
(215) 664-6595

Sportschannel/New England
10 Tower Office Park, Suite 600
Woburn, MA 01801
(617) 933-9300

Sportschannel/New York
150 Crossways Park West
Woodbury, NY 11797
(516) 364-3650

Titan TV
Sub of: Titan Sports, Inc.
1055 Summer Street
PO Box 3857
Stamford, CT 06905
(203) 352-8600

USA Network
1230 Avenue of the Americas
New York, NY 10020
(212) 408-9100

WTBS-Sports
Turner Broadcasting
1050 Techwood Drive Northwest
Atlanta,, GA 30318
(404) 827-1717

■ **INDIVIDUALS**

Red Barber
3013 Brookmont Drive
Tallahassee, FL 32312

John B. Brickhouse
WGN Continental Broadcasting
2501 West Bradley Place
Chicago, IL 60618

Bob Broeg
60 Frontenac Estates
St. Louis, MO 63131

Jack Buck
KMOX Radio
1 Memorial Drive
St. Louis, MO 63102

Dick Button
888 7th Avenue #650
New York, NY 10106

Harry Caray
Wrigley Field
Chicago, IL 60613

Howard Cosell
150 East 69th Street
New York, NY 10021

Don Drysdale
78 Colgate
Rancho Mirage, CA 92270

Joseph F. Falls
Detroit News
Detroit, MI 48231

Joe Garagiola
6221 East Huntress Drive
Paradise Valley, AZ 85253

Curt Gowdy
9 Pierce Road
Wellesley Hills, MA 02181

Bob Griese
3250 Mary Street
Miami, FL 33133

Jim Kaat
PO Box 86
Glen Mills, PA 19343

John "Red" Kerr
c/o WMAQ Radio
Chicago, IL 60604

Ralph Kiner
17 Legrande Avenue #17
Greenwich, CT 06830

Tony Kubek
3311 North McDonald
Appleton, WI 54911

Martin Liquori
5904 NW 57th Way
Gainesville, FL 32605

Tim McCarver
1518 Youngford Road
Gladwynne, PA 19035

Don Meredith
2222 LTV Tower
Dallas, TX 75201

Lindsey Nelson
International Creative Management
40 West 57th Street
New York, NY 10019

Parry O'Brien
3415 Alginet Drive
Encino, CA 91316

Richard O'Connell
49 Cedar Road
Belmont, MA 02178

Jim Palmer
PO Box 145
Brooklandville, MD 21002

Ara Parseghian
1326 East Washington Street
South Bend, IN 46601

Jimmy Piersall
1105 Oakview Drive
Wheaton, IL 60187

George Plimpton
541 East 72nd Street
New York, NY 10021

Phil Rizutto
912 Westminster Avenue
Hillside, NJ 07205

Kyle Rote
1175 York Avenue
New York, NY 10021

Vin Scully
1555 Capri Drive
Pacific Palisades, CA 90272

Duke Snider
3037 Lakemont Drive
Fallbrook, CA 92028

Bert Randolph Sugar
6 Southview Road
Chappaqua, NY 10514

Joe Theisman
5912 Leesburg Pike
Baileys Crossroads, VA 22041

Bob Uecker
Milwaukee Brewers Publicity Office
County Stadium
Milwaukee, WI 53214

Bill White
71 Cannonhill Road
Chalfont, PA 18914

SPORTS MEDICINE CLINICS ▬▬▬

ALABAMA
UAB Preventive Medicine
Stress Testing Laboratories
1717 11th Avenue South
Birmingham, AL 35205
Dir: L. Thomas Sheffield, MD

Lifestyles Sports Injury Clinic
951 Downtowner Boulevard
Mobile, AL 36609
Dir: Lynn Van Ost, RN, ATC

ALASKA
Denali Sportsmedicine Center
1867 Airport Road
Fairbanks, AK 99701
Dir: Cary S. Keller, MD

ARIZONA
Center for Sports Medicine and Orthopedics
4220 North 19th Avenue
Phoenix, AZ 85015
Dir: Peter M. Altieri

ARKANSAS
Arkansas Sports Rehabilitation Institute, Inc.
5606 West 12th Street
Little Rock, AR 72204
Dir: Terry Bunker, PT, ATC
Gordon Elland, PT, ATC

CALIFORNIA
San Diego Sports Medicine Center
6699 Alvarado Road
San Diego, CA 92120
Dir: E. Lee Rice, DO

STAAR Institute
11170 Warner Avenue
Fountain Valley, CA 92708
Dir: Alan M. Strizak, MD

National Athletic Health Institute
575 East Hardy Street
Inglewood, CA 90301
Dir: Ronald Mackenzie, MD

FASTRAC Institute
Loma Vista at Brent
Ventura, CA 93003
Dir: Paul Feuerborn, RPT
Robert O'Hollaren, MD

SPORTSMED Medical Clinic
39039 Paseo Padre Parkway
Fremont, CA 94538
Dir: Eugene Wolf, MD
Rodney A. Silveira, MS, RPT

CANADA
Canadian Academy of Sport Medicine
333 River Road
Vanier, Ontario, Canada
K1L 8H9

COLORADO

Fort Collins Orthopedic Association
1200 East Elizabeth
Fort Collins, CO 80524
Dir: Jack Harvey, MD

Aspen Club Sportsmedicine and Fitness Institute
1450 Crystal Lake Road
Aspen, CO 81611
Dir: Barry Mink, MD
Bruno Balke, MD

CONNECTICUT

East Harford Physical Therapy and Sportsmedicine Center, PC
28 North Main Street
West Hartford, CT 06107
Dir: Henry M. Balavender, PT

DELAWARE

Delaware Rehabilitation & Sports Medicine Center
2002 Foulk Road
Wilmington, DE 19810
Dir: John E. Hocutt, Jr., MD

DISTRICT OF COLUMBIA

Executive Fitness Center
Westin Hotel
2401 M Street N.W.
Washington, DC 20037
Dir: Maureen P. Smith

FLORIDA

Southeastern Sports Medicine Therapy
1333 South Miami Avenue
Suite 110
Miami, FL 33130
Dir: Paul D. Turbedsky, MS, ATC

Human Performance & Rahabilitation Clinic
Imperial Point Medical Center
6401 North Federal Hwy
Fort Lauderdale, FL 33308
Dir: R. D. Willix, MD

Palm Beach Institute of Sports Medicine, Inc.
880 Northwest 13th Street
Boca Raton, FL 33432
Dir: Dana Van Pelt, PT, ATC

Sports Medicine Boca Raton
690 Northwest Thirteenth St.
Boca Raton, FL 33432

Florida Center for Orthopedic Rehabilitation
500 9th Street North
Petersburg, FL 33705
Dir: J. Paul Melton, RPT

GEORGIA

Medical & Sports Rehabilitation Associates, Inc.
2151 Fountain Drive
Suite 204
Snellville, GA 30278
Dir: Robert E. DuVall, RPT

Sports Medicine Clinic, PC
615 Peachtree Street N.E.
Atlanta, GA 30308
Dir: Fred L. Allman, Jr. MD

Emory Health Enhancement Center
George W. Woodruff Physical
Education Center
600 Asbury Circle
Atlanta, GA 30322
Dir: Gerald F. Fletcher, MD

Sports Medicine Education Institute, Inc., and Northside Sports Medicine Center

993 Johnson Ferry Road N. E.
Atlanta, GA 30342
Dir: Ronald G. Peyton, MS, PT, ATC

HAWAII

Honolulu Medical Group

Sports Medicine Dept.
550 South Beretania Street
Honolulu, HI 96813
Dir: Robert L. Smith, MD

IDAHO

Idaho Sports Medicine Institute

1188 University Drive
Boise, ID 83702
Dir: Kirk J. Lewis, MD

ILLINOIS

Suburban Sports Medicine Center

420 Lee Street
Des Plaines, IL 60016
Dir: Lowell Scott Weil, DPM

Marianjoy Rehabilitation Hospital

26 West 171 Roosevelt Road
Wheaton, IL 60187
Dir: Richard F. Harvey, MD

University of Chicago Sports Medicine Clinic

950 East 59th Street
Chicago, IL 60637
Dir: Bruce Reider, MD

INDIANA

Methodist Sports Medicine Center

1919 North Capitol
Indianapolis, IN 46202
Dir: Richard J. Cota

Community Hospital Center for Sports Medicine

5626 East 16th Street
Indianapolis, IN 46218
Dir: Jerry Svendsen

IOWA

University of Iowa Hospitals

Sportsmedicine Clinic
Dept. of Orthopaedics
University of Iowa Hospitals
Iowa City, IA 52242
Dir: John P. Albright, MD

KANSAS

Salina Family Physicians, PA

617 East Elm Street
Box 1847
Salina, KS 67401
Dir: Ronald E. Hunninghake, MD

KENTUCKY

Lexington Fitness and Sports Medicine Clinic

2332 Broadway
Lexington, KY 40502
Dir: W. Ben Kibler, MD

LOUISIANA

Sports Medicine Section

Dept of Orthopedic Surgery
Ochsner Clinic
1514 Jefferson Highway
New Orleans, LA 70121
Dir: Charles L. Johnson, MD

Orthopaedic and Sports Medicine Center
7443 Picardy Avenue
Baton Rouge, LA 70809

MAINE
Sports and Orthopedic Rehabilitative Therapy
404 State Street
Bangor, ME 04401
Dir: Larry LoPointe

MARYLAND
Union Memorial Sports Medicine Center
Union Memorial Hospital
201 East University Parkway
Baltimore, MD 21218
Dir: William H.B. Howard, MD

MASSACHUSETTS
Sports Medicine, Inc. at the Cooley Dickinson Hospital
30 Locust Street
Northampton, MA 01060
Dir: Barbara W. Dolan, MS, RPT

START Inc.
91 School Street
Springfield, MA 01105
Dir: Stephen A. Black, MEd, PT

Sports Medicine Clinic/John J. Monahan, MD
University of Massachusetts Medical Center
55 Lake Avenue North
Worcester, MA 01605
Dir: Arthur M. Pappas, MD
John J. Monahan, MD

Sports Medicine Merrimack Valley
800 Broadway
Route 97
Haverhill, MA 01830
Dir: Richard A. St. Onge, MD

Sports Medicine Division
Children's Hospital Medical Center
300 Longwood Avenue
Boston, MA 02115
Dir: Lyle J. Micheli, MD

Sports Medicine Brookline
830 Boyleston Street
Brookline, MA 02167
Dir: William W. Southmayd, MD

MICHIGAN
Saint Mary's Hospital Sports Medicine Center
200 Jefferson SE
Grand Rapids, MI 49503
Dir: Ann Brashear

MINNESOTA
University of Minnesota Sports Medicine Institute
Mayo Memorial Building
Box 319, 420 Delaware Street
Minneapolis, MN 55455
Dir: Robert E. Hunter

MISSISSIPPI
Physical Fitness Institute
Box 10024
Southern Station
University of Southern Mississippi
Hattiesburg, MS 39406
Dir: David E. Cundiff, PhD

MISSOURI

Missouri Bone and Joint Sports Medicine Institute
12255 DePaul Drive
Suite 310
Bridgeton, MO 63033
Dir: Linnie M. Love

MONTANA

Havre Clinic Sports Medicine Program
20 West 13th Street
Havre, MT 59501
Dir: Robert Whipple, MD

NEBRASKA

Sports Medicine Program
Dept. of Orthopedic Surgery and Rehabilitation
University of Nebraska Medical Center
42nd Street and Dewey Avenue
Omaha, NE 68105
Dir: W. Michael Walsh, MD

NEVADA

Las Vegas Institute of Physical Therapy and Sports Medicine
3650 South Eastern Street
Suite 100
Las Vegas, NE 89109
Dir: Keith Kleven

NEW HAMPSHIRE

Dartmouth-Hitchcock Medical Center
Hanover, NH 03755
Dir: Robert E. Porter, MD

NEW JERSEY

Health Through Exercise and Rehabilitation
160 East Newman Springs Road
Red Bank, NJ 07701
Dir: Phillip C. Dunphy, PT

Sports Medicine Princeton
385 Princeton Avenue
Princeton, NJ 08540
Dir: Paul Van Horn, MD

Institute for Medicine in Sports
A Hamilton Hospital Associate
1881 Whitehorse Hamilton Square Road
Hamilton Center for Health
Hamilton Square, NJ 08690
Dir: G. Patrick Connors

NEW MEXICO

Tom Young's Total Health Center
2250 Wyoming NE
Albuquerque, NM 87112

NEW YORK

Lenox Hill Hospital Institute of Sports Medicine and Athletic Trauma
130 East 77th Street
New York, NY 10021
Dir: James A. Nicholas, MD

Mt. Kisco Sports Medicine Group
155 Kisco Avenue
Mt. Kisco, NY 10549
Dir: Phillip W. Rhoades

University Hospital Sports Medicine Service
Dept. of Orthopedics
T18 HSC 080
SUNY Stony Brook
Stony Brook, NY 11794
Dir: Stuart B. Cherney, MD

NORTH CAROLINA
Sports Medicine Clinic
1822 Brunswick Avenue
Charlotte, NC 28207
Dir: David S. Johnston, MD

NORTH DAKOTA
Red River Valley Sports Medicine Institute
110 Professional Building
100 South 4th Street
Fargo, ND 58103
Dir: Mark A. Lundeen, MD

Sports Medicine Dept.
Dakota Clinic, Ltd.
1702 South University Drive
Fargo, ND 58108-6001
Dir: James F. Johnson, MD

OHIO
Sports Medicine Grant
340 East Town Street
Suite 8-100
Columbus, OH 43215
Dir: Raymond J. Tesner, DO
Randall F. Baker

Sports Medicine Center of the Center for Health Promotion
Riverside Hospital
1600 North Superior Street
Toledo, OH 43604
Dir: Ann Murray, RN, MSN

Ohio Regional Centre for Sports Medicine
3187 West 21st Street
Lorain, OH 44053
Dir: M.C. Kolczun II, MD

Cleveland Clinic
9500 Euclid Avenue
Cleveland, OH 44106
Dir: John A. Bergfeld, MD

Work Physiology Laboratory
Dept. Zoological and Biomedical
Sciences
Ohio University
Athens, OH 45701
Dir: Fredrick C. Hagerman, PhD

OKLAHOMA
Welfit Health Services
2325 South Harvard
Tulsa, OK 74114
Dir: Charles R. Welden, MPH

OREGON
Thomas J. Carlsen, MD
2275 Northeast Doctors Drive
Bend, OR 97701

PENNSYLVANIA
Indiana University of Pennsylvania
Room 108
Memorial Field House
Indiana, PA 15705
Dir: Ralph Sweithelm, LPT

PUERTO RICO
Sports Medicine Clinic
Box 8600
Fernandez Jumos Station
Banturce, PR 00910
Dir: Victor I. Vargas, LPT
Dwight Santiago, MD
Sigfredo Rodriguez, MS

RHODE ISLAND
Garden City Sports Medicine and Fitness Center
170-C Hillside Road
Cranston, RI 02920
Dir: Heinrich Doll, BA

SOUTH CAROLINA

Spartanburg Family YMCA
266 South Pine Street
Spartanburg, SC 29302
Dir: Barbara L. Gibbs

SOUTH DAKOTA

Orthopedic and Sports Medicine Clinic, PC
1301 South Ninth, Suite 600
Sioux Falls, SD 57105
Dir: John J. Billion, MD

TENNESSEE

Dept. of Health Promotions
Methodist Hospitals of Memphis
1325 Eastmoreland
Memphis, TN 38104
Dir: Neil Sol, PhD

TEXAS

The Cooper Clinic
12200 Preston Road
Dallas, TX 75230
Dir: Kenneth H. Copper, MD

Sportsmedicine Center
St. Joseph Hospitals
1350 South Main, Suite 2000
Fort Worth, TX 76104
Dir: Joe Fritz

Hermann Hospital Center for Sports Medicine
1203 Ross Sterling Avenue
Houston, TX 77030
Dir: James E. Butler, MD
Will Risser, MD
David Yukelson, PhD

Travis Sports Medicine Centre
6655 Travis, No. 400
Houston, TX 77030
Dir: Steve L. Brown, LAT

Texas Rehab Associates Inc.
3000 Medical Arts
Austin, TX 78705
Dir: Spanky Stephens

UTAH

Utah State University Wellness Center
Logan, UT 84322-7000
Dir: Lanny J. Nalder, PhD

VERMONT

Human Performance Center
Castleton State College
Castleton, VT 05735
Dir; Robet E. Grace EdD

VIRGINIA

Center for Health and Sports Medicine
National Hospital for Orthopedics and Rehabilitation
1577 Spring Hill Road
Vienna, VA 22180

Center for Sports Medicine
National Hospital for Orthopedics and Rehabilitation
2455 Army Navy Drive
Arlington, VA 22206
Dir: Vanessa L. Mirabelli, PT

WASHINGTON

The Sports Medicine Clinic
1551 Northwest 54th Street
Seattle, WA 98107
Dir: Keith D. Peterson, DO

Division of Sports Medicine
University of Washington
242 Hec Edmundson Pavilion
Seattle, WA 98195
Dir: Roger V. Larson, MD

WEST VIRGINIA
Wheeling Hospital Sports
Medicine Center
Medical Park
Wheeling, WV 26003
Dir: Bob Ullum, LPT

WISCONSIN
University of Wisconsin Hospital
Sports Medicine and Fitness Center
3313 University Avenue
Madison, WI 53705
Dir: Brad Sherman, ATC

University of Wisconsin Sports Medicine and Fitness Center
3313 University Avenue
Madison, WI 53705.
Dir: William G. Clancy, Jr., MD

Gunderson Sport Medicine Clinic
1836 South Avenue
La Crosse, WI 54601
Dir: Richard L. Romeyn, MD
Mark E. Julsrud, DPM

WYOMING
Teton Village Clinic
Jackson Hole Orthopedic Services
Jackson, WY 83001
Dir: John A. Geagin, MD

STATE GAMES DIRECTORY

NATIONAL CONGRESS OF STATE GAMES
National Congress of State Games
PO Box 8336
Boston, MA 02114
(617) 727-3227

ALABAMA
Alabama Sports Festival
339 Dexter Avenue
Montgomery, AL 36130
(205) 261-4496

ALASKA
Great Lns FMWA
PO Box 91872
Anchorage, AK 99509
(907) 243-2820

COLORADO
Colorado State Games
PO Box 300282
Denver, CO 80203
(303) 782-9400

DISTRICT OF COLUMBIA
The Capital Games
3468 Mildred Drive
Falls Church, VA 22042
(703) 536-9063

FLORIDA
Sunshine State Games
1111 East Tennessee, Suite 201
Tallahassee, FL 32308
(904) 488-0148

ILLINOIS
Prairie State Games
500 Skokie Boulevard, Suite 444
Northbrook, IL 60062
(312) 291-9666

INDIANA
White River Park State Games
251 North Illinois, Suite 910
Indianapolis, IN 46204
(317) 237-2200

IOWA
Iowa State Games
200 East Grand
Des Moines, IA 5030

KENTUCKY
Bluegrass State Games
PO Box 1405
Frankfort, KY 40601
(800) 722-2474

MARYLAND
Maryland State Games
3430 Courthouse Drive
Ellicott City, MD 21043
(301) 992-2480

MASSACHUSETTS
Bay State Games
PO Box 8336
Boston, MA 02114
(617) 727-3227

MICHIGAN
Great Lakes State Games
Meyland Hall
Northern Michigan University
Marquette, MI 49855
(906) 227-2888

MINNESOTA
Minnesota Amateur Sports Commission
900 American Center Building
150 East Kellogg Boulevard
St. Paul, MN 55101
(612) 296-4845

MISSOURI
Show Me State Games
PO Box 809
Jefferson City, MO 65102
(314) 751-0916

MONTANA
Big Sky State Games
PO Box 2318
Billings, MT 59103
(406) 245-8106

NEBRASKA
Cornhusker State Games
PO Box 84211
Lincoln, NE 68501
(402) 476-7575

NEW JERSEY
Garden State Games
16 Roosevelt Avenue
Deal, NJ 07723
(201) 381-0666

NEW YORK
Empire State Games
Agency Building #1
Albany, NY 12238
(518) 474-8889

NORTH CAROLINA
State Games of North Carolina
PO Box 12727
RTP, NC 27602
(919) 361-1987

NORTH DAKOTA
Prairie Rose State Games
1424 West Century Avenue #202
Bismarck, ND 58501
(701) 224-4887

OKLAHOMA
Sooner State Games
4545 North Lincoln Boulevard,
Suite G
Oklahoma City, OK 73105
(405) 235-4222

OREGON
Oregon State Games
PO Box 1182
Oregon City, OR 97045
(503) 635-3019

PENNSYLVANIA
Keystone State Games
31 South Hancock Street
Wilkes-Barre, PA 18702
(717) 823-3164

SOUTH CAROLINA
Palmetto State Games
2600 Bull Street
Columbia, SC 29201
(803) 734-4650

TEXAS
**Texas Amateur Athletic
Foundation**
11442 North Interstate Highway 35
Austin, TX 89853
(512) 835-1434

UTAH
Utah State Games
PO Box 71
Cedar City, UT 84720
(801) 586-2950

WASHINGTON
**Washington State Games
Foundation**
1001 4th Avenue Plaza, Suite 3135
Seattle, WA 98154
(206) 682-4263

WISCONSIN
Badger State Games
1402 Regent Street
Madison, WI 53711
(608) 251-3333

WYOMING
Cowboy State Games
310 Elm Street
Pine Bluffs, WY 82082
(307) 245-3219